The Breaking OF Bread
AND THE
Breaking OF Boundaries

Studies in Biblical Literature

Hemchand Gossai
General Editor

Vol. 161

———————

This book is a volume in a Peter Lang monograph series.
Every volume is peer reviewed and meets
the highest quality standards for content and production.

———————

PETER LANG
New York • Bern • Frankfurt • Berlin
Brussels • Vienna • Oxford • Warsaw

MINKYU LEE

The Breaking OF Bread AND THE Breaking OF Boundaries

A Study of the Metaphor of Bread
in the Gospel of Matthew

PETER LANG
New York • Bern • Frankfurt • Berlin
Brussels • Vienna • Oxford • Warsaw

Library of Congress Cataloging-in-Publication Data

Lee, Minkyu.
The breaking of bread and the breaking of boundaries:
a study of the metaphor of bread in the gospel of Matthew / Minkyu Lee.
pages cm. — (Studies in biblical literature; Vol. 161)
Includes bibliographical references.
1. Bible. Matthew—Criticism, interpretation, etc.
2. Bread—Biblical teaching. I. Title.
BS2575.52.L44   226.2'064—dc23   2014022626
ISBN 978-1-4331-2768-7(hardcover)
ISBN 978-1-4539-1405-2 (e-book)
ISSN 1089-0645

Bibliographic information published by **Die Deutsche Nationalbibliothek.**
Die Deutsche Nationalbibliothek lists this publication in the "Deutsche
Nationalbibliografie"; detailed bibliographic data are available
on the Internet at http://dnb.d-nb.de/.

The paper in this book meets the guidelines for permanence and durability
of the Committee on Production Guidelines for Book Longevity
of the Council of Library Resources.

© 2015 Peter Lang Publishing, Inc., New York
29 Broadway, 18th floor, New York, NY 10006
www.peterlang.com

Printed in Germany

Contents

Editor's Preface

More than ever the horizons in biblical literature are being expanded beyond that which is immediately imagined; important new methodological, theological, and hermeneutical directions are being explored, often resulting in significant contributions to the world of biblical scholarship. It is an exciting time for the academy as engagement in biblical studies continues to be heightened.

This series seeks to make available to scholars and institutions, scholarship of a high order, and which will make a significant contribution to the ongoing biblical discourse. This series includes established and innovative directions, covering general and particular areas in biblical study. For every volume considered for this series, we explore the question as to whether the study will push the horizons of biblical scholarship. The answer must be *yes* for inclusion.

In this volume, Minkyu Lee examines the use of *bread* and the act of *breaking bread* as metaphors in Matthew's Gospel. Lee argues that this use of *bread* in Matthew shapes and represents Matthew's "communal identity and ideological vision." The author contends that while much of the scholarly focus with regard to Matthew's use of bread has been Christological in orientation and in light of the Eucharist, the use of bread is instrumental in understand the identity of the Matthean community. Lee notes, "the Gospel of Matthew re-defines and represents its own identity and the boundary of community, especially when Jesus breaks bread to share with others including Gentiles and the marginalized." Employing metaphor theory and incorporating narrative criticism, together with the concepts of hybridity and Third Space, the author establishes a strategy for interpretation. This study is certain to generate ongoing discourse, and will not only further expand the biblical horizon, but will do so in a direction that invites further conversation.

The horizon has been expanded.

Hemchand Gossai
Series Editor

Abbreviations

AB	The Anchor Bible
ABc	Analecta Biblica
ABD	The Anchor Bible Dictionary
ABS	Academia Biblica Series
ANTC	Abingdon New Testament Commentaries
APOTE	The Apocrypha and Pseudepigrapha of the Old Testament in English
BECNT	Baker Exegetical Commentary on the New Testament
BDAG	A Greek-English Lexicon of the New Testament and Other Early Christian Literature. 2nd and 3rd edn.
BR	Biblical Review
BS	Bibliotheca Sacra
BTB	Biblical Theology Bulletin
CBQ	Catholic Biblical Quarterly
EBC	The Expositor's Bible Commentary
IBCTP	Interpretation, A Bible Commentary for Teaching and Preaching
ICC	The International Critical Commentary
Int	Interpretation
IBS	Irish Biblical Studies

JAAR	Journal of the American Academy of Religion
JBL	Journal of Biblical Literature
JETS	Journal of the Evangelical Theological Society
JSNT	Journal for the Study of the New Testament
JSNTS	Journal for the Study of the New Testament Supplement Series
JSOTsup	Journal for the Study of the Old Testament Supplement Series
JSPS	Journal for the Study of the Pseudepigrapha Supplement Series
LNTS	Library of the New Testament Series
NCBC	The New Cambridge Bible Commentary
NICOT	New International Commentary on the Old Testament
NIGTC	The New International Greek Testament Commentary
NT	Novum Testamentum
NIBC	New International Biblical Commentary
NIDB	The New Interpreter's Dictionary of the Bible
PTMS	Princeton Theological Monograph Series
SBL	Society of Biblical Literature
SBT	Studies in Biblical Theology
SCJ	Studies in Christianity and Judaism
SJ	Studies in Judaism
SJSD	Supplements to the Journal for the Study of Judaism
SNTSMS	Society for New Testament Studies Monograph Series
SNT	Supplements to Novum Testamentum
SP	Sacra Pagina
SVC	Supplements to Vigiliae Christianae
TDNT	Gerhard Kittel and Gerhard Friedrich (eds.), *Theological Dictionary of the New Testament.* (trans. Geoffrey W. Bromiley; 10 vols; Grand Rapids: Eerdmans)
VT	Vetus Testamentum
WBC	Word Biblical Commentary
WUNT2	Wissenschaftliche Untersuchungen zum Neuen Testament. 2. Reihe

1

Introduction

The Purpose of the Project

Literature in the meaning of the word, as Terry Eagleton argues, is an ideology that has the most intimate relationship to questions of social power.[1] If one sees "literature" in *functional* rather than *ontological* terms, the criteria of what counts as literature would be an ideological expression in which the literary work represents one's own concerns and the values of the society one lives in. The ideology here is not so much about a physical means of enslavement but "a mental one, operating in terms of ideas, beliefs, cultural practices and religion,"[2] which reveals some kind of relation to the maintenance and reproduction of social power or a vision of socialization. All these social and mental phenomena appear in literature, including in biblical literature.

Especially in the light of the *functional* perspective on literature, the meaning and usage of specific foods in the text reflect various components of culture, identity, and even an ideological vision.[3] The image of a specific food is derived from the historical experience of a community and common knowledge, which are crucial elements for the formation of communal identity and self-consciousness. For instance, when one eats turkey on Thanksgiving Day, most North Americans know the meaning of eating turkey together and its cultural background. Likewise, Israel has special images and experiences of specific foods such as manna, quail, and bread. So these foods are not just nutritional supplies for satisfying human hunger when they are used as metaphors in biblical literature. Rather, the usage of food exhibits symbolic and metaphoric meaning for representing cultural identity and ideological vision beyond their literal expression.

This project will investigate the Matthean use of *bread* (ἄρτος) and the act of the *breaking of bread* as metaphors, which are not only intertwined within Matthew's narrative plots, but also function to represent Matthew's communal identity and ideological vision. In the Gospel of Matthew, bread (ἄρτος) and its relevant feeding scenes appear in five principal places: Jesus' temptation (4:1–4), the Feeding of the Five Thousand (14:13–21), the Canaanite woman (15:21–28), the Feeding of the Four Thousand (15:29–39), and Jesus' Last Supper (26:26–30). In the history of Matthean scholarship, these narrative units have been mostly interpreted independently in light of the themes of Christology and the form of Christian Eucharist, while not drawing scholarly attention to the motif of bread and the cultural conception or symbolic image of bread in the Matthean narrative context. However, when bread is recognized as a metaphor, it reveals a significant literary motif and interpretive frame for the Gospel of Matthew as a whole.

The metaphor of bread in Matthew's Gospel implicitly connects to Israel's indigenous sense of identity and religious imagination, while presenting the reconstruction of the communal identity of the group of Jesus' followers that is the Matthean community, through the metaphoric act of the *breaking of bread*. The Israelites had a common sense of identity and self-consciousness, which were formed by their own experience with God in the past, especially the unleavened bread and manna in the wilderness: *bread from heaven*.[4] The common knowledge and experiences of bread have led the Israelites into a common "religious imagination"[5] in solidarity through the generations. As Juliana Claassens argues, the memory of the Passover meal and God's provision in the wilderness provided some features in Israel's religious imagination, which formats and germinates Israel's communal identity.[6] In Jewish culture, even up until first century Judaism, bread and other specific foods in the communal feast or banquet have important functions to bond people in solidarity in the sense of Jewishness and to keep the originality of the Jewish heritage, while intensifying group identities and demarcating the ideological boundaries from others.

Therefore, the memory and historical-cultural experience of food are part of the cognitive knowledge of the Israelites and sources of a conceptual metaphor in reference to feeding languages or food/bread. Through the connection to the Passover meal, manna, and other common memories and experiences around bread including ritual meals, one can examine the metaphoric conceptions and socio-religious image of bread in Jewish tradition, which formed the cognitive conceptual knowledge of the Jewish reader. Thus, the reader can apply these metaphoric conceptions to the interpretation of Matthean bread and its relevant narratives: how bread as metaphor functions in the Matthean narrative; how Matthean bread as literary motif communicates with the reader's cognitive conceptions and exhibits its own meaning; and how these narratives in Matthew represent Matthew's communal identity and reflect the community's ideological vision.

Through the bread Jesus provides, the Gospel of Matthew re-defines and represents its own identity and the boundary of community, especially when Jesus breaks bread to share with others, including Gentiles and the marginalized (14:13–21; 15:21–28, 29–39) and identifies himself with the bread (26:26–29) as a sacrificial life-giving source, which was broken and given to others. Furthermore, while the metaphor of bread and the breaking of bread as a narrative strategy keep the Jewish indigenous socio-religious heritage, Matthew breaks down multiple boundaries of religion, ethnicity, gender, class, and the false prejudice in order to establish a new identity and ideological vision. From this perspective, one can see Matthew's own rhetorical claims with the metaphor of bread in the context of Matthean community in struggles between formative Judaism and Roman Imperial ideology, while signifying the destruction and reconstruction of communal identity and ideological vision beyond multiple boundaries.

If we extend our reading frame beyond its literal expression and see a narrative function and cultural conceptual value of the bread as a metaphor, it is not only a powerful narrative strategy for Matthew to represent and express communal identity and ideological vision, but it also becomes an effective hermeneutic lens for the reader to interpret Matthew's Gospel in a new way. So the purpose of this book is 1) to analyze the literary motif of bread, the rhetorical functions of bread as a metaphor, and its strategic narrative function in the Gospel of Matthew; 2) to re-read the Gospel of Matthew as a whole; and 3) to investigate the context of the Matthean community and their identity, as reflected in the metaphor of bread and the Matthean feeding narratives. Through this research, this book will provide another hermeneutic apparatus and lens to interpret Matthean feeding narratives and the references to ingestion in the Gospel of Matthew as a whole. The book presents another way to see how the Matthean community established an identity and communal vision amid the conflicts between formative Judaism and Roman Imperialism in the first century C.E.

Previous Studies

In the history of New Testament scholarship, many scholars have paid special attention to the references to food and meals in the light of the themes of Christian sacramentalism and Eucharist, while giving little consideration to the cultural concept of the food and the literary motif in its narrative context. A review of scholarly works on bread and other references to ingestion will clarify the purpose of this project and show the direction of the hermeneutic lens and strategy that I use in this volume. Furthermore, the review of Matthean scholarship will guide the way of research on the identity of Matthean Community in its own context. This section will briefly deal with the previous scholarly works, concerning both references to ingestion in the New Testament and the context of community in the Gospel of Matthew.

Bread and the References to Ingestion

Previous scholarly works on ingesting scenes with common meals and particular foods, such as bread and wine, have not extended their concerns to the cultural conception or symbolic image of bread, nor have they tried to see the motif of the bread metaphor as a narrative strategy in the Gospel. Basically, the references to food and the scenes of meals in the Gospel of Matthew have not attracted considerable attention from scholars, compared to the other Gospels. I think that is probably due to the lack of prevalence of these references in Matthew's Gospel. In the history of Matthean scholarship, many scholars have interpreted the two feeding narratives and other references to eating at Jesus' last supper in the light of the description of Jesus' messianic identity and its absolute sovereignty, and the Eucharistic interpretation. Namely, conventional pictures and studies of the bread and wine, especially in the context of group meals of early Christianity are taken to be mostly relevant to a liturgical form of the Christian mass or Eucharist.

Most of all, scholars have paid special attention to the occurrence of key words around references to bread: 'took,' 'blessed,' 'broke,' and 'gave' in two feeding narratives (14:13–21; 15:29–39), which are similar to the words of institution of the Lord's Supper (26:26) and Paul's account (1 Corinthians 11:23–24). For instance, Francis W. Beare interprets the two feedings of the multitudes as an "eschatological sacrament" with three verbs – εὐλόγησεν (blessed), κλάσας (broke) and ἔδωκεν (gave) – connecting to Jesus' Last Supper,[7] and he identifies these feeding stories with the Messianic banquet motif in Isaiah 25:6 and 55:1.[8] Through the bread and feeding scenes, Jesus' messiahship and his impending kingdom are declared in public, and the new covenant is established through the Eucharist.[9] Luz and Harrington also affirm that Matthew is careful to place the feeding narratives as the wilderness banquet in line with the last Supper and the Church's Eucharist,[10] in which those of Jewish and Christian heritage are reminded of their own family and church meals and gatherings.

All references to bread are not only identified with Jesus' body but also with the ritual of breaking, distributing, taking, and eating, signifying Jesus' spiritual presence at the Eucharist as traditionally established by early Christianity. In this interpretation, ingesting terms are mostly relevant to Christian sacramentalism and support the institutionalization of Christian ritual activity by finding valuable new meanings in the biblical passages. These scholarly works produce many fruitful meanings for Christianity. At the same time, however, these studies confine the extent of biblical ingesting narratives to the realm of Christian liturgy, thus limiting the meaning of the bread and wine. So, biblical references to common meals, foods, and their relevant narratives seldom deviate from a particular Christian perspective and traditional understanding.

Some scholars have attempted to study the literary motif of the language surrounding these food narratives and the symbolic usages of bread in Jewish religious ceremonies, while describing the portrait of Jesus as being in line with Moses.[11] However, most cases of interpretation are framed by the insistence on institutionalized sacramentalism and Christian Eucharist; and many scholars concentrate more on the Gospel of John and Pauline literature rather than the Gospel of Matthew. For instance, Borgen argues that the identification of Jesus with bread in the Gospel of John is an intentional distinction from the manna in the desert for the Mosaic age, so Jesus' feeding of the people in the wilderness must be understood as the Eucharistic bread for the feast in God's kingdom. Borgen suggests that the Johannine Gospel contrasts the external bread of the past, given by Moses, with the spiritual bread of the present, given by Jesus.[12] In this work, Borgen does not stray from the realm of sacramental meanings and traditional understandings of the text. More recently, Jane Webster concentrates on food as a literary motif and metaphor, and investigates the narrative context of meals and language drawn from ingesting scenes throughout the Gospel of John, in which food is identified with Jesus in many places.[13] According to Webster, the ingesting references—as metaphor—in the Johannine narrative context describe Jesus as a provider of food and drink, which always expresses the bestowal of salvation upon others; so that all languages of ingestion convey the soteriology of the Johannine Gospel consistently as a whole. This study extends the meaning of the references on food and the ingesting motif beyond the traditional Euchristic meaning.[14]

In more recent studies, some scholars have studied the biblical ingesting scenes as meals, in general, rooted in the social context of the Jewish and Greco-Roman world. For instance, Hal Taussig and Dennis Smith studied the early Christian experience of communal meals as a Christian social practice and rhetoric, which can correspond to the Hellenistic social gathering around meal, such as symposia, to the ritual practice as an identity performance, and to the meals of resistance to Roman Imperial power.[15] However, this study did not focus on the biblical literary motif and its interpretation, concentrating rather on the Christian meal in general and its ritual value from a social scientific perspective.

Overall for the previous studies on references to ingestion and their language, such as bread and wine in the New Testament, the vast majority of scholarly works mostly concentrate on the spiritual and symbolic meaning of the Eucharist in light of sacramentalism. These interpretations are meaningful enough and valuable; however, the prevalence of such interpretations does not mean that the text must only be interpreted this way. Rather, if one concentrates on the literary motif of food, its narrative context, and the cultural conception and imagery of bread as a metaphor, the meaning of references to ingestion would be multiplied, presenting another reading frame and hermeneutic lens. So in this book, I investigate the literary motif of bread and its relevant ingesting scenes in the Gospel of Matthew. I will concentrate on the rhetorical functions of bread as metaphor and its narrative strategy, paying special attention to the socio-cultural conception and the symbolic images of bread, and I will re-read Matthew's narratives as a whole through the metaphor of bread beyond the traditional meaning of Eucharist.

The Gospel of Matthew and Community

Among diverse aspects of Matthean studies, scholarly work in recent years can be largely divided into two perspectives: Matthew's relationship to formative Judaism and to the Roman Empire. First, in the past decade of Matthean studies, analytical perspectives have mostly concentrated on the relationship of Matthew's Gospel to first century Judaism in Palestine. In this case, some Matthew scholars such as Daniel Harington,[16] J. Andrew Overman,[17] and Dale C. Allison, Jr.,[18] were primarily influenced by Anthony J. Saldarini, whose main thesis states that Matthew's group[19] was "a fragile minority still thinking of themselves as Jews and still identified with the Jewish community by others."[20] Saldarini does not see a sharp distinction between the Jewish community and Matthew's group even after the destruction of the temple; rather, Matthew participated in the same social setting as formative Judaism. Furthermore, in a chaotic period for the Jewish community,[21] a minor group of Jews who followed Jesus emulates dominant groups such as the Pharisees with its own interpretation of Scripture and the belief in Jesus as teacher and Messiah. Here Jesus' polemics are mostly used as a delegitimizing strategy against the dominant institution. According to Saldarini, Jesus' polemics clearly show an engagement in inner-Jewish traditions, which might work during the chaotic period of the regrouping and reformation of group identity, but Jesus' polemics were about keeping Jewish indigenous socio-religious heritage, not anti-Judaism. In this perspective, Matthew's group can be understood by sociological concepts such as social deviance, voluntary associations, sect formation, and the like. Of course, not all Matthean scholars agree with this perspective; Ulrich Luz, Graham N. Stanton, and Donald Hagner argue that Matthew has made a definitive break with Judaism.[22]

Second, some scholars have paid special attention to the fact that the ethos of the early Christian community is forged in a process of interaction with the dominant values of the pagan world, especially Rome. These Matthean scholars examine Matthew's relationship to the wider world of the Roman Empire.[23] In recent years, Warren Carter wrote an influential monograph, *Matthew and Empire: Initial Explorations*,[24] proposing that the character of Matthean community life represented the resistance and the main alternative to Roman imperial domination.[25] Carter tries to find all these elements in Matthew's texts with special attention to the way in which Jesus is presented in Matthew as an alternative to Empire. For instance, the kingdom of God and God's presence in Jesus as an agency are taken to be direct challenges to the Roman imperial pretentions and claims. In this perspective, Matthew's Gospel and its communal vision and identity can be understood in light of the political and social realities that challenged the social structures imposed and maintained by Roman Empire.

Both perspectives—the perspective that sees a relationship to formative Judaism and the perspective that prefers to focus on the relationship to the Roman Empire—are meaningful and open up new and diverse insights into the themes of Matthew's Gospel and the community out of which it came into the progress of early Christianity. Obviously, not only the colonial situation but also the chaotic religious reforming situation of Judaism influenced the formation of Matthew's community and its Gospel. In this book, I will integrate both perspectives to situate the Mattthean community in a position of struggle between formative Judaism and the Roman Empire. I will examine how Matthean bread as metaphor rhetorically reveals the context of the Matthean community and forms its communal identity in-between formative Judaism and the Roman Empire.

Methodologies

This project mainly uses a contemporary Metaphor Theory as its theoretical and critical framework, while integrating narrative criticism and two concepts of postcolonial theory—*Hybridity* and the *Third space*—into my hermeneutic strategy.

Metaphor Theory

David Tracy affirms that "the study of metaphor may well provide a central clue to a better understanding of that elusive and perplexing phenomenon our culture calls religion."[26] In fact, he sees all religions as grounded in various metaphors, which are revealed "through linguistics and generic strategies" as a rhetorical function in their religious texts.[27] All these metaphors are rooted in "physical and cultural experience" and human cognition according to the postmodern theory of metaphor insisted on by George Lakoff, Mark Johnson and Mark Turner.[28] From this understanding, the metaphors in a certain religion must reflect a community's ideological vision and identity, based on communal historical memory and experience. This understanding of metaphor as a basic premise and reading method will guide this study, dealing with the metaphor of bread in particular and its metaphorical conceptual structure in the Gospel of Matthew.

While the classical view has seen metaphor as a matter of language and its figurative literary function, contemporary theory affirms that metaphor is fundamentally conceptual and a matter of thought in nature, not linguistic. This means that metaphor must be based on the mechanism through which humans understand abstract concepts and perform reasoning. Lakoff and Mark Johnson's *Metaphors We Live By* provoked much discussion, shifting the focal point on the conception of metaphor: *from semantic or linguistic point to conventional conceptual domain; from an analogy in literature to the cognitive reasoning and correspondences in our experiences.*[29] Basically, Lakoff asserts that a metaphor is not a figure of speech or a linguistic object, but rather it is a conventional concept or cognitive organization revealed in human language, structured by understanding and experience. Namely, "our ordinary conceptual system [based on the experience]…is fundamentally metaphorical in nature."[30] Our concepts are structured by "what we perceive, how we get around in the world, and how we relate to other people."[31] These concepts progressively build mechanisms of comprehension in our "internal lexicon" in the process of understanding and language acquisition.[32] They ultimately become our conventional knowledge and "idioms," which are sometimes neither literally true nor serve a figurative use,[33] but they work to communicate, based on common experience and knowledge.[34] Thus, the metaphor and its expressions as conception not only pervade our ordinary language, including thought and experience as well as speech and text, but they also reveal human cognition and conventional conceptions of the world.

In this regard, Lakoff and Johnson use the term 'metaphor' to designate "metaphorical concept."[35] Lakoff insists not only that everyday conventional language is metaphoric in origin, but also that those metaphors are comprehended by "a huge system of thousands of cross-domain mappings"[36] that are "sets of conceptual correspondences."[37] He defines metaphor as a "mapping across conceptual domain."[38] Namely, in our conceptual structures, an *experience/understanding* transfers from one domain of concept to another field in different terms. In this respect, Lakoff's metaphor as structure mapping is technically structured in the relation between a *source domain* and a *target domain*.[39] The *source* means the thing or object that sends the message; the *target* means the recipient of the message. One of the important points is that the mapping in conceptual correspondence between the *source domain* and the *target domain* is based on the *conventional conceptual structure*, formed by common experience and understanding, meaning that the metaphor as structure mapping is based on a fixed part of our conceptual system. He affirms, "mapping should not be thought of as processes" to produce a new relationship between source and target, but rather it is "a fixed pattern of ontological correspondences across domains."[40] Based on this, Lakoff believes that metaphorical mappings not only obey "the invariance Principle," but also are grounded in conventional concept and in everyday experience and knowledge. Thus, a particular metaphor and its relevant statements point to the conceptual structures shaped by our language.

In this regard, metaphors are the means of equation between two words, carrying out a change and making a new meaning. For instance, in the metaphoric expression, "*Life is a Journey*," *life* and j*ourney* are equated, or *life* is changed into a *journey*, or *life* takes on a new meaning in light of the meaning of *journey*. Here, the juxtaposition of two disparate images, such as *a life* and *a journey*, seeks resolution and common ground. In this regard, *a Journey* serves as the source (vehicle) domain to carry the meaning of *life*, which is usually called the *target* or *tenor*. It is in this metaphoric structure, for example, that "Dante begins his *Divine Comedy*, stating: In the middle of life's road, I found myself in a dark wood." Here, by virtue of the *Life Is a Journey* metaphor and mapping the conceptual structure, "the speaker found himself in a condition of being 'lost,' that is, without clear purpose in life or a clear path to his purpose."[41] All readers who recognize the concepts of *life* and *journey* and their relevant conceptual structure can easily comprehend the meaning of the metaphor in Dante's text.

Language reveals the structural metaphors that not only organize our thoughts and experiences but also produce relevant literal expressions and idioms, fitting the normal everyday way of talking and thinking about the subject. Lakoff and Johnson offer many examples of structural metaphors, such as a series of metaphors for ideas. In these examples, the metaphor '*Ideas are Food*' structures how we think about human ideas and how we experience the rephrase of an idea in our culture:

> *Ideas are Food*
> What he said *left a bad taste in my mouth.*
> All this paper has in it are *raw facts, half-baked ideas, and warmed-over theories.*
> I just can't *swallow* that claim.
> That argument *smells fishy.*
>
> *Ideas are Plants*
> The *seeds* of his great ideas were *planted* in his youth.
> She has *a fertile* imagination.
> Here's an idea that I'd like to *plant* in your mind.
>
> *Ideas are Products*
> We've *generated* a lot of ideas this week.
> He *produces* new ideas at an astounding rate
> His intellectual *productivity* has decreased in recent years.[42]

With respect to other conceptions and experiences, the structural metaphor extends the conventional network in a figurative or imaginative way[43] and produces various metaphors in coherence, such as *Ideas are Resources, Ideas are Money, Ideas are Cutting Instruments, and Ideas are Fashions*:

> *Understanding is Seeing; Ideas are Light-Sources; Discourse is a Light-Medium*
> I *see* what you're saying. The Argument is *clear.*
> It *looks* different from my *point of view.*
> Now I've got the whole picture.
> It's a *transparent* argument. The discussion was *opaque.*[44]

The interaction between two disparate words within the conceptual structure of one's cognitive knowledge functions not only to map the metaphoric structure in the text and speech but also to produce a new meaning of the metaphor. Paul Ricoeur argues that metaphor as a whole is dependent on the *interaction* in tension between two parts: "between *tenor* and *vehicle*, between *focus* and *frame*, and between principal subject and secondary subject."[45] This tensional relationship works within the context of a whole sentence, even a whole book, and the terms do not restrict or reduce each other in terms of the domain of rhetoric and discourse. Rather, they reciprocally work together to convey a new meaning and to reach the metaphorical truth. Ricoeur stresses that the analysis of statements and words renders them not just complementary but also reciprocal. "The statement-metaphor has as 'focus' a word whose meaning is changing, the change of meaning of the word has as 'frame' a complete expression whose meaning is in tension."[46] From this perspective, metaphor is not substituting a deviant word for revealing another proper (or fixed) meaning, but the metaphor as a strategy of discourse functions to convey a new meaning by the interaction between *frame* and *focus* and between *source domain* and *target domain* within the context of the whole sentence. Therefore, the metaphor is not a mere ornament of rhetoric but has a special and unique function for conveying new meanings and even truth.

The tensional interaction also extends to the act of reading, drawing the reader's experience and conception into the tension of two disparate images and the mapping process. When we read a certain metaphor in a text, "our unconscious conceptual system functions like a 'hidden hand' that shapes how we conceptualize all aspects of our experience,"[47] and this "hidden hand" offers a clue or source for mapping an abstract meaning of the metaphor. Actually, one's specific memory and experience influence one's cognitive conceptual system and build up an image and a metaphor on a surface of language. In this regard, Lakoff argues, "metaphors are rooted in physical and cultural experience."[48] The metaphor functions as a vehicle for understanding a concept and one's imagination in a specific culture by virtue of experience. The metaphor is not just a matter of language or words: it is more than that, covering human cognition and conceptual systems based upon a specific cultural context. In this respect, one can also comprehend a particular cultural identity and ideology in a specific metaphor through mapping the structure of the conceptual metaphor.

The metaphor as a strategy of discourse functions to convey a new meaning by the interaction between two disparate words: *frame* and *focus/ source* and *target* within the context of whole sentences and entire book. These metaphors themselves are basic to the conceptual system on which language and culture are based, no matter whether it is poetic or conventional language. According to Ricoeur, the metaphor is a kind of "strategy of discourse by which language divests itself of its ordinary descriptive function in order to serve its extraordinary function of re-description."[49] This function of metaphor always works by tensional interaction and within a conventional human conceptual system.

In this book, I argue that metaphor, especially the bread-metaphor in the Gospel of Matthew, is a part of a literary compositional strategy. I will investigate the conventional usage and meaning of bread in Hebrew Scripture and Jewish tradition; so that one can find possible cognitive conceptions of bread and metaphoric structure in tensional interaction. Then I will examine how the bread metaphor expresses its tensional interaction with other words for carrying a new meaning in the Gospel of Matthew, and how the narrator uses the bread metaphor as a literary strategy that develops throughout the whole story of Matthew's Gospel.

Other Methods and Hermeneutic Perspectives

First, I will place my methodological frame into the larger framework of literary criticism, more specifically narrative criticism. Narrative criticism is the most widely practiced of all literary approaches in Gospel studies, even in postmodern biblical studies. One of the most critical investigations in literary criticism and its approach would be "plot analysis,"[50] which usually studies the key features of development in the story line and discourse. Within the plot line, one can analyze the event, characters, conflicts of characters, and the setting of the narrative background in detail. Characters in a narrative are acting through a plot, responding to a climax, developing relationship, and expressing emotion. Furthermore, all these things are situated in and proceed through narrative setting, time, order and space. Through the analysis of the literary features of the text, one can conjecture a certain discourse and meaning presented by the text itself.

Narrative criticism concentrates on the meaning that is ascribed to the implied reader.[51] Namely, major interpreting work is mostly derived from the perspective of the reader who receives a text; especially the implied reader corresponding to the implied author and *his/her* expected intention in the text. So, I will take the starting point of reading Matthew with a premise that the Gospel of Matthew is a clearly defined historical literary document, which has a certain purpose to be read in a certain community. Based on this premise, I will investigate Matthew's narrative in narrative criticism with the metaphor of bread in order to find the meaning of the text as a whole, which is ascribed by the implied reader.

The implied reader is the reader presupposed by the text itself.[52] The implied reader is not a real reader but an imaginary person who is envisioned to respond to the text with whatever knowledge and understanding. The meaning is usually discerned by describing a range of what are called "expected responses" or expected understandings of the implied reader,[53] which is only revealed through the texts. In this book, the implied reader is expected to be Jews who know Jewish tradition, Israel's cultural features, and the political situation under the Roman Empire, but they are not expected to know the doctrinal propositions developed from later Christianity.

Second, as another reading strategy, I engage with two postcolonial concepts—*Hybridity* and *Third Space*—among many other postcolonial concepts. Homi Bhabha has developed the concept of "third space" from literary and cultural theory to describe the construction of cultural identity within the social context of colonialism and any other cultural binaries. Basically, Homi Bhabha affirms that there can be no cultural singularity or pureness to cultural enunciation because all cultures are mobilized. When two cultural entities encounter one another, "these two places [will] be mobilized through a third space," which represents both the general conditions of indigenous identity and the specific application to the contexts. Namely, for Bhabha, the relation of the first space (the indigenous) to the second space (the colonial) reveals a form of opposition that corresponds to asymmetrical power relations.[54] In this oppositional power relation, both determine either the way of negation or negotiation and produce a different cultural identity in the alternative space for the subject of enunciation.

The third space is a "productive space of the construction of culture as difference," functioning as a mode of articulation "in the spirit of *alterity* or *otherness*," which engenders new cultural identity and new possibility.[55] Bhabha argues that the third space is an "interruptive, interrogative, and enunciative" space, highlighting cultural difference that represents new forms of cultural meaning and production beyond the limitations of existing boundaries and colonial cultural imposition. Through the process of oppositional relation, the act of interpretation and understanding unconsciously produces the recognition of "an ambivalence," toward the cultural systems and inherent originality; and the interpretation reproduces new meaning and cultural identity and enunciates cultural difference in the third space, challenging the validity and authenticity of any essentialist cultural identity. Thus, Bhabha calls this space an "ambivalent space of enunciation"[56] and affirms:

> The intervention of the Third Space of enunciation, which makes the structure of meaning and reference an ambivalent process, destroys this mirror of representation in which cultural knowledge is continuously revealed as an integrated, open, expanding code.[57]

The third space functions to create an alternative space for "subject peoples" through the production of a new cultural entity and structure beyond the collision between the indigenous and the colonial. Furthermore the third space displaces histories and envisions new cultural-political initiatives. In this regard, Bhabha states:

> This third space displaces the histories that constitute it, and sets up new structures of authority, new political initiatives, which are inadequately understood through received wisdom….[third space] gives rise to something different, something new and unrecognizable, a new area of negotiation of meaning and representation.[58]

Ultimately the third space as a discursive space negates the purity of culture, primordial fixity, and any other colonial cultural imposition and continually represents the process of articulation of culture's hybridity. So Bhabha clearly affirms:

> It is that Third Space, though unrepresentable in itself, which constitutes the discursive conditions of enunciation that ensure that the meaning and symbols of culture have no primordial unity or fixity; that even the same signs can be appropriated, translated, rehistoricized, and read anew.[59]

In this discursive third space of enunciation, the colonized relocate and re-inscribe their identity as the hybrid subject. Namely, the third space functions as a generative home of hybridity.[60] The term hybridity itself refers to "the cross-breeding of two species by grafting or cross-pollination to form a third, 'hybrid' species."[61] Hybridity is a helpful concept to articulate the multiple and complex range of cultural activities and productions taking place in negotiating identity in the postcolonial context between the colonizer and the colonized. In postcolonial theory, hybridity refers to "the creation of new trans-cultural rather than multicultural forms within the space produced by colonization where people, indigenous, immigrated, settled, colonizing and colonized, live and move."[62] So the hybrid identity of the subject emerges from the interweaving of elements of the colonizer and colonized and it challenges the validity and authenticity of any essentialist cultural identity. Here the meanings and symbols of culture, according to Bhabha, have "no primordial unity or fixity" because of the hybrid nature of culture. In this regard Bhabha insists, "*Hybridity* is a problematic of colonial representation [sign, symbols, texts, discourse] and individuation that reverses the effects of the colonialist disavowal, so that other 'denied' knowledge enter upon the dominant discourse and estrange the basis of its authority—its rule of recognition."[63]

Thus, hybridity is a response that destabilizes colonial fixity, rigidity, and cultural imposition, so that hybridity functions as a "mechanism by which the alienated subject is enabled to challenge oppressive authority."[64] Robert Young argues that hybridity makes "difference into sameness, and sameness into difference, but in a way that makes the same no longer the same, the different no longer simply different."[65] In that sense, hybridity is "a breaking and joining at the same time, in the same place" that consists of "a bizarre binate operation, in which each impulse in qualified against the other, forcing momentary form of dislocation and displacement."[66] The concept of hybridity does not reduce tension, which might have the effect of justifying colonial interventions, but it rather tends to increase tension in order to challenge the system of authority and weaken the sense of colonialism.[67] In this regard, one clearly sees that hybridity allows the colonized to question the power and authority of colonial discourse by highlighting its hybrid identity and alteration, thereby disrupting the claim of personal purity, singularity, or cultural purity.

In postcolonial theory, hybridity in the third space neither subsumes the culture of the colonizer or colonized nor merely merges the two. Hybridity also does not imply a separate third culture but rather a process of continuous construction or formation and deconstruction of cultures by alteration, which is one of the best strategies to resist the colonizer. This is the nature of culture and cultural difference, what Bhabha effectively calls the location of culture. In this nature of culture defined by hybridity and third space, the power of the dominant discourse must be challenged as meaning and identity are opened. Furthermore, cultural discourse and identity can be re-presented, re-historicized, and re-inscribed with a different relationship to the dominant view.

These two conceptions, *Hybridity* and *Third Space* in postcolonial theory, will provide a crucial reading framework to investigate the Matthean community's altering and deviant position of identity and communal ideology *in-between* formative Judaism and the Roman Empire. In the later part of this book, I will identify Hybridity with the character of the Matthean community and will place Matthew's community within the postcolonial conception of the third space, in which Matthew places and represents their new communal identity through the metaphor of bread. Here one can see that Matthean bread and the breaking of bread as metaphor represent and "constitute the discursive condition of enunciation,"[68] beyond the colonial cultural impositions and indigenous Jewish culture.

Overview

The thesis of this book is that Matthean bread and the act of breaking of bread as metaphor reveal Matthew's communal identity that was newly reconstructed by the minority group of deviant Jews *in-between* formative Judaism and the Roman Empire. When Jesus breaks the bread, the metaphor of bread as a source of Matthew's rhetorical claim represents its ideological vision as an alternative community beyond the socio-religious boundaries toward the nation (Gentile)—framed by Hybridity and third space—subverting and deconstructing the hegemony of the dominant groups of formative Judaism[69] and the imperial ideology of Rome.

The following chapter focuses on the Jewish understanding of bread or food and its socio-religious role and imagery within the historical context. In second temple Judaism, particular foods in ritualized meals and festivals carried significant roles to preserve communal identity and social bonding, while reminding people of social memory of cultural history and the origins of Jewish heritage. In this chapter, I investigate the socio-religious function of the bread/food and festive meals in Jewish history and its literature, while examining the Jewish social memory on a specific food and festive meals that functioned to form a common sense of historical awareness. Obviously, a specific social memory formulates the cognitive conception in relation to language and its relevant metaphoric structure, so here one can find some metaphoric conceptions on the bread/food and commensality, which were maintained by written record and verbal recall. These conceptions of metaphor of bread/food will function as a hermeneutic apparatus for reading the Gospel of Matthew.

Chapter 3 examines the metaphor of bread and its narrative effects in two feeding narratives of Matthew's Gospel, 14:13–21 and 15:29–39. In light of the metaphoric conceptions of bread in Jewish tradition, the bread that Jesus breaks and shares with the crowds is not just food for hunger, but rather the bread together with Jesus' breaking action as a metaphor signifies *the establishment of Jesus' community* and *formation of communal identity*. The similarities and differences in these two repetitious stories sharpen the metaphoric meaning of the bread representing Matthew's communal identity and ideological vision. I investigate how the differences of the two feeding narratives intensify the meaning of the bread metaphor and its breaking action and how the metaphor of bread in the two feeding scenes reveals the context of the Matthean community and their identity. In addition, the identity of Matthew's community will be reviewed in terms of the postcolonial concept *Third Space*, in which Matthew's community as a voluntary association places its socio-religious identity in-between formative Judaism and the Roman Empire.

Chapter 4 continues the investigation of the metaphoric meaning of bread in Matthew's narrative plots, especially concentrating on the narrative of the Canaanite woman (15:21–28) and the bread at Jesus' Last supper (26:26–29). The bread of the Canaanite woman highlights the narrative role of the bread metaphor and exhibits the radical transition from Jesus' narrow mission strategy (10:5–6, especially: "Go nowhere among Gentiles") to the last commission for making disciples of all nations (28:19). Here one can see the ultimate vision of Matthew's community, driven by the prophetic fulfillment of Matthew's Gospel. Furthermore, Matthew officially legitimizes and corroborates Matthew's communal identity and ideological vision through presenting the bread metaphor again at Jesus' Last Supper, in which Jesus identifies himself with the bread. The bread metaphor as a narrative strategy functions to promulgate the legitimate identity and alternative vision of Matthew's community. In this chapter, the identity of Matthew's community will be redefined by the postcolonial conception, Hybridity, in which the Matthean community relocate and reinscribe their identity and ideological vision in-between formative Judaism and the Roman Empire.

Bread/Meals in Second Temple Judaism and Relevant Social Memories

As Lakoff and Johnson argue, the metaphor derives from a human cognitive concept formed by previous understanding and experience in our daily routine life,[1] which can structure one's understanding mechanism and hermeneutic lens. Therefore, the analysis of the Jewish background and socio-religious imagery of the *bread/food* and *meal* are significant in order to observe the cognitive conception of the bread and its relevant conceptual metaphoric structure. According to Israel's historical experience, the bread/food, such as the unleavened bread and manna, had a significant function to form a common sense of identity and self-consciousness, which led the Jewish people into a common "religious imagination"[2] and identity in the formation of Israelite society. Furthermore, the customs of meals and commensality signify a certain human behavior and ideological vision among social group in relation to one another and in relation to God. Israelites especially ritualized certain historical events with the bread/food in order to commemorate past events across the generations, so that they keep the social memories, and embody the past experience into their present life and communal identity. In second temple Judaism, some particular foods and the religious ritual customs of meals, such as pilgrimage festivals, were strictly observed as a means of maintaining a historical sense of identity, while functioning to bond people in solidarity in their sense of Jewishness.

The bread/food and ritual festive meals with the specific social memory formulate the cognitive conception and its relevant metaphoric structure. Obviously, something in social memory, maintained through written record and verbal recall, functions as a meaning-making and hermeneutic apparatus in human society. In this chapter, I investigate how second temple Judaism describe and recognize food and meals in relation to their socio-religious identity. Here one can find that particular foods and meals function as identity markers in second temple Judaism, and most imagery and conceptions of foods are derived from Jewish social memory and historical knowledge. I examine the source of memory and Jewish heritage of the bread/food, concentrating on the Passover meal, manna at Israel's wilderness experience and other banquet imageries; I also look for the socio-cultural functions of bread/food and commensality in human relation in the history of Israel. This chapter presents some possible conceptions and symbolic imagery of the bread/food and meals and makes a conceptual metaphoric structure.

Food and Meals in Second Temple Judaism

Food and Meals and Jewish Communal Identity

As David Sutton affirms, food is not just a matter of nutrition but an important source of historical knowledge, which forms social structure, national identity, and religious beliefs.[3] In Jewish history, meals and a specific memory of particular food indeed had a significant function to preserve communal identity, while reminding and connecting people to the history and the origin of Jewish heritage. Especially, under the unsecured social context of the foreign rules and Hellenization in second temple Judaism,[4] Jews and their socio-religious heritage were constantly being challenged to reconsider the nature of their identities in relation to foreigners. In this context, Jews divided into a variety of competing groups or sects; Jewish ritual practice and belief were always contested among groups or sects.[5] At the same time, food and the religious ritual custom of meals, such as the rite of purity or the Jewish dietary law and the pilgrimage festivals, were strictly observed as means of maintaining historical commonality. The Jewish legal code on food/meals and its observation indeed functioned to bond people in solidarity in their sense of Jewishness and to keep the origin of Jewish heritage and communal boundary in each sect.

No one group or sect in formative Judaism[6] could claim to represent the norm for orthodox Judaism in the years following the fall of Jerusalem in 70 C.E. Even before and after the intertestamental period,[7] there were many groups and sects within Judaism, interpreting and studying the Torah in their own context and perspective, practicing the religious festive rites and ceremonies, and even writing their hope and vision in literary form. Each sect developed certain religious ideas within Judaism and sought the legitimacy of their own communal vision among various groups within Judaism.[8]

In this context, each sect and group of Jews preserved their appropriate identity, connecting to the origin of Jewish heritage in terms of the covenant of God in order to achieve group legitimacy. Among their covenantal rules, the dietary law and other festive meal customs were highlighted and interpreted in their own way, and people strictly observed them. As Gillian affirms, food functions as a means of social bonding and preserving communal identity:

> God's covenant was binding not just on the nation but on all the individual Israelites who made up the nation. Individuals, interpreting God's word differently, were bound to embody it in different forms, and, as we have seen, food was one of the most important of these forms. It was logical, therefore, that Jewish sectarians would choose to express and maintain their doctrinal differences through food.[9]

Jewish people not only needed to preserve their identity with legitimacy but also had to keep a safeguard against ritual impurity and to maintain a certain position of separation from people and things that were regarded as unclean-ness and the other.

In late second temple Judaism, the significant matter of the food/meals was how/what people ate in ritual meals, even in daily meals at home, and with whom Jewish people ate. Jews were expected to begin a day and any meal with hand washing, as a practice that was meant to purify one from any impurities; some Jews would not even share a meal table with anyone who sinned[10] and was like a Gentile (e.g., Tobit 1:10–12).[11] The Pharisees in particular, as is seen in Gospel accounts, strictly sought to preserve ritual purity "not only in matters relating to temple worship, but also to every day relationships–in the home, in business and in the communities."[12] Although there was a large ritual apparatus to preserve ritual purity and common identity as a Jew, common meals in everyday life and even special festive meals were significant ways to maintain and represent the communal identity, not only from a socio-cultural perspective but also from a religious point of view. The Pentateuchal law code, such as Leviticus 11, 17–26 and some other strict dietary law (e.g., Deuteronomy 8, 14, 26), insisted that the purity of Israel as a chosen or separated nation is kept by the eating of clean food, the proper observance of festivals, and what constitutes the covenant with God. In this way, the Jewish belief affirms that the Jews as distinct from other groups of pagan, sanctify the everyday physical lives and harness to serve God, as chosen one within the covenant with God,[13] while keeping their communal identity and Jewish cultural-religious heritage. After the destruction of Jerusalem, a washing of the hands before eating bread (a rabbinic ordinance) became enforced even more.[14]

One can find many examples of food/meals in the Gospel accounts when Jesus eats and drinks with the other. Jesus is pictured at meals in the homes of opponents[15] and at table with his followers including sinners and the marginalized;[16] he shares a meal with the crowd and a last meal with disciples, and even after resurrection, Jesus appears in the context of a meal. Many cases of Jesus' meals cause controversies with Jewish religious leaders in the light of Jewish conventional law on food and meals; and the Gospels emphasizes Jesus' ministry of meal and feeding for the breaking of boundaries and exclusive prejudices in Jewish conventional belief. From this perspective, one can see that food and meals, especially the matter of how/what one eats and with whom one eats, were significant matters in second temple Judaism and first century formative Judaism.

Furthermore, Jewish festive meals had a significant role in preserving Jewish identity in second temple Judaism. Festivals that most Jews strictly observed required a pilgrimage to Jerusalem;[17] that pilgrimage was associated with Passover; the spring barley harvest festival of *Pesah*, Pentecost; the early summer wheat festival of *Shavuot*, and the Booths; the autumnal harvest festival of *Sukkot*. The origin of these festivals derives from the historical experience of ancient Israel and its commemorating process, which strongly influenced the communal identity of Jews. In this respect, the observance of the festive meals itself represents the indigenous identity of Judean that differentiates them from all other lands and cities, "as holy Israel is different in genus from all other social entities in humanity,"[18] having a special relationship with God. Jacob Neusner states:

> In Rabbinic Judaism pilgrimage means a voyage to the Holy Land, and, in the Land, it means the ascent to Jerusalem,…the sole focus of pilgrimage is Land, Jerusalem, Temple, and the purpose of pilgrimage is to present offerings to God and to partake of the [meal]…in the Temple courtyard: to eat meat /[meal] with God.[19]

On these pilgrim festivals, there are three requirements: appearing before God, keeping a feast/meal to the Lord, and rejoicing.[20] This means that all Israelites were summoned at Jerusalem to be seen by and rejoice with the Lord, not only commemorating a particular historical event but also celebrating the formation of Israel and the covenant with God. The act of rejoicing is highlighted and executed by the eating of a meal together. Jacob Neusner affirms:

> Rejoicing on the festival means eating meat at God's place, in the condition in which God eats his meals as well: cultic cleanness. It is then that the Israelite appears before God and is seen by God. The nexus of the encounter is the meal, in which the Israelite accepts the rules of cleanness that pertain to God's table, the altar.[21]

Before the destruction of the Temple in 70 C.E., the Passover feast was the primary sacrificial-ritual meal among pilgrim festivals.[22] The Passover also was commemorated as a national holiday of thanksgiving for the exodus from Egypt.[23] As Josephus describes, a huge number of pilgrims came to Jerusalem during festival for keeping this national ritual celebration;[24] Jesus also came to Jerusalem to keep the Passover in the Gospel accounts. In the Passover meal, people consume particular foods such as the unleavened bread, bitter herbs, and the paschal lamb for the commemoration of the Exodus (e.g., Mishnah *Pesahim* 10:5; c.f., Exodus 12). It clearly shows that the Passover meal with these specific foods not only celebrates their experience of liberation from the life of slavery in Egypt but also functions to embody the historical knowledge and its relevant identity in the present life of participants. Rosenblum argues, the Passover is a metonymic food in early rabbinic Judaism; it can be eaten only by "us," so that "the moment that the Passover is ingested, one is embodied as part of Israel."[25] Namely, the consumption of these symbolic foods marked one as distinctly Jewish, indicating the identity status of the person. Even a converted non-Jew can be embodied in Israel through the consumption of this archetypal Jewish food in early rabbinic Judaism.[26] The festive meals—and particular foods—with pilgrimage had a significant function not only to remind Israelites of their historical experience and common knowledge but also to maintain the communal identity of Jews.

Even after the destruction of the Temple in 70 C.E., the festive meal and its ritual process have not ceased, but they have continued and even strengthened, transformed into a domestic celebration called the *Passover Seder.*[27] Although Jewish people commemorated the Temple's sacrificial service and historical event at the domestic dining table without a pilgrimage to Jerusalem, people viewed the domestic table as a substitute for the Temple's altar with the blessings of the divine presence.[28] Before the destruction of the Temple, the synagogue emerged as a site of communal worship, supported by the family home in numerous rituals; however, after the destruction of the Temple, the home functioned as a prime ritual center,[29] in which not only the meal recalled temple ritual and the history of Israel at the table, but also Jewish men and women took upon themselves priestly roles.[30] In the meal at home, Jews focus on "God's graciousness in providing food to the world, praise him for giving Israel a holy land rich in agricultural produce, and petition him to rebuild Jerusalem, the heart of the land."[31] The meal more effectively functions to preserve their communal identity as Jews and envisions the restoration of their future. So, despite the destruction of the Temple, the food/meals continually functions to preserve Jewish communal identity and even more effectively commemorate their historical events and knowledge and maintain their identity throughout generations.

From this perspective, food/meals is not just a matter of nutrition but an important source to preserve the socio-religious boundary and communal identity in second temple Judaism. Through commemorating a particular historical event, some mnemonic foods and the acts of eating have a significant role in maintaining Jewish indigenous identity and its legitimacy and in solidifying people in a common sense of identity.

Food and Meals in Literature: Identity Demarcation

Alongside other factors such as circumcision and the keeping of the Sabbath, a particular food, its relevant dietary law, and the festive meals in Jewish culture had an important role in intensifying the sense of commonality and demarcating the communal boundaries and identity from others. These socio-religious roles of the food/meals are clearly found in Jewish literature. In second temple Judaism, the dietary law and food-related literary descriptions are found in various documents, which constructed a religious cultural boundary and sustained "the identity of displaced Judahites" during the post-exilic period.[32]

Most of all, the Jewish dietary law, especially food restriction in Leviticus and Deuteronomy was continued and kept by Israelites under the unsecured political situation in the second temple period,[33] even though its detailed prescriptions were differently approached by the contexts. The food and its relevant historical knowledge embodied the ethnical-national identity in Jewish history. For instance, in the story of Daniel, Daniel and his friends keep themselves from defilement and eating food provided by the Babylonian royal court through eating vegetables and water (Daniel 1:8–16). The consumption of inappropriate food or pagan food symbolically means not just defilement but a loss of native identity.

It is difficult to know exactly what Jewish dietary law is applied to the case of Daniel;[34] some commentators assume that the defilement comes from the consumption of the foreign king's rich food[35] or meat with blood (Isaiah 59:3; 63:3).

Although there is no clear-cut evidence here, the book of Daniel metaphorically shows the unyielding trust in God and the indigenous identity of Daniel and his friends. Towner insists that the text speaks only about the function of Daniel's refusal, not about its motivation; Daniel's act "had the effect of setting him and his companions apart from the common run of aliens and other students in the Babylonian academy of wisdom" and set out their identity away from the other.[36] From this perspective, Daniel's abstinence from particular foods clearly represents his avoiding assimilation with the foreign identity and keeps the legitimacy of his indigenous identity.

The consumption of particular foods and meals exemplifies the political ideal and the sustenance of substantial ideology. The eating and drinking in a meal relates to the matter of keeping the identity and apostasy.[37] The meal of foreign royal food involves not only an act of worship to an idol on a religious level but also apostasy from fidelity to Jewish identity in a political dimension. The book of Daniel, written about 170 B.C., supports the Maccabean revolt by presenting pious characters who keep their own identity before the political power. A similar level of discipline is found in the story of Judith: Judith brings her own food when she visits the Assyrian commander, Holofernes (Judith 10:5; 12:1–4), preventing herself from being defiled by the fare of the foreign commander;[38] then Judith chops his head off and delivers it back to the Israelites (12:10–13:10). During the Maccabean period, the dietary laws became more significant prescriptions for generating and sustaining Jewish identity in response to Hellenization:[39]

> But many in Israel stood firm and were resolved in their hearts not to eat unclean food. They chose to die rather than to be defiled by food or to profane the holy covenant; and they did die. Very great wrath came upon Israel.
>
> (1 Maccabees 1:62–64; cf. 2 Maccabees 6:7–7:42)

In this period, Jewish people resisted the decree of Antiochus Epiphanes IV, refusing to eat the unclean food in order to avoid defilement and keep their indigenous identity even though this entailed death. This theme of 1 Maccabees extended to the account of the Maccabean martyrs in the second book of Maccabees. Furthermore, the issue of food and defilement extends to the social relations between Jews and Gentiles strictly, as was prescribed in Torah and prophetic literatures.[40] For instance, the book of Jubilees shows that eating with Gentiles causes to pollute the identity of Jews because Gentiles eat unclean food that is offered to foreign gods and idols:

> Separate thyself from the nations, and eat not with them. And do not according to their works and become not their associate. For their works are unclean, and all their ways are a pollution and an abomination and uncleanness. They offer their sacrifices to the dead and they worship evil spirits, and they eat over the graves, and all their works are vanity and nothingness.
>
> (Jubilees 22:16–17)

By this point, one must realize that the food issue and the dietary law are an important touchstone for keeping Jewish identity.

These dietary laws and food issues as an identity marker are closely associated with the communal meal and feast in second temple Judaism. Namely, alongside the dietary laws, the matter of eating with whom and participation in the communal feast has a significant function for maintaining communal identity and cultural boundary. Most of all, commensality is closely associated with "covenant" in Israel's religious history.[41] The covenant is annually commemorated through the Passover feast in the first month of the year (Exodus 12:47). The Passover common meal not only celebrates the past deliverance of Israel, but also commemorates God's covenant and teaching (Exodus 12; 13:8–10), through which the Israelite expects the future salvation and unceasing relationship with God. Commensality in Jewish society functions to maintain the covenant with God and the communal identity. So, when people participate in a communal feast and share a table fellowship officially, it implicitly acknowledges that they are under the same covenant. Namely, the participation in a communal feast signifies the acceptance of common obligation in the covenant and sharing of the same identity.

For instance, in Jesus Ben Sira, eating and drinking together is described as symbolic of sexual love and marriage, which reflects covenantal relationship.[42] Sirach warns not to break marital relationship through having a meal with another's wife: "Never dine with another man's wife, nor revel with her at wine; lest your heart turn aside to her, and in blood you be plunged into destruction" (Sirach 9:9). Further, Sirach describes Israel's acceptance of God's wisdom and covenant in light of eating and drinking at the feast provided by God:

> He who holds to the law will obtain wisdom. She will come to meet him like a mother, and like the wife of his youth she will welcome him. She will feed him with the bread of understanding, and give him the water of wisdom to drink. (Sirach 15:1–3)

At this point, Gillian Feeley-Harnik argues that meal gathering in Jewish tradition provides some of the clearest examples to identify the parties (sects) to an agreement and confirm their common obligation in the covenant, which leads the parties in a common identity.[43]

Furthermore, the communal meal, which is implicitly associated with God's covenant, solidifies not just on the national identity but also on all the individual Israelites.[44] The significance of commensalism is exposed in Jewish sects during the second temple period, maintaining their own doctrinal perspective and identity through food and communal meal gathering. For instance, the Dead Sea Scrolls clearly show how the Qumran community manages the communal meal and organizes the meal system in order to sustain communal identity. Basically the Qumran community describes their life that "they shall eat in common and bless in common and deliberate in common" (1QS 6:2–3). As Philip Davies argues, eating and drinking together within the community (*Yahad*) does not have to be understood "as a gesture of fellowship, or indeed as a quasi-sacrificial act," but it functions as a physical control over what members eat and drink, through which the Qumran community maintains the integrity of the sectarian society and the actual boundary of the community.[45] The community set the regulation of exclusion from the meal for a specific time with a reason, through which the members were disciplined: "If one of them has lied deliberately in matters of property, he shall be excluded from the pure Meal of the Congregation for one year and shall do penance with respect to one quarter of his food" (IQS 6:24–25; cf. 1QS 7:15–20).

Namely, one of the punishments for several violations of community rules is exclusion from the meal for a stipulated time because violations were regarded as a source of ritual impurity. The meal at Qumran signifies the messianic banquet through which members of the Qumran community believed that it was living on the verge of the days to come (1QSa 2:11–22).[46] Schiffman sees that the communal meals at Qumran "were connected with the future expectation of community and stemmed from the deep messianic consciousness."[47] Exclusion from the communal meals means being deprived of the opportunity to enact in the present age the messianic banquet, which is the communal consciousness and future vision. It clearly presents that Qumran meals are explicitly cultic and their participants are consumed by the desire to remain in the boundary of community, avoiding any contagious impurity and excluding from the community. Even the prescription of the entrance of new members relates to one's coming into contact with the food and drink at the common meal of the community (1QS 6:13–23).[48] In this respect, the communal meals at Qumran themselves function to preserve the rule of community and to secure the boundary and the solidarity of community. Only members who follow the sectarian law could partake of the communal meals with their fellows at the same table in the Qumran community.

Thus, the commensality and the meal in Jewish sects function as a "boundary marker,"[49] setting the community apart from other groups.[50] The communal feast, banquet, or their specific foods in Jewish culture have an important function for intensifying group identities and for demarcating the ideological boundaries in second temple Judaism. All these socio-religious functions of food/meals derive from the historical experience of ancient Israel and its relevant conception of Jewish heritage, so I move to study Israel's social memory of bread and food in the next section.

Social Memories of Bread and Meals

MacDonald argues that memories are formed within communities through the commemorating process, and food is one of the ways in which communities structure communal identity, reflecting on the past.[51] Particular foods and festive ritual meals are the central means of remembering what God has done and the special relationship with God in Israel's history. Namely, meals contain certain foods, associated with particular seasons or historical events, as the Passover meal contains unleavened bread and paschal lamb associated with the Jewish historical experience of Exodus. The ritual act of eating solidifies people in a sense of common identity and connects them not only to past experience and present lives but also to the future vision through one's cognitive knowledge. Anthropologist David Sutton affirms:

> The role of food plays as a mnemonic for the passing of time and the seasonal cycles.… food is equally important in creating *prospective memories*, that is, in orienting people toward future memories that will be created in the consumption of food. What is notable here as well is the interdependence of ritualized memory and everyday memory in relation to food.[52]

The food is a vehicle for memories that are "important both as expressions of social relations and as constructions of identity," not only for the individual but also on the level of the community.[53]

The mnemonic images and conceptions of food and meals in Jewish culture derive from the historical experience of ancient Israel and its social memory. One of the most memorable events involving food issues in Jewish history is the Passover at the Exodus and its following event of God's provision of food, *manna* and *quail.* Also one of the most significant pilgrim festive meals that most Jewish people strictly observed was the Passover; even after the destruction of the Temple, the ritual process of Passover and its theological discourse were kept at home and continued to serve as a means of preserving Jewish religious cultural identity in Rabbinic Judaism.[54]

In this section, I investigate sources of social memory of food/bread and meals, tracing back to the crucial experience of food in ancient Israel's history and its description of the biblical heritage. I specifically concentrate on Passover, manna, messianic banquet, the relationship between the bread and the word of God, and other descriptions of the symbolic action, "the breaking of bread," while paying special attention to the mnemonic image of bread and its theological discourse.

Passover Meal with Unleavened Bread

Unleavened Bread and Passover

In the Hebrew Bible tradition, bread was a special symbol in relation to God and the formation of Israel's socio-religious identity. Bread clearly appears with the festive meal of Passover in the book of Exodus where God instructs the Israelites to eat special foods prior to their departure from Egypt. In the book of Exodus, chapters 12 and 13 describe how the Israelite has been instructed by God for the night before the actual exodus and the ritualizing procedure for remembrance of this experience. When God informed Moses that, in the tenth plague, God would slaughter the firstborn and firstlings of Egypt and lead the Israelites out of Egypt, the Passover regulations were given to Moses:

> They shall take some of the blood and put it on the two doorposts and the lintel of the houses in which they eat it. They shall eat the lamb that same night; they shall eat it roasted over the fire with **the unleavened bread** and bitter herbs. (Exodus 12:7–8)

Pesah, which is Passover sacrifice, must be slain and its blood was smeared on the outside of the doorposts and lintel. And a family has gathered and eaten the lamb as roasted over the fire with the unleavened bread. Here, the blood has "an apotropaic function,"[55] when the Egyptian firstborn and firstlings were slain. Then, the Israelites were begged to leave quickly out of Egypt, and they took unleavened bread at night in haste. This is because they had not enough time to allow the dough to knead and ferment in their hasty exodus out of their enslavement in the land of Egypt.

In two chapters of Exodus, 12 and 13, one can see repetitious descriptions of Passover regulation, so one can divide two chapters into 3 parts in light of each separate description of Passover.

A 12:1–13—God's instruction to Moses
A1 12:14–20—Instruction for celebrating Passover as a ritual
A2 12:21–23—Moses' transmission to the elders of Israel

C 12:24–28—Moses' instruction for Ritualization[56]

B 12:29–32—The Tenth Plague
B1 12:33–42—Real Exodus

C1 12:43–49—God's another instruction of Passover
C2 13:3–10—The Festival of Unleavened Bread

Group **A** contains a pre-Exodus Passover instruction and God's instruction for celebrating Passover as a perpetual ordinance. Group **B** is a scene of real Exodus, which actively shows Israelites baked unleavened bread of the dough and clearly explains the reason for unleavened bread: "they were driven out of Egypt and could not wait, nor had they prepared any provisions for themselves" (12:39). Group **C** as post-Exodus Passover direction shows the developed version of Passover ritual, especially regarding the regulation on ritual cleanness for the participants, and the feast of unleavened bread.

The Exodus accounts associate the Passover and its paschal lamb, referring to God's passing over the house of Israel, with the festival of unleavened bread more concretely when Moses instructs the leaders of the Israelites. Although God's first direction in **A** briefly describes the consumption of roasted lamb with unleavened bread at the eve of exodus, **A** and **B**, real exodus, do not reveal its association with the feast of unleavened bread. However, in **A1**, **A2** and in **C1**, **C2**, the instruction of Passover as a perpetual ordinance clearly describes the regulation of the festival of unleavened bread.[57]

> Seven days you shall eat unleavened bread; on the first day you shall remove leaven from your houses, for whoever eats leavened bread from the first day until the seventh day shall be cut off from Israel....you shall observe the festival of unleavened bread, for on this very day I brought your companies out of the land of Egypt... (Exodus 12:15, 17)

Many scholars have debated on the existence of two separate festivals that may have existed even before the exodus from Egypt, tracing their independent origins and discovering how they have been combined later in the Bible.[58] Some scholars such as Cernea and Segal argue that the patriarch Abraham already observed the Paschal sacrifice well before Israel's exodus.[59] Cernea insists that certain actions could have existed prior to a certain event in social history; and it became "the means through which new ideas crucial to the definition of the community."[60] In this view, the spring festival for the protective paschal celebrations of transient breeders combined with the agricultural first-fruit festival of the unleavened bread, while applying into the idea of the Exodus, which was the crucial event for the formation of Israel's communal identity. This chapter will not explore this scholarly debate further, especially concentrating on the significant role of the un-leavened bread on the Israelites' experience of the Exodus. What I want to high-light on the Passover is that the origin of Passover was combined with two crucial entities: the paschal sacrifice and the feast of Unleavened Bread. Namely, from the beginning of the Passover legend, not only does the biblical account contain the eating of roasted paschal lamb with the unleavened bread, which symbolically represents the urgent situation of the exodus; but also the role of the unleavened bread is reinforced in the process of ritualization of Passover festival as a perpetual ordinance. Thus, the unleavened bread can be recognized as a symbolic source of the formation of Israel's identity.

Ritualization: *Maintaining Identity*

In Exodus 12 and 13, God commanded all Israel to keep Passover as "a day of re-membrance" (12:14) throughout the generations. The scripture uses the verb זכר, 'to remember' (12:14; 13:3), by which the Israelites are usually reminded of God's redemptive works and through which a people forms the foundation of historical memory and communal identity. "Biblical memory recalls the past in order to influence the present."[61] When a specific event is celebrated repeatedly as a per-manent ordinance, not only does it function to renew the mnemonic tradition through the generations, but it also actualizes its meaning and historical motif in participants' minds psychologically.[62] So Childs argues "a real event [of exodus] occurred as the moment of redemptive time from the past initiated a genuine en-counter in the present"[63] Spaulding observes the function of commemoration in the methodology for her research on Jewish social memory and states:

> The past becomes immanent in the present, not merely something to be remembered in thought alone, but to be enacted and lived. This produces a personal identification with the collective past as well as with those of the collective present who are also participating in the commemoration.[64]

Thus, as Paul Ricoeur argues, making a repetitive ritual and a textual record are linked with the formation of communal identity and group memories.[65] From this perspective, the Passover event and the process of its ritualization must reveal the socio-political role that embodies the social identity of Jew and maintains communal identity through the generations, while consuming the Paschal lamb and unleavened bread together in Jewish culture.

In the book of Exodus, chapters 12 and 13 cover not only the Passover event and its instruction but also the establishment of the Passover ritual as a permanent institution. In 12:14, God instructs the Israelites to keep Passover as a "festival to the Lord" throughout the generations, observing it as "a perpetual ordinance" with unleavened bread for the remembrance of God who delivered Israel from Egypt. The book of Exodus makes the reason for this ritual clear with the inquiry of children: "what do you mean by this observance?" and answers that:

> "It is the Passover sacrifice to the Lord, *for he passed over the houses of the Israelites in Egypt,* when he struck down the Egyptians but spared our houses" (12:27)

And the very next chapter presents another motif of the observance of the feast of unleavened bread and another regulation of the consecration of the firstborn (13:11–16) in the frame of answering children:

> "You shall tell your child on that day, 'It is because of *what the Lord did for me* when I came out of Egypt" (13:8)

> "You shall answer, 'by *strength of hand the Lord brought us out of Egypt,* from the house of slavery. When Pharaoh stubbornly refused to let us go, the Lord killed all the firstborn in the land of Egypt, from human firstborn to the firstborn of animals" (13:14–15)

These passages clearly show that all the reasons for eating Paschal lamb and unleavened bread throughout the generations are about the remembrance of what the Lord did for the Israel when they came out of Egypt. Passover as a permanent ritual exhibits an intrinsic attribute of God in the relationship with Israel such as God's favor, protection, or bounty toward Israelites.[66] Furthermore, the observance of it as a ritual serves the function of carving the historical experience of the ancestors into the spiritual mind and heart of all descendents of Israel. Exodus says all the commemorating process "shall serve for you as a sign on your hand and as a reminder on your forehead, so that the teaching of the Lord may be on your lips… You shall keep this ordinance at its proper time from year to year" (13:9–10). In this respect, one realizes that in the book of Exodus the Israelites firmly establish the rite of Passover with unleavened bread, and the ritual functions as a means of formatting their self-understanding in the relationship with God and of maintaining their communal identity.

Other documents in the Old Testament show that the ritual ceremony is to be observed annually, be developed by the cultural context, and functioned to maintain Jewish socio-religious identity. Leviticus 23:4–8, in a list of the appointed festivals, presents the Passover offering and the seven-days festival of unleavened bread on the fourteenth day of the first month. The book of Numbers 9:1–15; 28:16–25 lists sacrificial festivals with concrete instruction: the Passover offering and the feast of unleavened bread. Obviously, Passover ritual with the unleavened bread became a major part of Israelites' spiritual life. Each post-exodus text shows a developed version of Passover instructions. Passover ritual is not only concretely associated with the feast of unleavened bread but also highlights more on the role of seven days of restriction of leavened bread. On the other side, the instruction of the paschal lamb and the specific way in which the blood was manipulated is weakened.[67] The book of Numbers adds a prescription on the participants of the rituals, concerning the ritual impurity or physical distance from unclean-ness (9:9–11) and the various burnt offerings (28:17–25). Furthermore, Numbers warns the Israelites about the possibility of excommunication from the community as a penalty:

> "But anyone who is clean and is not on a journey, and yet refrains from keeping the Passover, shall be cut off from the people for not presenting the Lord's offering at its appointed time; such a one shall bear the consequences for the sin"
>
> (Number 9:13)

During the whole journey through the wilderness to the Promised Land in the wilderness, Israelites keep the Passover rites as well as the eating of unleavened bread. Specifically, they circumcise all the people who came out of Egypt (Joshua 5:1–9), and then they are eligible to partake of the Passover rite and the eating of unleavened bread, right after crossing over the Jordan River and having crops in the land of Canaan (Joshua 5:10–12).

Deuteronomy 16:1–8 reviews the Passover ritual, associating the unleavened bread with the haste of the exodus. Deuteronomy concentrates more on the seven days of unleavened bread than the Passover offering. J. B. Segal argues that Deuteronomy 16 treats the paschal sacrifice as "the opening ceremony" of the week restricted to the unleavened bread.[68] Furthermore, Deuteronomy locates the Passover rites in the special place, which "God will choose" (v. 7). This place is probably a public sanctuary or a shrine. The Passover ritual was prescribed as a family gathering and a domestic ritual celebration in the previous documents, however, Deuteronomy clearly changes the character of this ritual by appointing a specific location beyond the domestic area. According to Bokser, the Deuteronomist demonstrates that the Passover rite has been upgraded to the part of a "national gathering- though families might celebrate together in that central location."[69]

The Passover rite including the unleavened bread comes to have a significant role at the official national level, forming and maintaining the identity of the Israelites. In a later book, 2 Kings 23:21–24, Josiah reforms and re-prescribes the Passover rite, which has not been performed properly.[70] Josiah commands all the people to keep the Passover rite to the Lord in Jerusalem (v. 23). Namely, Josiah officially claims the domestic rite of Passover as a national ritual, which opens a new phase in the history of the festival.[71] 2 Chronicles 35:1–19 elaborates more on the shifted version of Josiah's Passover, in which Josiah appoints the priests and Levites to a certain role in performing the Passover ritual together with the seven days of unleavened bread. The Passover rite begins to be supported by the kingship and religious authorities. The Passover in Jerusalem as national ritual is described more concretely in 2 Chronicles 30:1–27, in which King Hezekiah proclaims a decree for people from all over the country gather in Jerusalem in order to "keep the Passover to the Lord the God of Israel, at Jerusalem" (v. 5). So, a lot of people gather at Jerusalem, eat the Passover offerings (vv. 15–20), and observe the festival of unleavened bread (v. 13, 21). Both the 2 Kings and the 2 Chronicles accounts demonstrates that the Passover rite has been upgraded to a national ritual, which is centralized in Jerusalem.[72]

From all these accounts, the Passover event and the process of its ritualization are not just presenting Jewish cultural history; but rather they exhibit that the social memory of the unleavened bread and its ritual meal function to embody the socio-religious identity of Israel within an indigenous historical perception of God and maintain their communal identity through the generations.

New Year: *New Beginning*

The unleavened bread with Passover signifies a new beginning of the freed-life under God's complete care out of the bondage of Egypt. As a basic motif of forming a primitive Jewish identity, the Passover rite and the unleavened bread have a significant meaning: *New beginning of life with God.*

When the first Passover was instituted by God's commandment, the book of Exodus clearly states, "this month shall mark for you the beginning of months; it shall be the first month of the year for you" (Exodus 12:2). This means that the month containing Passover must be "the head of months of year," which discerns a "qualitative distinction"[73] that clearly exhibits the line of demarcation between two qualitatively different entities by the terms "before" and "after." The month with Passover must be a moment of the New Year (season) or New Beginning. The Scripture implicitly demarcates a new beginning of the history of the Israelite from the moment that all Israelites experienced God's redemptive work at the exodus. Furthermore, it could be a moment of creation of a calendar. Nahum M. Sarna argues that the Priestly writer ignores the measure of months until Exodus 12, and the calendar by month was not instituted in Genesis,[74] so this is the establishing moment of a new calendar. According to William Propp, the implication may be applied for the completion of the unfinished creation through the birth of the Israelite nation, freed from Egypt, and "the concomitant establishment of a calendar."[75] The new beginning of Israel by creating a calendar entails an implicit proclamation of God's sovereign power over Israel, which has signaled the end of Pharaoh's reign.

Many scholars agree that the Passover is a New Year festival that was held in the spring. The first month of the year is obviously in the spring. All Pentateuchal festivals with unleavened bread begin in the spring (Exodus 23:14–16; 34:18–22; Leviticus 23; Number 28:16–29; 39; Deuteronomy 16).[76] J. B. Segal compares the aspects of Passover with the general pattern of New Year festivals in the Near East, even with the primitive culture of Canaan.[77] Then he argues that many aspects of Passover are peculiar to the spring festival, even within the frame of the Israelite religion. This means that Passover as a ritual "conform[s] fully to the spirit and practice of that annual turning-point in the life of the people."[78]

In this point, the Passover ritual has some special metaphoric meaning for the Jewish community as a special turning point or creating moment in their lives. One of the interesting features of ancient New Year festivals in the Near East, according to Segal, is the recitation of epics of world creation.[79] The association of the New Year festivals with Creation in ancient times shows how ancient people endow a special meaning on the New Year festival and what they believed and invoked a fertility at the destinies of new beginning. Segal argues that the recital practice of the creation epics at the New Year was an old custom among the Israelites.[80] The cycle of reading Torah, which begins with the story of Creation, is parallel to the annual cycle, so the recital of epics of Creation at the New Year implicitly reflects the new birth of something. Israelites read the Torah publicly "every seventh year" as a schedule for remission and atonement (Deuteronomy 31:9–13), and they read the Torah publicly again when they began new life with the reconstruction of the Temple after the exile (Nehemiah 8:1–3, 9). Ezra 6:19–22 briefly mentions Passover and the feast of unleavened bread when Israelites were returned to their original land from exile. It was indeed a new phase of the history of Israel, re-creating a community, so the Passover celebration, associated with the creation theme, functions as a demarcation of the beginning of a new phase of history at the dedication of the reconstructed temple.

Ruth Fredman Cernea sees Exodus serving as a "creation myth" of the Jews, forming a new community.[81] As the creation story in Genesis concerns the coming into being of a physical universe and humanity, the story in Exodus represents a new physical status of Israelite, coming out of the slavery in Egypt and creates a new communal relationship with God, which can be a basic source of self-definition for Jews as a community.[82] In the book of Genesis, there is an absolute separation and distinction between nothing and something created. Likewise, Exodus shows clear distinction between absolute slavery in Egypt and absolute freedom in the Promised Land in light of the creation of a new society. All these creating moments are commemorated by the Passover ritual and the unleavened bread. From this perspective, the ritual of Passover with unleavened bread not only signifies the destruction of the first born of Egypt and the dramatic escape from Egypt, but it also represents the new-born of Israel and the beginning of their new relationship with God in which Israelites find the motif of their self-identity as a community.

Manna: Bread from Heaven

Bread from Heaven

Right after the escape from oppression in Egypt, during the journey through the Sinai Peninsula, the Israelites realized that they encountered enormous problems securing existence in the wilderness as an autonomous community. While remembering the stable life with plenty of food in Egypt, they were starving and in desperate need of food. For instance, the Israelites had a concern about how they could secure the food for daily survival and how they could survive without an internal or external order of community and communal identity. When the Israelites complained to Moses, leading them out of Egypt, God performed a miracle to feed all the Israelites by providing *manna* in the morning and *quail* in the evening. Moses tells the Israelites, "it is the bread which the Lord has given you to eat" (Exodus 16:15). Although God provided the appropriate food to the Israelites in the wilderness, the wilderness experience itself shows Israel's struggles to survive and find the appropriate life-giving source. Furthermore, the life in the wilderness shows Israel's efforts for enabling and maintaining socio-political and religious integrity,[83] but it also implicitly reveals the process of the forming of a communal identity as an autonomous community.

The manna has a significant role in integrating Israel's historical perception and identity. The book of Exodus describes manna as the "bread from heaven" (16:4; cf. Psalms 78:24) that God has provided. The Israelites name it manna when they are asking about what it is in v. 15.[84] Every time Moses explains about manna, he calls it the "bread from heaven." Manna is described as "a fine flaky substance, as fine as frost on the ground" (v. 14) and is like a coriander seed, white, and the taste of wafers made with honey (v. 31). This can be baked or boiled to eat. Some scholars see manna as natural phenomena, such as gum resin from tamarisk tree or the scale of insects from tree.[85] The most interesting point however is that no matter what the real manna was, in the Israelites' commemorative remembrance, not only were there various ways to cook and make bread, but also the Israelites recognized it as bread coming down from heaven. In Numbers 11:8, the taste of manna is like "cakes baked with oil." In other documents, the Psalmist also describes that God rained down upon the Israelites "the grain of heaven" and "bread of angels" (Psalm 78:24–25; 105:40). In the experience of the Israelites and their religious cognition, manna is bread, a basic life-giving resource given by God from above, no matter whether it was associated with the lofty trees. *Manna* only was commemorated for the nourishment of divine being and God's sustaining presence, complete care for forty years in the wilderness.

Manna, the bread from heaven has a significant role in mediating between God and Israel and in representing God's complete presence in the lives of the Israelites, through which the Israelites establishes a communal identity. As Passover and the unleavened bread reminds the Israelites of the God who liberates them out of Egypt, the bread from heaven is associated with the God who provides a life-giving resource, manna in the wilderness. Both breads can be a mediating source, which can lead the Israelite into commemorating what God has done and who God is for him/her. Manna possibly represented a continuation of the unleavened bread.[86] Manna, the bread from heaven replaces Israel's not enough hasty unleavened bread in the wilderness. Then, the day after the manna ceases, Israel celebrates the festival of unleavened bread under the leadership of Joshua (Joshua 5:11–12). Both are bread that signifies a God who liberates, provides, sustains, and is with the Israelite in the wilderness.

God's Complete Care

The anxiety of unsecured life and survival in the wilderness is exposed by the Israelites' complaints. The Old Testament (Exodus and Numbers) brings God's complete care for Israel's fears and complaints into relief, and draws the Israelite into a special relationship with God. Here *manna,* the bread from heaven, has a significant role as a mediating source between God and Israel and as a representation of God's complete presence in the lives of the Israelites, through which Israel established a communal identity. The fear of the Israelites and the outcry of people are expressed by frequent, repetitious usage of the word, "complain" in the book of Exodus 16:1–12.[87] A certain section in the book of Exodus, 15:22–18:27 is interwoven with the theme of *complaint/answer.*[88] Carol Meyers sees this section as setting forth the crises and resolution in light of physical and cultural survival in the wilderness.[89] While the Israelites keep complaining to Moses in reminiscence of the fullness of Egypt, God faithfully responds to their murmuring with the miraculous resolution and the provision of food. God is indeed sustaining the Israelites in the wilderness.

In Exodus 16:1–12, as a center of the interwoven repetitious theme of *complaint/answer*, Israelites murmur about the lack of bread, which is the most important resource in their daily lives: "The whole congregation of the Israelites complained against Moses and Aaron" (vv. 2–3). Moses and his freedom-giving leadership is the object of people's protest:[90] "for you have brought us out into this wilderness to kill this whole assembly with hunger" (v. 3). The Israelites are murmuring against Moses who brought them out of Egypt into landless crisis; however, this biblical account states that God understands these complaints to have been directed toward God, not to Moses and Aaron.[91] The complaints are almost never followed immediately by God's response,[92] because Moses has his role as a transmitter between God and the Israelites; however, God's answer not only clearly reveals God as the only objective reality of the theme of *complaint/ resolution*, but it also implicitly draws the Israelite into a direct relationship and trust in God. The Scripture brings the main issue to the surface of the narrative: God must be the object of complaints. Exodus 16:1–12 repeatedly reminds the readers that God is their only liberating and sustaining resource, working through and behind Moses. So, verses 1–12 repeatedly call to mind God's presence:

> "In the evening you shall know that it was the Lord who brought you out of the land of Egypt" (v. 6)
>
> "in the morning you shall see the glory of the Lord." (v. 7)
>
> "because the Lord has heard the complaining that you utter against him" (v. 8)
>
> "Draw near to the Lord, for he has heard your complaining" (v. 9)
>
> "the glory of the Lord appeared in the cloud." (v. 10)
>
> "then you shall know that I am the Lord your God" (v. 12)

Through the thematic repetition of complaints/resolutions, God establishes a new direct relationship with the Israelite, with which the Israelites can form a communal identity and sustain a community autonomously. The biblical account highlights God's presence and God's complete care in every moment of the Israelites' journey through the wilderness, so the account of Israel's experience of manna, the bread from heaven, as a continual sign of God's presence and complete care, is not just a miracle story but a significant fuse for establishing a new close relationship between God and the Israelites. As Bruckner states, God used Israel's error of complaining faith to invite them to "draw near" (v. 9) to see and know that God is the real actor providing real life-giving substance (v. 12)[93] and to realize that a new relationship has begun. The fullness of life in Egypt, provided by the bondage of Pharaoh, is replaced by the bread from heaven provided by God who sets them free and takes complete care of every step of the Israelites, even in the landless life in the wilderness.[94]

Forming legitimate rules and commemorative ritualization beings to firm the new relationship. As the experience of the water crisis, Marah (15:22–27), God testes the Israelite with concrete instruction about manna (16:13–20); taking an *omer* for each person and each day. On the sixth day they can gather twice as much, and on the seventh day as the Sabbath, no manna will come down. The test becomes "the vehicle for the introduction of a community observance,"[95] and this is the first place to present the legend for Sabbath in the Bible. The seventh day is proclaimed as a "day of solemn rest, a holy Sabbath to the Lord" (v. 23). God is inviting the Israelite into direct relationship through the test. Observing God's instruction on Sabbath, the Israelite participates in God's sovereignty and creating authority. As God's creation comes from chaos (Genesis 1:2) to Sabbath (Genesis 2:1–4), God's creating authority brings the Israelite from a chaotic life in Egypt and wilderness to the place in which God's complete care and nourishment are given.[96]

Furthermore, the Israelites keep a secure relationship with God and their communal identity as an autonomous entity through the observance of God's instruction and the commemoration of manna. The description of manna in Exodus 16 shows the way of using manna as a commemorative ritual (vv. 33–34) like Passover.

> "Take a Jar, and put an *omer* of manna in it, and place it before the Lord, to be kept throughout your generations." (v. 33)

The manna jar is probably placed in a shrine, and it is for future generations to see. Although the manna jar has not survived throughout history, it was a visible memorial to the manifestation of God's presence and complete care in the history of Israel (v. 32). When they are in a place of poverty, disease, and the crisis of death in wilderness, God is there, having a special relationship with the Israelites, sustaining them and providing full life-giving resource. Thus, the commemoration of manna serves as a means of reminder, not only of God's instruction and relationship, but also of established communal identity as an autonomous nation throughout the history of Israel.

God who Provides Food: *Nursing Imagery*

The usage of food, particularly bread, and its image in the Bible are strongly related to the image of God's provision. In both Jewish and Christian tradition, the central metaphoric concept of food is based on the story of God's provision of manna and quail to Israel in Exodus 16 and Numbers 11. Israel's experience of manna and quail in the wilderness not only presents a special relationship between God and Israel, but it also reveals how Israelites understand and imagine the attributes of God in their relationship. As mentioned above, many occasions in the book of Exodus place God's instruction in the test that makes the Israelites recognize the presence of God who brought them out of Egypt. The act of God's provision of food firms up the identity of the relationship between God and Israel. In this regard, the biblical narratives in Exodus 16 and Numbers 11 and its later interpretation of manna are not just a miraculous story or historical legend, but these become the essential symbolic image of God and a basic source of communal identity. Furthermore, throughout the process of commemoration of the manna, the bread itself is a metaphor for God who provides life-giving source.

Most of all, the metaphor of God-given bread exhibits nursing imagery of a mother and provides a description of God's complete care in the wilderness,[97] in light of the relationship between mother and baby. God's provision of food to Israel in the wilderness expresses Israel's understanding of their special relationship with God, which clearly forms Israel's religious imagination. The relationship between God and Israel is based on the metaphor of God as mother who feeds and Israel as a baby who completely relies on the mother. A baby drinks and takes his or her nutritional needs from the mother's breast. Likewise, Israel has enough manna to eat in the wilderness every day from God's favor (Numbers 11:1–15; Exodus 16:1–36). Based on this understanding, Claassens affirms, "the metaphor of a mother nursing her baby provided a fitting description of God's complete care in the wilderness."[98]

From this perspective, one can find a feminine image of God in the Old Testament. A female metaphor of nursing to describe God's care clearly appears in the book of Numbers 11:1–15. In this narrative, one of the interesting points is that the people in need of food complain and cry out, not directly to God, but to God's appointed leader, Moses. The people's dissatisfaction with food and complaints lead Moses to ask a question about his own role as a leader in vv. 10–13. The narrator effectively draws the reader's attention to the role of leader and the role of God. Moses strongly appeals to God:

> "Did I conceive all this people? Did I give birth to them, that you should say to me, 'Carry them in your bosom, as a nurse carries a sucking child to the land that you promised on oath to their ancestors? Where am I to get meat to give to all this people?" (vv. 12–13)

One can easily see in Moses' appealing question that the two themes, *food* and *the role of leader*, are intertwined throughout the passages.[99]

Another interesting point is that the narrator uses a maternal image and the female metaphor of nursing in Moses' appealing questions. In a series of rhetorical questions, the narrator uses the feminine metaphoric terms, "conceived" (הרה), "give birth" (ילד), "nurse" (האמן), "suckling" (הינק), and "bosom" (חנק). These terms cause the reader to imagine that the role of leader in this context is based on the maternal image. Of course, the verb, "nurse" (האמן) can be problematic because it is masculine in its form; however, this verb directly links with "sucking child" and the context in the previous line, "did I conceive all this people?" so that the nurse has to be understood as feminine.[100] From this point, Moses sees his given role as the substitute mother or nurse for God's children; however, he is denying this role as the substitute mother with strong appeal to God. Moses is realizing that he is not able to feed them by himself, and he is complaining that God is not fulfilling his duties as mother, so his rhetorical question indirectly urges God to step in and fulfill God's maternal duties as the real mother by providing food and care.[101] Namely, Moses is complaining that this is not his job, but God's. Ultimately, God takes his duty and fulfills the function as a mother, providing sufficient food. Claassens affirms that this passage in the book of Numbers describes "God as the one who functions as a mother and the one who nurses Israel by providing food enough for each day."[102] God appears as a mother, described by the female metaphor of nursing, and God's provision of manna for the life of the Israelites in the wilderness can be regarded as a maternal duty of God.

God's maternal image is also found in Deuteronomy 32:7–14, which presents the evidence of God's caring fidelity toward Israel. This passage is dominated by a rich series of verbs with God as active subject: fixed, sustained, shielded, cared, fed, guided, set, nursed–all are applied to Israel's well-being in the wilderness.[103] In v. 13, "[God] nursed him with honey from the crags, with oil from flinty rock." In this passages, the verb, "ינק" means nurse or suckling an infant at mother's breast again. The verb "nurse ינק" is the same in Numbers 11:12, "suckling child," which represents God's maternal metaphor of nursing that I mentioned above. It is also same with the verb "nurse, ינק" in Exodus 2:9: "Pharaoh's daughter said to her, 'take this child and *nurse* it for me.'" In this point, Deuteronomy 32:13–14 describes God's caring fidelity with the maternal metaphor of nursing.

In the wilderness, Israel was not able to secure their daily life and future. The only way to live was to trust God fully for each day's food, totally relying on God, as a baby has to be reliant on the mother. A female metaphor of a mother nursing her child is a fitting illustration to understand Israel's religious imaginations of God who provides manna every day in the wilderness. Numbers 11 and Deuteronomy 32 not only represent the feminine image of God as a mother, but also give the reader a crucial hint to interpret and understand the history of God's provision of food in light of the maternal image of God who nurses and feeds as mother. Although some of the other texts referring to God's provision do not use a feminine lexical form, the reader can apply the maternal duties of a God who feeds and nurses to those texts, so when God provides manna and quail (Numbers 15:1–11; Exodus 16:1–36) in the wilderness, it can be understood that God is taking his duty and fulfilling the function of mother of Israel.

From this perspective, the metaphor of God's provision does not exhibit just nourishment for God's people, but it represents the formation of communal identity through food, particularly the bread God provides in the light of intimate relationship. The experience of God's care through the bread and God's provision in the wilderness became the foundation of the self-identity of the Israelites. In this regard, the bread can be a germinator of the formatting process of Israel's identity.[104] For instance, whenever the Israelites celebrate the Passover meal with unleavened bread, they remember their own experience in Egypt, Sinai, and the wilderness, which created their communal identity and united them into one community. The principle of the Passover meal plays an important role in shaping and maintaining Israel as one community.[105] The matter of whether one observes the Passover meal or not, and whether one knows about the bread or not, could be criteria of exclusion and inclusion in community. This means that the bread and the image of God who feeds reveal a metaphoric function of building socio-religious identity in people's self-consciousness and communal identity.

The Breaking of Bread in Human Relationship

With the conception of God's provision and human dependence on God, bread is used to show hospitality and share a meal with the other in the Bible, especially when it is used with the symbolic action of "the breaking of bread."[106] The action of "the breaking of bread" represents three meanings in a social perspective: *the end of hostility, making a covenant, and the formation of community.* First of all, in the Middle East, "the breaking of bread," referring to the sharing of a meal (Exodus 2:20), with one's former enemy is an important symbol of the end of hostilities.[107] Basically, the sharing of bread signifies the provision of hospitality for the other, in which one can break any hostile boundaries and form a welcoming atmosphere in the nature of the relationship. For instance, in Genesis Abraham ran out from the tent entrance to serve the messengers and said:

> My Lord, if I find favor with you, do not pass by your servant. Let a little water be brought, and wash your feet, and rest yourselves under the tree. Let me bring a little bread, that you may refresh your selves, and after that you may pass on–since you have come to your servant. (Genesis 18:2–5)

In the account of Sodom and Gomorrah, the hospitality of serving a meal and bread is highlighted by Abraham's interaction with the angelic figures who announce the birth of Isaac. Abraham convinces his visitors to stay not in the town square as they intended but in his house, and he serves a feast: "he made them a feast, and baked unleavened bread, and they ate" (19:1–3). Here the alacrity with which Abraham responded to the needs of his guests by serving a feast and sharing bread was to link the characteristic of warm hospitality to the patriarch and to his descendents.[108]

After Isaac negotiated with Abimelech over ownership of the wells at Beersheba, he said, "You will do us no harm, just as we have not touched you and have done to you nothing but good and have sent you away in peace. You are now the blessed of the Lord," (Gen 26:29) and Isaac made them a feast and they ate and drank together (v. 29). The festive meal with old family rival Abimelech functions as a sign of reconciliation after their quarrel over the use of the well. Namely, the sharing of a meal together signifies the termination of the hostile relationship and the belonging together in same peace (v. 29, 31); and hostility, antagonism, and any boundaries disappear through the breaking of bread and the sharing of a meal.

Second, sharing one's own bread with others also occurs when one makes a new covenant.[109] Through the breaking of bread and sharing a meal, people on different sides put themselves together under the same rules and contracts. In the book of Genesis, the festive meal sharing precedes the actual swearing of the oath when Isaac makes reconciliation with Abimelech (Genesis 26:28). Interestingly, the ultimate object of the meal is similar to the meal that Jacob and Laban observed when they took their swearing oath with the meal (Genesis 31:46, 54). Victor Hamilton argues that the meal is not simply for reconciliation but "an integral element of the covenant-making process, in which, in a sense, the individual offering the meal admits the other individual" into a covenantal relationship.[110] Genesis describes the scenes at the moment of swearing:

> Jacob swore by the fear of his father Isaac, and Jacob offered a sacrifice on the height and called his kinsfolk to eat bread; and they ate bread and tarried all night in the hill country. (Genesis 31:54)

They eat the bread together as a sign of making a covenant between them. Furthermore, when Joshua sees the bread of the others and shares their bread, he "made peace with them, and made a covenant with them" (Joshua 9:15). Strangers want to make a treaty with Israel while saying:

> Here is our bread; it was still warm when we took it from our houses as our food for the journey, on the day we set out to come to you, but now, see, it is dry and moldy. (Joshua 9:12)

The sharing bread and partaking of others' provision signify the establishment of a new covenant and treaty in the nature of the relationship between two parties. Obviously, making a covenant means the removal of any hostile boundaries that existed before and the creation of a good relationship under the same legal boundaries. Eating together in the breaking of bread is a symbol of belonging together, and the breaking of bread is a significant symbolic action for the initial step for making a new covenant.

Third, the breaking of bread not only signified, but also actualized the formation of community.[111] The formation of Israel's religious identity derives from the experience in the wilderness in Exodus, through which Israelites realized complete dependence on God and have a covenantal relationship with God.[112] Israel's life in the wilderness represents how Israel perceives God and how they understand themselves as a community under God's complete care.[113] The life in the wilderness is mainly celebrated by a group meal, the Passover feast, and the remembrance of God's provision of manna, so the bread, especially the unleavened bread and the bread from heaven (manna), are significant substances for reflecting Israel's communal identity. Actually, in the Jewish community, the breaking of bread, referring to sharing a meal in the Passover feast or other rituals, not only commemorates God's liberating power, complete care, the provision of life-giving source, and the covenantal relationship, but also creates the community and maintains its communal identity. Through the commemorating process, the bread consistently carries the semiotic value of the community of Israel and the metaphorical and symbolic significance of the foundation of Jewish community.

Thus, sharing a meal and its symbolic action, the breaking of bread is exclusive in that any foreigner or uncircumcised person cannot be allowed to participate. This is because the breaking of bread is not just sharing in a performance, but a symbolic act of formation of community and its identity. Therefore, if one shares the bread, which has a special meaning of the past, one would share the identity and be included symbolically. In this perspective, the breaking of bread signifies the openness of the community instead of exclusiveness,[114] if it happens. The meaning of "the breaking of bread" and sharing a meal represent breaking any hostile boundaries and social barriers symbolically.

Messianic Banquet

God Will Provide Again

One of the remarkable features of the metaphorical usage of food or communal meal in Jewish tradition is the description of the so-called messianic banquet.[115] The term messianic banquet normally refers to a divine festive meal to signify an eschatological vision;[116] and its motif is associated with apocalyptic tradition, which was widely dispersed throughout prophetic literatures and second temple Judaism. Dennis Smith argues that the apocalyptic motif in the messianic banquet originates in mythological heritage from the ancient Near East in light of the numinous quality of symbolic foods.[117] For instance, as the "tree of life," signifies special life-giving qualities (Genesis 2:9),[118] the messianic banquet in apocalyptic literatures utilizes the image of numinous foods, such as water, wine, bread, fish, and the like, and their provision in order to represent the gift of eternal life at the end of times.[119] As was stated, the bread from heaven, manna, as a divine substance is associated with the symbol for the provision of God for maintaining the life and the new stage of life.[120]

Most of all, the description of the messianic banquet signifies the restoration of Israel and associates it with the metaphor of God's provision. While the memory of God's provision in the wilderness forms Israel's religious imagination and communal identity, the famine in Israel's experience is associated with God's ceasing to feed and signifies the judgment of God. (e.g., Joel 2:12–17; Amos 4:6–12). In line with this, Claassens argues that the eschatological metaphor of God's renewed provision of life-giving source not only reveals the restoration and renewal of all creation but also signifies the redemption of the Israelites and the hope that God will change Israel's immediate future.[121] In this vision, the messiah is deemed to be appearing as a protagonist who provides numinous food again.

In fact, several prophetic texts use the metaphor of God's provision of food as a symbol of restoration. For instance, in the book of Jeremiah 31:1–14, the prophet proclaims the word of God about the vision of the deliverance of Judah with a description of God's provision of "the grain, the wine, and the oil" and newborn flock (Jeremiah 31:12). In Joel 2:1–27,[122] in response to Israel's laments, God shows his pity on Israel and promises to send them grain, wine, and oil (vv. 18–19), which signifies the restoration of God's people. These prophetic passages of Israel's restoration clearly express that God is the explicit subject of the restoration (e.g., Jeremiah 29:14; 30:3; Ezekiel 16:53; 37:22–28; Amos 9:13–15), providing life-giving resources and transforming their life of famine to a life where they are fruitful and satisfied.

God's provision of food as a symbol of restoration inevitably leads the Israelites into their commemorative image of the presence of God, who liberated and nursed them in the wilderness (e.g., Exodus 16; Numbers 11). 2 Baruch 29:8 envisions a new manna, saying "it shall come to pass at that self-same time that the treasury of manna shall again descend from on high, and they will eat of it in those years, because these are they who have come to the consummation of time."[123] The messianic provision of life-giving food evokes the relationship with God as a provider and God's attentive nature, as the ancient Israelite had experienced in the wilderness. Claassens affirms, "God's provision of food serves as an illustration of God's presence."[124] She argues that the description of God's renewed provision of sufficient food in Joel 2:22–27 is enough to enlighten people to recognize "the giver as their God" in their journey of life.[125] Here one can recognize that while the experience of suffering and agony, described as a famine, corresponds to the absence of God or hostile presence, the presence of God with the provision of sufficient food corresponds to the sign of God's favor of restoration. Thus, the prophetic description of God who will feed again, which is associated with the motif of the messianic banquet, expresses not only Israel's belief of God's attribute of attentive presence in their lives but also their hope for the restoration of Israel.

The Ultimate Triumph and Vindication

The belief in the God who will feed again and in God's attentive presence in the banquet is also exposed in the apocalyptic vision of Israel's ultimate victory in battle and its joyous celebration. Dennis Smith found the origin of the theme of banquet in certain ancient Near Eastern creation myths, which normally describe a great battle in the divine sphere.[126] Paul Hanson insists that apocalyptic literature presents the motif of battles and victory over enemies; the banquet in this motif is fulfilled to celebrate victory and deliverance once the battle has been won.[127] In this regard, the messianic banquet itself signifies the ultimate victory and its joyous celebration of deliverance and restoration. A classic description of the messianic banquet in Isaiah 25:6–8 clearly reveals the mythical motif of banquet, in which God hosts a glorious banquet on Mount Zion as the redemption of Israel:

> On this mountain the Lord of hosts will make for all peoples
> A feast of rich food, a feast of well-aged wines,
> of rich food filled with marrow, of well-aged wines strained clear.
> And he will destroy on this mountain the shroud that is cast over all peoples
> The sheet that is spread over all nations; he will swallow up death forever.
> Then the Lord God will wife away the tears from all faces,
> and the disgrace of his people he will take away from all the earth
> for the Lord has spoken (Isaiah 25:2–8)

In Isaiah 24 27, an apocalyptic vision begins with God's judging activity and the destruction of enemies, reflecting to the divine battle in Near Eastern myth. Then, God will "reign on Mount Zion and in Jerusalem, and before his elders he will manifest his glory" (24:23). On the mountain, God will reveal God's presence with the victory over enemies in battle. In this vision, God appears as a provider of life-giving resources, hosting "a feast of rich food, a feast of well-aged wines, of rich food filled with marrow, of well-aged wines strained clear" (25:6). With the most plentiful supply of foods (cf. 2 Baruch 29:5–6), God reveals his presence by hosting a feast for all people to celebrate the victory over the evils and iniquity of the world.

Representing the ultimate victory, the messianic banquet expresses the divine reversal in the presence of Messiah, judgment and the restoration of the God's chosen people. For instance, 1 Enoch clearly shows the Lord's triumph, the following judgment, and the provision of food:

> And He will deliver them to the angels for punishment,
> To execute vengeance on them because they have oppressed his children and his elect

> And they shall be a spectacle for the righteous and for his elect:
> They shall rejoice over them, because the wrath of the Lord of Spirits resteth upon
> them,
> and his sword is drunk with their blood
>
> And the righteous and elect shall be saved on that day,
> ......And the Lord of Spirits will abide over them
> and with that son of Man shall they eat
> and lie down and rise up for ever and ever. (1 Enoch 62:11–14)[128]

The Lord of Spirits and the Son of Man execute vengeance and the judgment against "the kings and the powerful" (46:4; cf. 38:4; 53:3; 63:1), who have denied the name of the Lord and committed sins and evil (45:5); here the judgment entails the divine reversal: those who enjoy power in the present will be judged and destroyed, conversely those who are powerless and rejected in the world of iniquity now will rejoice "on that day."[129] Those who hunger now will feast in the future with the Lord (cf. 1 Enoch 60:24). Collins sees the "kings and the powerful" as Gentile rulers, and the "righteous" refers to a much narrower group of Jewish people who are vindicated by God.[130] As it is in the Isaianic vision, the ultimate victory and judgment appear with the commensality provided by God and the divine reversal, God's deliverance (cf. Isaiah 25:6–9; Joel 2:24–26; 3:18).

The most significant point in this vision is that, while God's judging activity or divine battle is prior to the banquet, the feast provided by God and the commensality are the main features of this vision and signify the restoration and new life. Namely, the attribute of God who provides food plays a significant role in the description of apocalyptic vision in the form of messianic banquet where the whole community eats together. The food is definitely not ordinary food but life-giving resource for the restored life of God's people. In this regard, the messianic banquet, associated with the metaphor of God's provision of life-giving source, is a striking means of the expression of the apocalyptic vision of God's ultimate restoration and the socio-religious imagination of a future lived in final victory over the chaotic world; whereby Israelites envision the new age and new communal life under God's complete provision.

Bread and the Word of God: Ideology

Female Wisdom and the Gift of Life

The metaphor of God's provision of food can also be found in wisdom literature, in which Wisdom is personified and feminized; thereby wisdom tradition not only highlights nursing imagery of God as mother who completely cares for her children, but the banquet of Wisdom also signifies the gift of new life with God's wisdom. Proverbs 9:1–6 presents a scene in which Wisdom prepares a luxurious banquet and invites people to come share in her bread and drink of her wine:

> Wisdom has built her house; she has hewn her seven pillars.
> She has slaughtered her animals, she has mixed her wine,
> She has also set her table
> She has sent out her servant-girls, she calls from the highest places in the town,
> "You that are simple, turn in here!" to those without sense she says,
> "Come, eat of my bread and drink of the wine I have mixed.
> Lay aside immaturity, and live, and walk in the way of insight
> (Proverbs 9:1–6)

Grammatically, from the beginning of Proverbs, "Wisdom is a female entity."[131] In Proverbs 9, the female Wisdom builds a house with seven pillars (v. 1), which signifies completeness, perfection of knowledge (Proverbs 24:3–4), or affluence.[132] Wisdom herself "slaughtered her animals," "mixed her wine" and set the table (v. 2) preparing for a feast. The text describes what the female Wisdom is doing with special emphasis that all the foods and the feast are prepared by herself. She "sent out her servant-girl" for an open invitation and said "come, eat of my bread and drink of the wine I have mixed" (vv 3–5). The female Wisdom then explains the meaning of her invitation and consuming foods, (v. 6) and reinforces her exhortation that Wisdom is a gift of God and a gift of life: "for by me [wisdom] your days will be multiplied, and years will be added to your life" (v. 11).

The female Wisdom clearly presents that the food at her feast is not simply for hunger and the wine for thirst, but for the gift of life. With three imperatives, "come," "eat," and "drink" in vv. 5, 6, and 11, the female Wisdom proclaims that if the guests eat her food and the wine she has mixed, and if any one participates in her feast, they will receive the gift of life and knowledge of the Holy One (v. 10). Leo Perdue affirms that the female Wisdom invites the unlearned to come "to enjoy not a literal meal of meat and spiced wine but rather a festival of life" with the wisdom of God.[133] Further, the life given by Wisdom does not mean just human life, but a life of justice ruled by God's wisdom.[134] Michael Fox argues that listening to wisdom, living within her house, and participating in her feast represent and envision a "life time of learning" with God.[135] The eating of the food that the female Wisdom provides signifies the acceptance of the gift of new life and God's wisdom. In this manner, the female Wisdom not only presents her gifts of food as the content of wisdom of God, but also she is revealed as provider of foods of wisdom for the life. Namely, the female Wisdom is described as the one who provides numinous food for the people's new life, as God provided the food for the life of the Israelites in the wilderness.

Furthermore, in this passage, the female Wisdom is described as the "hostess,"[136] who is in charge of the preparation of the food and the place for the feast. Here the maternal image of Wisdom, especially as the female head of the house, is highlighted. The metaphorical invitation of this passage can be compared with Isaiah 55:1–2[137] in terms of giving a life:[138] "everyone who thirsts, come to the waters; and you that have no money come, buy and eat! Come, buy wine and milk without money and without price." In this passage, like Proverbs 9:1–6, imperatives "come," "buy," "eat," show the subject of the host who is in charge of the preparation of the foods. God as the *host/ess* invites people with his bountiful gifts of food and wine, and *he/she* reminds the people of the promise of returning home from exile (Isaiah 55:3–13). The foods that God offers are not for the appetite of the people, but for the promise of the gift of new life.

The food of life, which the female Wisdom offers in Proverbs 9, parallels with God's provision of food in Isaiah 55. Claassens insists that Proverbs 9 and Isaiah 55 use gifts of food as a symbol of God's word to invite the people to enter into a life with God.[139] At this point, God in Isaiah 55 can be identified with the female Wisdom in Proverbs 9 in terms of *the host/ess* who provides the foods and invites people to the life-giving feast. When the female Wisdom provides the foods for the life of the people, it evokes the reader's mind to the female metaphor of God who feeds and nurses for the life of people in the wilderness. As the hostess who invites people to come to share the foods, the female Wisdom and her role can be described with the maternal image like the metaphor of God as mother who feeds and nurses to give life.

Eating the Bread and the Word of God: *Ideology*

In the wisdom tradition, the commensality of the Jewish banquet function as the ideological manifestation of Israel's religious political identity, beyond the cultural customs or the apocalyptic expectation for restoration. The wisdom and food images in Hebrew scripture explicitly describe that the food God provides embodies God's word; the wisdom of God is identified with the food God provides. Gillian Freely-Harnik argues that the metaphorical expression of eating God's wisdom/food should establish a binding agreement and a covenantal relationship and represent the acceptance of ideological vision, among the eaters to abide by God's word.[140] In the ancient imperial world, offering a feast has played an important role in the manifestation of imperial ideology, expressing wealth, political power and status.[141]

The association of wisdom and food can be widely found in Hebrew Scriptures; the eating of the food God provides implicitly signifies taking in God's words and wisdom. Most of all, the manna, the bread from heaven, the most significant entity of Israel's communal identity, is not just food for satisfying hunger, but it represents God's wisdom for the Israelites, which lets them know that "one does not live by bread alone, but by every word that comes from the mouth of the Lord" (Deuteronomy 8:3).[142] In Proverbs 9:1–6 God invites people to participate in the wisdom banquet, enjoying luxurious foods; here the participation in her feast signifies listening to wisdom, consuming the ideology of her house, and envisioning a "lifetime of learning" with God.[143] Furthermore eating the food that the female Wisdom provides signifies the acceptance of the gift of new life and God's wisdom.

In second temple Judaism, the association of wisdom with bread or manna, water, and other foods by divine provision is widespread. For instance, Ben Sira says that for "whoever fears the Lord," Wisdom will "feed him with the bread of learning and give him the water of wisdom to drink" (Sirach 15:3). Sirach clearly describes that Wisdom "come[s] forth from the mouth of Most High and covered the earth like a mist… like the vine I bud forth delights, and my blossoms become glorious and abundant fruits" (Sirach 24:3–17); then Wisdom invites people saying, "come to me, you who desire me, and eat your fill of my fruits" (24:19). In the Odes of Solomon, "the Lord has multiplied his knowledge" through the provision of "the living water of eternity" which is given by "the Most High," so that those who have fallen are restored (Odes of Solomon 6:1–18; 11:7, 30; cf. 2 Esdras 8:4). The food provided by the divine being is not just a material food for human hunger but God's wisdom for sustaining human lives in relationship with God and for leading people into a new life, as is commanded in Deuteronomy 8:3.

The consumption of the food and bread or the participation in the wisdom banquet functions as a symbolic expression of the learning and acceptance of God's knowledge and ideological vision; at the same time its apocalyptic vision of restoration by the consuming of food manifests the ultimate legitimacy of God's ideology. As Terry Eagleton argues, ideology must play a substantial role in the shaping of the texts,[144] even the wisdom literature. In line with this point, Leo Perdue argues that the theology of the wisdom literature represents the major features of ideology that undergirded a certain worldview and socio-religious vision within early Judaism and the larger social structure of the ancient world.[145] Wisdom chooses kings, rules nations, and provides food, the life-giving source that people should live by (Deuteronomy 8:3); the food provided by the divine being is identified with God's word too. The *food/God's wisdom* must represent socio-religious ideological vision of Israel; and the consumption of the *food/wisdom* signifies the participation in the same ideological vision. For instance, in the book of Ezekiel, a more radical description about the consumption of God's word is found:

> He said to me, O mortal, eat what is offered to you; eat this scroll, and go, speak to the house of Israel. So I opened my mouth, and he gave me the scroll to eat. He said to me, Mortal, eat this scroll that I give you and fill your stomach with it. Then I ate it; and in my mouth it was as sweet as honey. (Ezekiel 3:1–3)

The prophet is commanded to deliver God's word to the house of Israel who refuses to hear (2:6–8). Then, God gives the prophet the scroll to eat; here the scroll signifies the word of God/Wisdom, a message sent to the house of Israel. The eating of the scroll is a test of the prophet's obedience, in contrast to the people (cf. 2:7–8).[146] Furthermore, the consumption of the scroll obviously means the acceptance of God's word and command and the prophet's comprehensiveness of God's ideological vision.

Dennis Smith also argues that the Jewish banquet tradition in Wisdom literature, especially in Ben Sira, functions in similar ways to what the Greek and Roman Empire express in their ethical value and ideology.[147] The description of the banquet in Ben Sira is quite parallel to the Greco-Roman meal customs, especially philosophical symposium.[148] Michael Fox insists that Wisdom's banquet is to be envisioned as a symposium of philosophers. The wise eat and drink, listen to wisdom, and discourse upon it.[149] In this regard, as Greco-Roman symposium functions as a cultural symbolic force to represent ethical value and ideology, Wisdom banquet represents the ideology of the providence of God and legitimizes their ideological vision. Furthermore, the acceptance of Wisdom's invitation signifies the participation in the life of wisdom/God's word and the ideological vision in God's kingdom.

Synthesis: Bread/Food and Metaphoric Conceptions

The *bread/food* functions to form a common sense of identity and self-consciousness, which leads the Jewish community into a common "religious imagination,"[150] in the formation of Israelite society. Meals and commensality also symbolize a certain human behavior and ideological vision among social groups in relation to one another and in relation to God. Specifically, Israelites ritualize certain historical events with bread/food in order to observe and commemorate past events throughout the generations, maintaining the social memories and embodying the past experience into their present life and their communal identity.

All human experiences and thoughts are filtered through metaphoric structures in the dialogic relation between the reader and the text when the reader reads a certain text. At the same time the human cognitive conceptions form metaphoric language and relevant meanings. In this regard, one can analogize that the bread/food and communal meals with the specific social memory in Jewish tradition form several cognitive conceptions of the reader and relevant metaphoric structure; and those metaphoric conceptions can be apply for reading the Gospels, evoking the reader's conceptual knowledge by certain metaphoric language, a context of narrative, atmosphere, and the like within the text.

According to Jewish experiences and tradition that I observed in this chapter, metaphoric conceptions on the bread/meals and their structure are analogized as follows:

The Bread is God's Life-giving Source
Bread is a sign of God's complete care/ nursing imagery
Bread is a sign of God's presence
Bread signifies God who provides
Bread is a fundamental source of Israel's Identity

The Breaking of Bread means sharing a meal
The breaking of bread is a sharing of bread
The breaking of bread is the end of hostility
The breaking of bread is a making a covenant
The breaking of bread an actual formation of community
The breaking of bread is blessing
The breaking of bread is a participation in an ideological claim

Eating/Sharing Bread is the Sharing of Communal Identity
Sharing Bread is the acceptance of the other
Sharing Bread is the breaking of Boundary

Participation in the Banquet is the Consumption of the Food God/Wisdom provided
Eating the meal/bread is learning God's word/knowledge
Eating the meal/bread is accepting God's wisdom/ ideology
Eating the meal/bread is the acceptance of God's authority
Eating the meal/bread is participation in God's sovereignty/ ideology

The Bread/ Food/ Meals are Identity Markers

3

The Metaphor of Bread in Feeding Narratives and Matthean Community

In Matthew's two feeding narrative units (14:13–21; 15:29–39), the narrator describes that, as God provides manna for the Israelites in the wilderness, Jesus actively engages the problem of the crowd's hunger with a compassionate heart. Furthermore, Matthew portrays Jesus as a "prophet like Moses" (Exodus 16: 13–35; Numbers. 11:7–9, 31–32) and Elisha (2 King 4:42–44), highlighting the miraculous event as a manifestation of God's sovereign power and Jesus' divine identity.[1] In the history of Matthean scholarship, most scholars see the narrative of the feeding of the five thousand as a miracle story revealing Jesus' identity as a supernatural heavenly being and upcoming messiah. To those scholars, the feeding narratives are primarily to be read in terms of Christology,[2] which means that most scholars have barely been concerned about the metaphoric meaning of bread and its relevant theme of Jesus' provision of life-giving source.

In Jesus' miraculous feeding scenes, the bread (ἄρτος) and the metaphoric image of God's provision of food evoke the reader's cognitive conceptions, which correspond to the Passover meal, manna, and other symbolic imagery of food/meals in Jewish tradition and social memory. Analogizing Matthean bread with Jewish metaphorical conceptions of bread, one can read the two feeding narratives in another way beyond the miraculous event. The differences and similarities in the two repetitious feeding narratives sharpen and highlight the metaphoric meaning of the bread, covering the plot of Matthew's Gospel as a whole. In this way, the reader can recognize that the bread is not just for human hunger; but rather the bread and Jesus' provision metaphorically signify the fulfillment of prophecy, the establishment of a new community, the restoration of Israel, and the messianic banquet extending beyond socio-religious ethnic boundaries. At the same time, binding all narratives in the Gospel of Matthew, bread and Jesus' feedings clearly represent the identity of the Matthean community, which strives for legitimacy in-between formative Judaism and the Roman Empire.

In this chapter, I investigate the narrative features and the literary motif of the bread metaphor in the two feeding narratives (14:13–21; 15:29–39). I also re-interpret these narratives within the context of Matthew's gospel as a whole in the light of Jewish conceptions of bread, while paying special attention to the similarity and difference between the two feeding scenes. I finally examine the rhetorical claim of Matthean bread, representing Matthew's communal identity and ideological vision.

Bread in the First Feeding Narrative (14:13–21)

The metaphor of bread in the first feeding narrative signifies the actual formation of Jesus' community integrating Jesus' teaching and ministry, which is the fulfillment of prophecy for the restoration of Israel. This section concentrates on special narrative features, the meaning of the breaking of bread and its application to Jesus' feeding narrative, while paying attention to the role of Jesus' first feeding in the context of Matthew's Gospel as a whole.

Significant Features of the Narrative

ἀναχώρεω (*withdrawal*)

The first feeding narrative (14:13–21) begins with Jesus' reaction to the death of John the Baptist (14:1–12). When Jesus hears the news of the execution of John the Baptist, Jesus "withdrew (ἀνεχώρησεν) from there (ἐκεῖθεν) in a boat to a lonely place apart." (v. 13). As compared with the Gospel of Mark 6:32, Matthew's narrator intentionally replaces the plural form, ἀπῆλθον with the singular form, ἀνεχώρησεν, adding here ἐκεῖθεν.[3] The Greek verb, ἀναχώρεω is usually used to express something Jesus does occasionally, including encounters with potential danger or conflicts in the Gospel of Matthew. This expression is a clue to understanding narrative flow and narrative strategy. Used in combination with "ἐκεῖθεν" (from there), a pattern develops[4] in Matthew for presenting the itinerant route of Jesus' ministry.

Basically, the term ἀναχώρεω in Matthew appears in the face of potential danger or hostility. Gundry deals with the appearances of this term in Matthew under the topic of Jesus' "flight from persecution."[5] When Jesus hears John has been arrested right after the temptation story, Jesus withdrew into Galilee, ἀνεχώρησεν εἰς τὴν Γαλιλαίαν (4:12); when the Pharisees plan to destroy Jesus at the counsel, "Jesus withdrew from there, ἀνεχώρησεν ἐκεῖθεν" (12:15); when he gets the news of the death of John the Baptist, "he withdrew from there, ἀνεχώρησεν ἐκεῖθεν" (14:13); right after the big debate with Pharisees and scribes, "Jesus withdrew to the district of Tyre and Sidon, Ἰησοῦς ἀνεχώρησεν εἰς τὰ μέρη Τύρου καὶ Σιδῶνος" (15:21). Most usages of the term ἀναχώρεω occur in the face of potential hostility with Jesus' intentional move to somewhere else.

Jesus' withdrawal is not just to flee from the potential persecution, but also to move intentionally and transition to fulfill his purpose. From this point, Deirdre Good observes the motif of ἀναχώρεω as a special feature of the Gospel of Matthew, presenting a "three-fold pattern of hostility/withdrawal/prophetic fulfillment," which Matthew seems to create.[6] In her observation, Deirdre Good attempts to find the motif of ἀναχώρεω in some passages of LXX, 1 and 2 Maccabees, and Wisdom literature.[7] For instance, the book of Exodus 2:15 uses ἀναχώρεω, when Moses withdraws from Pharaoh's hostile intentions and comes into the land of Midian.[8] Later Moses encounters God in the burning bush and leads the Israelites out of Egypt, the land of slavery. Here one can see a kind of narrative pattern in three forms: hostility from power, withdrawal from danger, and a specific action, which Deirdre Good calls "prophetic fulfillment."

In the Gospel of Matthew, the three-fold pattern fits with the narrative feature of Jesus' withdrawal. In Matthew chapter 4, when Jesus withdraws from the hostile plan of the Pharisees, Jesus goes to Galilee, living in "Capernaum by the sea, the territory of Zebulum and Naphtali" (4:13). As the narrator explains, this location fulfills the prophecy in Isaiah 4:14–16. Then, Jesus' prophetic teaching and performance follows in the Sermon on the Mount (5–7) and healing in Capernaum (8:5, 14). In chapter 12, after withdrawing from a hostile moment, Jesus heals people and lets them know that his ministry and teaching are a fulfillment of Isaiah's prophecy (12:15–17). Jesus also withdraws, when he becomes aware of a conspiracy to destroy him (v. 15). Here the narrator quotes the words of Isaiah 42:1–4, representing Jesus' ministry as a fulfillment of prophecy (12: 18–21): "Here is my servant, whom I have chosen, my beloved, with whom my soul is well pleased. I will put my Spirit upon him and he will proclaim justice to the Gentiles….And in his name the Gentiles will hope." Matthew's narrator foreshadows Jesus' ultimate ministry objective, the inclusion of Gentiles as fulfillment of prophecy.

Furthermore, in the first feeding narrative (14:13–19), Jesus' miracle, a prophetic action, occurs, right after he withdraws from potential persecution to deserted place (14:13). The feeding of the five thousand can be observed as a fulfillment of prophecy. Then, when Jesus withdraws from the controversy with the Pharisees and scribes to the district of Tyre and Sidon (15:21), Jesus encounters the Canaanite woman and applauds this woman's faith. The reader can recognize in this narrative as a fulfillment of the prophecy of 12:18 and 12:21. From this perspective, Matthew's intentional use of ἀναχώρεω as a narrative strategy, does not represent a "retreat from hostility"[9] or a description of Jesus' itinerancy, rather it reveals "withdrawal for fulfillment of prophecy."[10] Therefore, ἀναχώρεω presents a significant lens through which the reader interprets the first feeding narrative in the terms of prophetic fulfillment.

Location and Time

In Matthew's first feeding narrative in 14:13–21, the descriptions of location and time serve a significant literary function through which the reader recognizes that the feeding story is not just concerned with the miraculous performance of Jesus but also presents other metaphoric meanings, corresponding to the wilderness experience of ancient Israel. Encountering the news of the death of John the Baptist, Jesus and his disciples go out to "a deserted place," ἔρημον τόπον (v. 13). Interestingly, the narrator kindly explains the place again and includes the time through the words of disciples, "This is a deserted place, and the hour is now late" (v. 15). The repetitious description of the deserted place and the late time has a significant role to present a hint or an interpretational frame for the reader. Namely, using the special narrative setting including the place, time and atmosphere, the narrator evokes the reader's imagination and cognitive knowledge for exploring the narrative.

The Greek term ἔρημος, which is often linked with τόπος in the gospels,[11] can be translated "lonely place" or "isolated place" according to the context of the narrative, in which Jesus intends to isolate himself for a moment from where people can easily find him.[12] Furthermore, according to this narrative context, the reader should not imagine this place as a real desert[13] because the place is obviously by the Sea of Galilee,[14] and the place is described as being close to the village in which people can buy food (v. 15). At the same time, the term ἔρημος itself literally must be related to the expression of the place in "desert," which alludes to ancient Israel's wandering in the wilderness and God's feeding with manna.[15] The term ἔρημος could be associated with the wilderness in Jesus' temptation story (4:1–11)[16] in the narrative context of Matthew, in which the reader begins to typologically identify Jesus with Moses. Obviously, Jesus wants to isolate himself from the conflicts for a while; however, he does not need to go to a deserted place to take a rest. The narrator intentionally places Jesus into the deserted place as a narrative strategy for evoking the reader's cognition and presenting metaphoric background for Jesus' feeding scene.

In the Jewish tradition, wilderness[17] not only designates a certain place but also presents an evocative symbol with various meanings.[18] Primarily, the wilderness represents the place of the forty-year sojourn and Israel's life and experience on their journey to Canaan, which decisively forms Israel's communal identity.[19] In the wilderness, Israel is chosen by God, makes a covenant with God, experiences God's liberating power and gracious provision of food, and even rebels against God and sometimes is punished by God. All these experiences in the wilderness not only shapes Israel's identity but also provides contents of the evocative symbol the wilderness. In this manner, the term ἔρημος itself or the retelling of the wilderness experience function as a lens through which Israel interprets the contemporary contexts of life (e.g., Nehemiah 9:9–21; Psalms 68:7–10; 78:12–41; 105:26–45; 106) and the eschatological vision (e.g., Isaiah 24–27; Jeremiah 31; Ezekiel 40–47; Revelation 21:1–22). For the reader who is familiar with the experience of ancient Israel's wilderness sojourn, the term wilderness itself is not just the designation of an area of unsettled and uncultivated land, but it functions as an evocative symbol with various meanings.

In this regard, the narrator's repetitious guidance, "a deserted place" (e;rhmon to,pon; vv. 13, 15) is enough to remind the reader of Ancient Israel's sojourning in the wilderness of Sinai in Exodus,[20] a theme that is relevant to the experience of Israel. Against this background and the feeding theme, the narrative evokes the memory of a Passover meal, particularly unleavened bread the ancient Israelite ate, and later the manna that God provided in the wilderness.

In addition, the description of time in v. 15, which actually represents "evening"[21] time, causes the reader to flashback to the night of the Exodus, especially the meal of unleavened bread, or a typical Jewish evening meal, in the context of the first feeding narrative. The narrator indicates the time was "late (ὀψίας)" and expresses the time of day, probably "evening meal,"[22] which is already passed (v. 15; ἡ ὥρα ἤδη παρῆλθεν),[23] indicating a much later hour than the time of evening meal. The description of time differs from Mark 6:36, which describes the time just as a late hour (ἤδη ὥρας πολλῆς). There is no precise time-description in both texts. However, Matthew's variant description clarifies the lateness and shows the urgency of the crowds' need for some food. The narrator reports, however, that the people have no food except five loaves and two fishes (πέντε ἄρτους καὶ δύο ἰχθύας,14:17). The only way to get food is to go out to a village and buy some food (14:15). Here the late hour of evening mealtime, especially when the multitudes are gathered, alludes to the night of Israel's deliverance from Egypt and the Passover meal to which people gathered to observe the feast (Exodus 11:4; 12:1–27).[24] The crowd without food in the wilderness also alludes to the complaining situation of Israelites in the Sinai wilderness (Exodus 16:3; Numbers 11:4). Both the crowds and the Ancient Israelites have been fed in full by God.

Thus, the description of location and time is significant as a strategic narrative device, which leads the reader to interpret the first feeding narrative in light of the socio-religious functions and meaning of Israel's wilderness experiences of the Passover meal and God's provision of manna.

Character of Jesus and the Crowds

In the feeding narrative, Jesus is described as a merciful messiah, who has compassion on the crowd and willingly cares for the problems of the people. As the emotion of compassion normally makes the one involved identify with the situation of others who are in need, Jesus offers a special action for the other's benefit. The narrator expresses Jesus' emotion with the verbal terms σπλαγχνίζομαι (compassion) in v. 14, which is used before in 9:35–36 when Jesus sees the crowd as sheep without a shepherd. So, when the reader sees Jesus' compassion on the crowds,[25] the reader naturally flashes back to Jesus' compassionate emotion in 9:35–36; "they were harassed and helpless like sheep without a shepherd." This emotional description of Jesus alludes to the Old Testament picture of God's people as not having a shepherd and God as a shepherd (e.g., Numbers 27:17; 1 Kings 22:17; Psalm 23). In this allusion, the verbal term σπλαγχνίζομαι represents Jesus' messianic character rather than the mere depiction of sympathetic emotion.[26]

Furthermore, Jesus' compassion with the analogy of the shepherd/sheep relation evokes Ancient Israel's wilderness experience in light of God's nursing imagery and the metaphor of God's provision of food. In the first feeding narrative, the description of Jesus' emotion and Jesus' use of the imperative δότε "you give them something to eat," δότε αὐτοῖς ὑμεῖς φαγεῖν (v. 16) lead the reader to the allusion of Ancient Israel's experience of God's feeding in the wilderness because God willingly fed them. This allusion gives the reader a special lens to understand the first feeding story. The verbs σπλαγχνίζομαί θεραπεύώ and Jesus' feeding the crowds as a shepherd reflect the relationship between God and Israel in the light of God's maternal imagery – nourishing her son[27] – revealed in God's provision of manna and quail in the wilderness.

In this analogy, Jesus' active compassionate character is intensified by a contrast to the passive reaction of disciples. The disciples asked Jesus to finish his work for the day, and said, "send the crowds away so that they may go into the villages and buy food for themselves" (v.15). Jesus said, "No! You give them something to eat." I think this is surely a weird and unfair instruction. How could the disciples feed the crowd in the wilderness without any preparation? It is probably more reasonable that, as the disciples suggested, the crowd go into the villages and buy some food for them. However, through this weird instruction, which indirectly exposes Jesus' intention to give them something special, the narrator highlights Jesus' compassionate active character, corresponding to God who feeds Israel in the wilderness. At the same time, the narrator brings out the main subjects: the feeding, eating, and the bread, which are related to the reader's historical memory.

The character of the crowds (ὄχλος) in the first feeding narrative is also a significant narrative feature, through which the reader understands the metaphoric meaning of Jesus' feeding. ὄχλος or ὄχλοι are typically found in Greek literature, expressing "a crowd of men milling around or closely pressed together."[28] In the Gospel accounts, the term is usually used for denoting an anonymous background to Jesus' ministry[29] and the groups of people who voluntarily gathered around and followed Jesus as an audience. From the beginning of Jesus' ministry, Matthew's narrator describes that "great crowds followed him from Galilee and the Decapolis and Jerusalem and Judea and from beyond the Jordan" (4:25), and they were taught by Jesus (5:3–7:29), being witnesses to Jesus' healing and compassionate ministry (8–9). However, the crowds in Matthew's Gospel are a shifting, unreliable, and unfixed group.[30] So, the components of the crowds are variable according to the narrative flow, and its various characters present significant clues for interpreting Jesus' ministry.

In the first feeding narrative, the crowds are plausibly composed of the Jewish people and the marginalized in Jewish society. According to the narrative of Matthew, Jesus begins his ministry at Galilee (4:12), the heart of Israel, moving out from Nazareth and Capernaum and he teaches and heals "throughout Galilee" (4:23). The narrator describes, "the crowds followed him from Galilee and the Decapolis and Jerusalem and Judea and from beyond the Jordan" (4:25). Most of these places are denoting "historic Israel"[31] and were actually Jewish territories. Compared to the Gospel of Mark in 3:7–8, interestingly Matthew's narrator omits from the lists "Idumea" and the region of "Tyre and Sidon," highlighting Jewish territory. Even until the first feeding narrative, the narrator places Jesus' ministry around Galilee; and Matthew's crowds always follow[32] the route of Jesus; and Matthew's Jesus keeps his mission instruction only for "the lost sheep of house of Israel" (10:5; 15:24). In this regard, the crowds at the first stage of Jesus' ministry are mostly composed of the Jewish people.

Furthermore, the crowds are mostly composed of the marginalized in Jewish society. Anthony Saldarini argues that the crowds in Matthew are "subgroups of Israel, thrown together for a time, mostly in need and potentially available to Jesus as followers," and typically the lower classes, illiterate, lived at a subsistence level.[33] In the first feeding narrative, the narrator describes that Jesus "healed their sick" (14:14), so that the reader can recognize many of the crowd are the sick people, without enough food for a day.

The Metaphoric Meaning of Bread in the First Feeding Narrative

Not Just for the Satisfaction of Hunger

As far as the bread is concerned, the reader must recall Jesus' first temptation story (4:1–4) because the bread (ἄρτος) appears for the first time here in the Gospel of Matthew. The bread in the temptation narrative offers a basic clue for interpreting Matthew's narrative in light of the metaphors of bread and eating and it intrigues the reader's interest about the meaning of the bread in this Gospel.

In the narrative of Jesus' temptation, the Spirit led Jesus into the wilderness (εἰς τὴν ἔρημον), and the narrator explains that Jesus fasted forty days and forty nights (v. 2). The location, τὴν ἔρημον, and the number forty allude to the forty years in the wilderness in which Israel was tested (Deuteronomy 8:2). They also directly correspond to Moses' experience of a forty-day fast (Deuteronomy 9:18) and Elijah's as well (1 Kings 19:8).[34] As was indicated, Israel's experience of wilderness is important for the formation of Israel's religious-ethnical identity. Many scholars have identified Matthew's Jesus with Israel or with Moses,[35] as a way of legitimating Jesus' identity and the Matthean community in light of the Israel's religious-ethnical identity: Jesus came into the wilderness to be tempted, just as Israel was tempted.[36] Through this analogical identification, scholars insist that Jesus relived Israel's wilderness experiences; yet Jesus succeeded while Israel mostly failed their tests.[37] In this respect, the discourse of Jesus' temptation story can be interpreted in the frame of the experience of Israel in wilderness.

The Gospel of Matthew mostly quotes from Deuteronomy 6 and 8 for Jesus' answers to the test. In the first temptation, based on Jesus' hunger, the tempter comes to Jesus and speaks, "if you are the Son of God, command these stones to become loaves of bread (ἄρτοι)" (v. 3). This test is probably not a test of Jesus' ability to perform a miracle because there is no audience to witness of it; but rather it tests how Jesus trusts in God nourishes and how Jesus understands the life-giving source in terms of food and bread. Daniel Harrington sees the background of the first temptation as God's feeding Israel in the wilderness (Deuteronomy 2:7). Although Israel's grumbling and craving for food caused God's provision of manna for them (Psalm 78:18–20),[38] they failed to recognize the real source of their life. According to Israel's wilderness experience, the bread in the first temptation is not about human hunger, but it rather signifies the faith in God's provision and its appropriate ideological vision, driven by the word of God.

If the reader knows Jesus' feeding story or the relevant tradition in early Christianity, the reader will realize soon that this test is very simple and easy for Jesus because Jesus performs a miracle in a similar situation in Matthew 14:13–21 and 15:29–39. However, Jesus refuses to do this here. The reader may ask questions: why did Jesus not make bread here, even though he did this in front of many people? Does the bread or the first test present a symbolic meaning in this text?

Jesus answers the tempter, "One does not live by bread alone, but every word that comes from the mouth of God" (v. 4). This is a quotation from Deuteronomy 8:3,[39] that implicitly signifies that Israel should know the word of God as true source of life[40] and that physical food would be supplied by God's complete care. For Jesus, the bread no longer means food that satisfied people's hunger and their lives because God would perfectly provide everything people needed. Rather, the bread here signifies something else: a true life-giving source that people should pursue. Namely, while the tempter wishes Jesus to believe that the bread satisfies human hunger, Jesus denies the tempter's suggestion and has no concern about physical hunger or satisfaction. Rather, Jesus is concerned about the true meaning of bread as a real life-giving source in the light of God's complete provision and God's teaching by the word in human lives. At this point, the reader might ask: what does the bread mean in Jesus' mind in Matthew's Gospel? The first temptation story invites the reader into the two feeding narratives in 14:13–21 and 15:29–39. The meaning of the bread as a true life-giving source and the true bread will be exhibited and manifested throughout Matthew's narratives, particularly the two feeding narratives and Jesus' Last Supper.

In this manner, the Gospel of Matthew implicitly affirms that the true life-giving source only comes from God, and the bread as a source for satisfaction of human hunger is not meaningful for Jesus' and humanity's true life. However, the word of God as our daily bread, a true life-giving source given by God, transcends the human conception of food for hunger and human life. All these discourses in the temptation story implicitly present the clue to understanding the meaning of bread in Jesus' feeding narratives.

The Bread as a Source of Formation of Identity

Entering the main part of Jesus' first feeding narrative, the disciples bring the only five loaves and two fishes they have: πέντε ἄρτους καὶ. δύο ἰχθύας (14:17). In comparison with the Markan narrative, Matthew seem to weaken[41] the quantity of food for covering the crowds, but concentrates on the entity of food, bread and fish in this narrative. The Markan narrator directly indicates the small quantity of food and its number by the dialogue of disciples and Jesus, so that the reader naturally pays attention to the small quantity of food. The disciples wondered about Jesus' asking to feed the crowds and said to Jesus: "Shall we go and buy two hundred denarii worth of bread, and give it to them to eat?" (Mark 6:37). Then Jesus asked them about how many loaves they have (6:38). However, the Gospel of Matthew omits this dialogue and just briefly reports what they have (v. 17). Here the reader focuses more on the entity of the foods they have than the deficiency of food.[42] Matthew's narrator attracts the reader's attention to what the crowd had and what they did with those foods: *bread and eating*.

As far as the bread is concerned in Jewish tradition, the symbolic imagery of bread and its metaphoric conception are linked to a fundamental source of Israel's identity in Ancient Israel's experience: God's complete care, provision of food, liberating power from slavery, and covenants with Israel, etc.[43] All conceptions of bread and the relevant discourse of Israel's identity analogize with the bread in Jesus' feeding action in Matthew. The loaves (ἄρτους) as a primary symbol are identified with God's provision of manna and with the Passover meal, especially unleavened bread, during the journey of Exodus. The fish reminds the reader of Israelites' complaining desire for fish of Egypt, which provoked God to send a substitute, quail meat (Numbers 11:4–5). So the fish is also related to God's provision of the quails on which Israel was fed in the wilderness (Numbers 11:31: 'quail *from the sea*').[44]

Based on the cognitive conceptual analogies between the *bread/fish* and the *manna/quail,* the reader realizes that the first feeding story is not only concerned about Jesus' miraculous power for satisfying hunger, but also it is about ἄρτος and the event of Jesus' feeding the entire crowd, which correspond to God's provision in the memory of Israel. Jesus' compassionate character (14:15) can be identified with God who willingly provided food in the wilderness and God who drew Israel to have a covenant with God. In addition, the act of eating bread together in the urgent situation, having no food at night in the deserted place, can reflect the unleavened bread of the Passover meal, which reminds the reader of their exodus experience.

In this regard, the bread/fish in Jesus' feeding narrative metaphorically functions to signify the divine provision of a life-giving source for the crowd in need, and liberating power, which is a significant medium for the formation of communal identity, as in Ancient Israel. Jesus is providing a new life-giving source for the crowds, a liberating vision with healing and feeding, and Matthew's Jesus is in the process of the formatting of a new communal identity, as Ancient Israel experienced. Consequently, the first feeding event not only evokes the experience of Ancient Israel, which is the foundation of Israel's identity or the process of forming a community, but it also signifies an actual event of formation of community, which can reflect Matthew's community and a ground of the forthcoming community.

The most powerful moment is at Jesus' blessing and breaking of the bread before the distribution of food. Jesus ordered the crowds to sit down on the grass. "Taking the five loaves and the two fish, he looked up to heaven and then blessed (εὐλόγησεν) and broke (κλάσας) the loaves, and gave (ἔδωκεν) them." (v. 19). The three verbs, "εὐλογέω" (bless), "κλάω" (break), and "δίδωμι" (give)" describe Jesus' symbolic action of feeding as a special messianic event, through which the metaphoric meaning of the feeding scene is intensified. First, the verb εὐλογέω is normally used to mean "utter the blessing," "blessing like cursing" as an object of belief in primitive religion,[45] and "give thanks to God."[46] According to cultural observance of Jesus' time, however, the significant feature of blessing in this narrative is like "a blessing at meal,"[47] especially a family meal. Based on the traditional belief that the whole world belongs to God (Psalm 21:4; 115:16), Jewish people strictly observe the rule that the head of house pronounces a blessing before the meal.[48] Even in the Passover meal, the main meal is begun by a blessing prayer over the unleavened bread and the accompanying breaking of bread.[49] The meal or sharing of bread itself symbolically connects to God's blessing and provision, acknowledging God's sovereign power and God's provision as a life-giving source. When Jesus "looked up to the heaven" before uttering a blessing, his action seems to ask God's complete care, as God provided the manna and quail in the wilderness. The narrator manifests God's metaphoric image as a provider and God's sovereign power in and through Jesus' compassionate action. Through the blessing, the people at the meal are solidified as a single community under God's provision.

Furthermore, the sequence of verbs remind the reader of Jesus' Last Supper meal[50] in Matthew 26:26; "Jesus took a loaf of bread, and after blessing it (εὐλογήσας) he broke it (ἔκλασεν), gave it (δοὺς) to the disciples," and of the celebration of the Eucharist in the early church. Luz argues that, with these verbs and formulations, the Jewish-Christian readers remembered their own family and church meals and the Lord's Supper.[51] The Matthean narrator describes this event as a Eucharistic meal, hosted by Jesus, through the sequence of Jesus' symbolic action. Jesus plays the significant role of host for solidifying the crowds as one communal entity, as the Eucharist functioned in the church. At this point, when Jesus blessed, broke the bread, and distributed it, the feeding scene functions not only as a ritual feast but also the ordinary communal meal and family meal. Thus, the entire crowd became a community, a family, and the people of God in the first feeding scene through eating the bread Jesus blessed and broke.

The Breaking of Bread: *Actual Formation of Community*

Right after Jesus utters blessing, he breaks the bread. The verb κλάω, which is used to describe Jesus' symbolic action of sharing a meal,[52] evokes the reader's cognitive knowledge of a socio-political and a religious meaning of the breaking of bread and sharing a meal in human relationship. In Palestine custom, the breaking of bread is a simple customary action to initiate the sharing of the common meal, whether it is an ordinary family meal or a ritual feast.[53] As the verb εὐλογέω identifies this feeding scene as a meal hosted by Jesus, Jesus' breaking of bread signals the commencement of the common meal of a communal entity in solidarity.[54] Some may think that it is a magical action for performing a miracle or a just action for the distribution of food. However, when Jesus breaks the bread by his own hand,[55] the breaking of the bread in this meal is not only an action for introductory process for sharing a meal, but it also has symbolical meanings in Ancient Israelite: *the end of hostility, making a covenant, and an actual formation of community.*

The symbolic action of the breaking of bread itself could be a literary source to signify the meaning of bread as a metaphor and its relevant conceptual structure. Namely, the breaking of the bread could be a *source domain* of metaphor, targeting to represent *the end of hostility, making a covenant, and the actual formation of new community.*[56] In these respects, when Jesus breaks the bread, the action itself functions as a metaphoric source of narrative, which evokes the reader's cognitive conception on the socio-political function of the bread in human relationships. Jesus' breaking action as a metaphor not only signifies the end of hostility where the crowds are gathered and solidified as a familial community, but it also proclaims the establishment of new community as a prophetic fulfillment.

First, in the first feeding narrative Jesus breaks the hostility and exclusive boundaries through the *breaking/sharing* of bread with the crowds. According to the narrative flow, the crowds in the first feeding scene must be composed of the sick and the marginalized that are desperate for help in Jewish society. Most of them were the marginalized who lived the agony of alienation from the major society and who were denied access to power both socially and religiously.[57] There was an invisible social hostility to the marginalized and boundaries between the classes. Actually, Matthew's gospel clearly describes a certain distinction between the crowds and the religious elites. However, Matthew's Jesus had compassion on them, healed their disease willingly, and he finally broke the bread with them. Interestingly, Matthew's account of Jesus' feeding clearly incorporates "women and children" (14:21), the social minorities in Jesus' time, into the community of Jesus-followers who were satisfied by Jesus' provision. Jesus' breaking action metaphorically means that Jesus invites all the marginalized into communal solidarity in God's complete care, as Ancient Israel experienced in the wilderness.

Second, the reader recognizes that the narrator metaphorically expresses that Jesus is also making a new covenant with the crowd through the breaking of bread. As the three sequential verbs parallel those of Jesus' Last Supper meal (26:26), the reader applies the meaning of the Last Supper as the establishment of a new covenant into Jesus' feeding moment.[58] Obviously, members of the Matthean community and the reader already know the meaning of Eucharist in the early church and Jesus' Last Supper meal: Jesus made a new covenant beyond the Jewish tradition (Matthew 26:26–29; Mark 14:22–25; Luke 22:14–20). In Jewish cultural tradition, commensalism was thought of not only as confirming intimate relationships and constituting kinship in a real sense[59] but also as constituting a covenantal relationship.[60] So, Jesus' act of feeding is itself connected to making a covenant. Interestingly, the narrator describes that Jesus feeds the crowds with only five loaves and two fishes (μὴ πέντε ἄρτους καὶ δύο ἰχθύας, v. 17). Some scholars see the number of the loaves has a symbolic meaning that the five loaves stands for the symbol of Torah, the five books of Moses.[61] So, Jesus' breaking of five loaves not only means the sharing of a meal but also signifies the establishment of new covenant.

Third, as far as the constitution of a covenantal relationship is concerned, the breaking of bread not only means to have a communal relationship but also signifies participation into a common ideology. Basically, the acceptance of the broken bread symbolizes the acceptance of the authority of Jesus.[62] When the crowds share the bread broken by Jesus' hand, the crowds tacitly accept the power and authority of Jesus and his teachings and ideology of the kingdom of God, as the Ancient Israelite completely accepted and depended on the sovereignty of God, the central ideological authority of the Passover and the gift of Manna in the wilderness.

In the wisdom literature, the food God provides is identified with God's word; the food embodies his wisdom (Proverbs 9:1–6; 10:11; 13:14; 14:27; 16:22; 24:13–14; Psalms 36:9; 42:1–3, 23; Isaiah 12:3; Jeremiah 17:13).[63] In this regard, when Jesus breaks the bread and shares the bread, Jesus' teaching must be established as a binding agreement, acceptance, and a covenant among the crowds. For the crowds, the breaking of bread and eating the bread means to participate in the common sense of value and ideology, especially Jesus' teachings in this context. The narrator clearly describes that Jesus gives the broken pieces of bread to disciples who distribute them to the crowds (14:19) and all people are satisfied (14:20). In this point, the breaking of bread and the sharing of bread are not just a matter of a communal relationship but represent to participate in an ideology and teaching.

Fourth, the metaphor of Jesus' breaking of bread in the first feeding narrative is eventually an actual formation of community. Through the act of breaking of bread, Matthew's narrator presents that Jesus promulgates the end of hostility among the crowds, makes a new covenant with them, and ultimately establishes a new community with the crowds that is mostly composed of Jews. In the first feeding scene, the reader flashes back to the foundation of Israel's communal identity, which is formed by the common experience of Exodus and the wilderness: Passover and Manna. Overlapping the ancient knowledge with the feeding narrative, one can retrospect the original process of the formation of Israel and the basic premise of Jewish identity in the covenantal (close) relationship with God. Then, the reader and the crowds compare and contrast their own conception and the theological theme in the feeding story, and recognize a new relationship with Jesus who provides food and complete care in the deserted place, which can correspond to what God has done in Ancient Israel. Especially, when Jesus breaks the bread and shares a meal with the crowds, the scene itself can be a germinator of formation of communal identity and the new community with a new ideology is established.

At the end of the feeding scene, Matthew's narrator clearly indicates that "the twelve baskets full of the broken pieces left over: ἦραν τὸ περισσεῦον τῶν κλασμάτων δώδεκα κοφίνους πλήρεις" (14:20). Matthew's narrator omits the reference to fish in the Markan narrative 6:43 (broken pieces and of fish): ἦραν κλάσματα δώδεκα κοφίνων πληρώματα καὶ ἀπὸ τῶν ἰχθύων. It seems that Matthew's narrator intentionally highlights the bread itself broken by Jesus' hand, weakening the significance of the fish in this context. However, the narrator leads the reader's attention to the left-overs: *twelve baskets*.

There is scholarly agreement on the number twelve that the symbolic meaning of the number δώδεκα is associated with the twelve tribes of Israel.[64] John Nolland sees that "the number twelve is probably symbolic: food for all Israel"[65] and the gathering of the fragments indicates the future ministry. In this point, Jesus' breaking of bread is ultimately for all of fractured Israel in the future, as Matthew reveals Jesus' mission strategy in 10:5–6. Jesus' breaking of bread represents the ultimate restoration of Israel as a new community which is formed by Jesus' complete care and his life-giving provision with a new covenant and ideology. In the Hebrew Bible, God's abundant provision, especially the renewed provision of food used as means of expressing the belief that God will restore the Israel community and their fortune.[66] When Israel lamented encountering a terrible situation, in response to the lament God provides abundant foods and comforts Israel (e.g., Joel 2:18–19). God's provision of food functions as a symbol of restoration.

Jesus said to the disciples, "Bring them here to me" (Φέρετέ μοι ὧδε αὐτούς 4:18), before he breaks the bread. "ὧδε, (here)" is the place Jesus withdrew from the dangerous place and society that does not accept Jesus' teaching and ideology. "ὧδε" indicates the deserted place which evokes the communal experience in the wilderness and the communal identity of Israel. With the terms "ἀναχώρεω," the narrator metaphorically presents that Jesus' prophetic fulfillment, the formation of a new community envisioning the ultimate restoration of Israel, is performed at the place of "ὧδε" where he withdrew and broke the bread. Consequently, the community of the crowds Jesus formed is the first result of Jesus' ministry toward the lost sheep of the house of Israel (10:52).

The Role of the First Feeding Narrative in the Context of Matthew's Gospel

Fulfillment of Previous Discourses and Teachings of Jesus

In light of the metaphoric interpretation, the primary significance of the first feeding narrative in the context of the Gospel of Matthew is to be seen in the role that it presents a consequence of fulfillment of Jesus' own discourse, teaching, and ministry in the previous chapters in Matthew. Namely, Matthew's narrator metaphorically describes the formation of a new community as the ultimate vision of the Israel's restoration through the breaking of bread by Jesus' hand in the first feeding and synthesizes previous discourse and teachings. The scene itself functions to show that Jesus is executing his prophetic purpose based on his teachings and ministerial instructions, in which the ideological vision of the kingdom of heaven is exposed.

After Jesus' baptism (3:13–17) and temptation in the wilderness (4:1–11), the Gospel of Matthew recounts Jesus' official ministry, proclaiming the good news of the kingdom (4:17). Before the feeding narrative, the reader recognizes four phases of activities that divide Jesus' ministry in Matthew: teaching, healing, mission instruction, and actual practice. Matthew's narrator concentrates on Jesus' teaching ministry in chapter 5–7, and chapter 8–9 recounts Jesus' healing activities. Then, in chapter 10, Matthew presents Jesus' specific mission instruction.

In the first phase of Jesus' ministry (chapter 4–13), all of the teaching, healing, and instructions are a foundation of Jesus' symbolic action: *the breaking of bread.* In addition, Jesus' teaching discourse seems to be addressed directly to the disciples (5:1–2), but the audience must be all of the crowds in the context of the Gospel (4:24–25). Actually, the crowds were described as astounded at Jesus' teaching at the end of his exhortations (7:28). In this regard, the crowds at Jesus' feeding scene, not all of them but many who keep following Jesus are already taught by Jesus and know the ideological vision of Jesus when he breaks the bread. Then, they participate in the community formed by Jesus in the first feeding scene.

Most of all, Jesus' teaching and Sermon on the Mount are not only relevant to his innovative understanding of the kingdom of heaven but also represent his ideological discourses for the alternative visional community, which people should accept and follow. Jesus' teaching is composed of four sections: the Beatitudes (5:3–16), Six Antitheses (5:17–48), Jesus' own teaching on authentic piety (6:1–7:12), and Exhortations to moral action (7:13–27). All the teaching discourses are Jesus' own interpretation of Torah and Jesus' own understanding of Jewish heritage, with which Jesus offers a new covenantal vision and the sense of socio-religious value in Jesus' time. Its setting on a mountain also describes Jesus as a Moses-like figure and even as the one who exceeds Moses as authoritative teacher who leads the people into new faith and new understanding of their Jewish traditions.[67] The teaching discourse and alternative interpretation of Torah have authority to challenge the contemporary religious thought, as Moses did. Furthermore, his teaching and preaching not only contain Jesus' ideological vision for the kingdom of heaven but also reveal Matthew's messianic vision for the restoration of Israel, the formation of new community.

Then the Gospel of Matthew leads the reader into the cluster of the miraculous healing stories[68] in chapter 8–9. Following Jesus' teaching discourses, the healing stories reveal Jesus' majestic power to heal as well as extraordinary compassion toward the people he met (9:36). In the cluster of healing stories, the crowds (8:1) and the people whom Jesus met and healed are all the marginalized who had a disease or were possessed by a demon. According to Matthew's narrative in chapters 8–9, Jesus intentionally meets with the marginalized in Jewish society and shows great compassion on them after he finished teaching the crowds. Matthew's narrator briefly explains Jesus' continuing ministry of teaching, preaching about the good news of the kingdom, and healing the sick (9:35).

Jesus regards the people he met as "harassed and helpless, like sheep without a shepherd" (9:36), as the narrator explains the motif of Jesus' compassion. The flock image of Israel is common in the Hebrew Bible, especially when the relationship between God and Israel is metaphorically expressed as the relation between flock and shepherd.[69] Compared with the usage of this imagery in Hebrew Bible, the expression appropriately indicates that Israel needs new leadership for the restoration of Israel after the destruction of temple at A.D. 70.[70] At the same time, in the healing narratives in Matthew and his work for the restoration, Jesus concentrates on the marginalized and "wishes to serve as their shepherd"[71] in order to restore their lives. So, Matthew's Jesus indirectly shows his messianic vision, quoting from Hosea 6:6: "I desire mercy, not sacrifice. For I have come to call not righteous but sinners." In this regard, Donald Senior affirms that "the healing stories are not simply a physical transformation of sick or possessed people; they extend beyond physical cures to profound spiritual transformation and healing whereby those who had been isolated or excluded are now drawn into the community and partake of its life."[72] The same compassion on the crowds is a motivation of Jesus' breaking of bread in the first feeding narrative. This is all about what Jesus has done as a healer in Matthew, which followed Jesus' teaching discourses.

Based on the teaching, proclamation of the good news for the kingdom, and healing activities, Jesus summons twelve disciples, gives them authority to do what Jesus had done, and sends them to the lost sheep of the house of Israel in chapter 10. Then Matthew recounts additional ministry of Jesus and teaching including controversies with Jewish leaders in chapter 11–13. Finally, Matthew's narrator metaphorically presents that Jesus establishes a new community with the crowds in the first feeding narrative (chapter 14) through Jesus' symbolic act of breaking of bread.

Thus, Jesus' first feeding the crowds can be seen as a prophetic action, synthesizing previous teaching and ministries. Especially, with Jesus' withdrawal (ἀναχώρεω) from the place of the death of John the Baptist (14:13), Matthew invites the reader to expect a following prophetic fulfillment and presents Jesus' prophetic action in the first feeding scene.[73] Obviously, the reader must be familiar with Jesus' teaching discourse and healing activities in the previous chapter, so that the reader may expect Jesus' prophetic action. So, the first feeding scene as a symbolic formation of community functions as a prophetic fulfillment of the previous discourse and teaching of Jesus.

Only for the Lost Sheep of the House of Israel

The narrative function of the first feeding scene as a prophetic fulfillment of previous discourse corresponds to Jesus' Mission instruction in chapter 10. Namely, the first feeding scene and the bread metaphor function as means of expressing the fulfillment of Jesus' own mission instruction. After the teaching and healing activities, Matthew's Jesus gives a specific instruction for Mission to his twelve disciples. In the Mission instructions, Jesus clearly urges them not to go anywhere in Gentile areas but only go to the Jewish territory (10:5–6). What the texts actually prohibits is 'the way of Gentiles' εἰς ὁδὸν ἐθνῶν and 'the town of Samaritans' εἰς πόλιν Σαμαριτῶν. According to Davies and Allison, the phrase εἰς ὁδὸν ἐθνῶν refer to "a road leading to a Gentile city," [74] so that Jesus' instruction very strictly prohibits reaching out even on the way toward the Gentile territory. Furthermore, interestingly Jesus never entered Samaritan territory in the Gospel of Matthew as a whole, in contrast to the Gospel of Luke and John. At the same time, Jesus urges his disciples to only go to τὰ πρόβατα τὰ ἀπολωλότα οἴκου Ἰσραήλ. 'The lost sheep' does not mean a certain 'lost' group or elements among Jewish people, but the whole phrase itself means that the object of Jesus' mission instruction is the Jewish people as a whole. However, compared to the references to ἐθνῶν and Σαμαριτῶν,[75] Jesus obviously confined his mission within the boundaries of Jews.

The mission instruction is very exclusive and limited within the boundaries of Jewish territory and it is even confined by ethnicity. Of course, the Gospel of Matthew extends Jesus' mission to the all nations in later part of Matthew 28:16–28. However, up to this stage of the first feeding scene, the reader clearly recognizes that Jesus' ministry and mission are confined by the strong focus on the restoration of Israel[76] and a particular socio-religious ethnicity: Jew. Actually, all of Jesus' instructions in chapter 10 follow the pattern and ways of Jesus' previous ministry, which he began in Galilee (4:12–16), teaching, proclaiming the good news of the kingdom, and healing the marginalized up to this point.[77] In his previous ministry, except in 8:28–34, Jesus has never crossed the borders of Israel until

15:21.[78] In addition, the narrator repeats this strict mission instruction through the mouth of Jesus in 15:24, reaffirming the limitation to "the lost sheep of the house of Israel" and applying it to Jesus' vocation. Up to this point, the reader realizes that the Gospel of Matthew intentionally highlights what Jesus has done as a messiah for the Jews and for their restoration and the ideology of Mission.

From the perspective of Jesus' mission instruction, the bread metaphor and Jewish crowds in the first feeding narrative are great examples of consequences of Jesus' mission and his prophetic fulfillment. From the beginning of Jesus' official ministry in Galilee (4:12–16) to the first feeding scene, Jesus keeps teaching, preaching, and healing people in the cities and villages in Jewish territory (9:35). All the time many crowds of Jews, which is mainly the marginalized, follow the itinerant ways of Jesus (5:1; 7:28; 8:16; 8:18; 9:25; 11:7; 12:15; 12:46; 13:1 14:13), and Jesus always has great compassion on them, hoping to serve them as a shepherd (9:36; 14:14). When Matthew's Jesus metaphorically establishes a new community with the Jewish crowd in Jewish territory through the breaking of bread, the reader realizes that Jesus is doing what he was supposed to do according to his mission and instructions, especially up to this point. Thus the first feeding narrative reveals the bread and Jesus' breaking of bread as a narrative strategy by means of metaphor and utilizes it as significant literary function to highlight Jesus' mission strategy and the prophetic fulfillment of Jesus' mission.

The Bread in the Second Feeding Narrative (15:29–39)

The second feeding narrative is very similar to the first one. In the feeding (vv. 32–39) scene, the reader recalls clearly the previous feeding story (14:13–21). The theme and meaning are also same, but the fundamental meaning of the feeding is extended and intensified here. The author's deeper intention of this repeated story is exhibited by some differences between two narratives. These differences intensify the metaphoric role of the bread and expand the boundary of Jesus' provision of food and his community.

Significant Features of the Narrative

Location: *Mountain*

It is impossible to trace Jesus' itinerant route and geographical location exactly with the sparse information in this narrative. However, in the second feeding narrative, the narrator clearly describes that Jesus performs the second feeding "on the mountain." Jesus left from the place he conversed with the Canaanite woman (ἐταβὰς ἐκεῖθεν, v. 29) and went up to the mountain (ἀναβὰς εἰς τὸ ὄρος, v. 29). To. ὄρος possibly reminds the reader of the same mountain as in 14:23 and 5:1.[79] The Gospel of Matthew places the important events in Jesus' life mostly on mountain sites: Jesus' temptation (4:8–10), the second feeding scene (15:29–39), the transfiguration (17:1–9), and the great commission (28:16). The specific place of Jesus' ministry—especially the phrase εἰς τὸ ὄρος—is very important for interpreting the theological meanings of each narrative.

In the Ancient Near Eastern world, the mountains were regarded as "the homes of the gods and sacred sites."[80] In the Old Testament the mountains, the Hebrew הַר associated with the LXX ὄρος,[81] sometimes implicitly express "the superior power of God over all things on earth" in prophecy and poetry (Psalm 90:2; 95:4; 65:6; Isaiah 40:12, etc).[82] To. ὄρος also represents a sense of God's nearness, associated with the mountains of Sinai, Zion, Ebal, and Gerizim.[83] At this point, Terence L. Donaldson's work[84] is very helpful for understanding the motif of τὸ ὄρος. So, I will mostly adopt his argument in this part. He critically observes the usage of τὸ ὄρος, both in the Old Testament and Second Temple Judaism, in light of the mountain of Sinai and Zion traditions by analyzing the importance of historical events, divine election, and the people's cultic life. First, the הר appears in juxtaposition with סיני or חורב and is used to designate "the site of the giving of the law" in Exodus, Leviticus, Numbers and Deuteronomy. (Exodus 3:1; 4:27; 18:5; 24:13; Numbers 10:33).[85] The Sinai event is one of the crucial accounts for the formation of Israel's self-understanding and their salvation history in the Old Testament. The most significant feature of the Sinai account is "the form of *Theophany*," in which God encounters his people on the mountain (Exodus 19:9, 18; 34:5).[86] Donaldson argues that the event is not just *theophany*, but a "covenant-making ceremony." Namely, the Scripture describes the Sinai event not just as a revelation of God, but the event clearly represents a crucial moment in which Yahweh willingly binds himself to the Israelites in covenant relationship. Then Donaldson emphasizes the Sinai event as "the basic presupposition for the rest of the Old Testament,"[87] which is the core of Israel's covenant theology. The Deuteronomic tradition keeps retelling the account, reminding the reader of Mount Sinai. Sinai does not just designate a geographical location, but it represents the root of the covenantal relationship with God and the formation of Israel's salvation history. From this point, "Sinai played a foundational role as the mountain association with Israel's constitution as a people."[88]

Second, in the Old Testament, הר is associated with Zion – צִיּוֹן, referring to the site of the temple or the city as a whole. Mostly Mount Zion is used synonymously with 'Jerusalem,' representing "the mountain of the house of the Lord" (Micah 3:12–4:2). In this Zion tradition, Donaldson finds two significant theological features: Zion as a present religious and political reality and Zion as an eschatological vision. First, Mount Zion is described as the place in which Yahweh chose to dwell[89] as political and religious center. In light of the covenant relationship with God, the covenant with David was established on the election of Zion, representing a shift from Sinai as the center of God's place in the wilderness experience to Zion as God's dwelling place and the center of worship (Psalm 68; 78; 132).[90] In terms of "throne, kingship, and sovereignty," the motif of Mount Zion exhibits the political-religious role of Zion within Israel.

For instance, in so-called "Royal Psalm,"[91] Yahweh declares the Mount Zion would not only be "the site of Yahweh's throne and the center of his rule" (Psalm 47; 48; 99:1–5; 146:10) but also the throne of King David and his line: "I have set my king on Zion, my holy mountain" (Psalm 2:6; 110:2; 132:11–18).[92] At the same time, the theme of Zion reflects its religious role as a center of worship. The Psalmist describes Zion as Yahweh's sanctuary (Psalm 78:67–71) and the place where the people participate in praise and worship (Psalm 15:1; 24:3; 99:9; 102:21), responding to Yahweh's election of Israel's King. The Israelites celebrated the election of the king in their territory and developed the motif of Mount Zion in their religious tradition. With this regard, Donaldson sees that, as Sinai was the site of Israel's constitution, Zion is "the living center of Israel's political and religious existence," revealing God's continuing presence with his people.[93]

Third, Mount Zion symbolically extended its theological role as a vehicle for eschatological hopes and ideals in a variety of changing circumstances.[94] In the prophetic literature, the Psalmists' conception of Zion is reflected in the eschatological vision of prophets, in which Yahweh restored Israel and set the throne of the King on Zion again as the center of the renewed Israel.[95] In this eschatological vision, God will gather the scattered Israelites into renewed relationship on Zion (Jeremiah 31:1–25) and re-establish and purify the Temple on the mountain (Ezekiel 40–48). In this holy place, people who gathered and are purified will serve Yahweh again (Ezekiel 20:33–44; Isaiah 35), and form a renewed community. Furthermore, Zion is described as the place in which Yahweh defeats and rules over the nations (Isaiah 24:23; 29:8; Joel 3:9–21; Micah 4:11–13). Zion would be the center of worship in which all nations participate and share in the eschatological blessing (Isaiah 25:6–10; 56:6–8).[96]

Thus, Zion will be the place of the realization of the eschatological messianic banquet. From this perspective, one can see the second feeding on the mountain place is not just showing a geographical location of Jesus, but a special narrative strategy for presenting a symbolic or metaphoric meaning of the bread and Jesus' provision of banquet.

Crowds: *Gentile*

According to the context of the second feeding narrative, the description of the crowds can be identified as *Gentiles*, which is different from the first one. However, the determination of the crowd's identity is indeed not easy. In the last decade, scholarly opinions have been equally divided on the ethnic identity of the crowd in the second feeding narrative. Some scholars would argue the Jewishness of the crowd,[97] and others concentrate on their Gentile character.[98]

Scholarly analyses of the question of ethnic character of the crowds in the second feeding basically examine two factors: the geographical route of Jesus' travel and the interpretation of the phrase, "τὸν θεὸν Ἰσραήλ" (15:31). Firstly, on the one hand, those who would see a Jewishness of the crowd stress that Jesus completely came out from the Gentile territory and came into the side of the Sea of Galilee, which is Jewish territory. For instance, Ulrich Luz argues that Mark's Gospel clearly shows that the second feeding story takes place on the eastern gentile shore of the lake with the specific description of the crowd's physical location: "Some of them have came a long way (distance), τινες αὐτῶν ἀπὸ μακρόθεν ἥκασιν" (Mark 8:3).[99] However, Matthew's narrator intentionally omits this description because Matthew's narrator wants to avoid any possible impression that the crowd might be Gentiles.[100] So, Luz affirms that the crowd in Matthew cannot be regarded as Gentiles. On the other hand, scholars on the side of Gentile character, such as Gundry, Carson, Harrington, Davies and Allison interpret that Jesus traveled into gentile territory northeast of the Sea of Galilee, comparing to the counterpart in Mark.[101] They connect the feeding episode to the foregoing Gentile mission. The description of Jesus' itinerary in Matthew 15:29–31 is very vague. So, both opinions are reasonable.

However, in light of the matter of the ethnicity of the crowd, Jesus' itinerant route or geographical location is not crucial. This is because Jesus never comes to find the place of the crowd, but rather the crowds always follow Jesus' route and strive to find where Jesus is in the Gospel narrative (cf. 4:25; 8:1; 15:21, 29–30; 19:2; 20:29). In this view, Jesus' geographical location cannot be a clue to answer the question of the ethnic character of the crowds.

Second, the interpretation of the phrase "τὸν θεὸν Ἰσραήλ" (15:31) is a compelling source to recognize the crowd as Gentiles for lots of scholars. When Jesus heals the crowd (15:31), the narrator describes that the crowd "glorified the God of Israel, (ἐδόξασαν τὸν θεὸν Ἰσραήλ)". Daniel Harrington argues that the phrase, "τὸν θεὸν Ἰσραήλ" is "a bit odd,"[102] if it was on the mouth of Israelites. Carson also insists that it "could be naturally said only by Gentile."[103] Further, Bruner observes and finds a similar phrase in the reaction of the Philistines in 1 Samuel 4:1–7:1.[104] Most scholars, who interpret the crowd as Gentiles, insist that this phrase technically represents the ethnic identity of the crowd.[105] If the crowds were Jews, the reader would expect "they glorified God,"[106] not "the God of Israel." Namely, the Gentile crowds employ the God of the other nation and praise that god, the God of Israel, when they are healed.

The recent study by J. R. C. Cousland presents a different opinion about the phrase "τὸν θεὸν Ἰσραήλ". Cousland argues that the designation "God of Israel" is most proper in the mouth of Israelites, evoking Jewish salvation history and reflecting Israel's cultic response to God.[107] He presents some examples of the usage of this phrase in Hebrew Scripture. Then Cousland clearly affirms that the most "occurrences of God of Israel and its variants in the Hebrew scriptures are not attributed to Gentiles."[108] Rather "Yahweh, God of Israel" encapsulates the covenantal relationship between Yahweh and his people Israel.[109] Furthermore, he insists the phrase "the God of Israel" naturally corresponds to "the House of Israel" (15:24).[110]

However, Cousland's argument is not entirely accurate as far as the phrase "the God of Israel" is concerned. Actually, in the Hebrew Scriptures, one can find both examples of "the God of Israel" in the mouth of Gentiles and by Israel, even if there is a difference of frequency. However, if one reads the second feeding narrative within the context of narrative flow, referring to other peculiar features of this narrative, the phrase "the God of Israel" is more fitting in the mouth of Gentiles.

The Breaking of Bread: Expansion of Matthew's Community

Breaking the Boundaries

The second feeding narrative (15:29–39) greatly parallels the first feeding narrative (14:13–21), so that the reader easily recognizes that the narrator presents Jesus' prophetic fulfillment again through the breaking of bread, signifying the establishment of a new community. As Janice C. Anderson argues, the repeated feeding stories, which are underscored by Jesus' verbal repetition and similar dialogue, serve to highlight "something that is typical of a character,"[111] events, and its theological discourse as a prophetic fulfillment.

As in the first feeding scene, Jesus heals the sick (15:30–31) and shows compassion on the crowds (vv. 32) by his compassionate willingness of feeding for the crowds. Jesus' compassion leads the reader to remember the image of God who provided the food in the wilderness. The feeding scene itself recalls Ancient Israel's experience of the Passover meal and manna, as the reader did in the previous narrative. In particular, the disciples' question to Jesus, "where are we to get so much bread in the wilderness?" (v. 33), reminds the reader again of the manna experience of Ancient Israel,[112] combining "wilderness" and "bread."

The narrator also highlights the motif of bread, which leads the reader's attention to the bread metaphor and its discourse. In the case of Mark's Gospel, the narrative presents two separate distributions equally, one for bread and the other for fish (Mark 8:6–7). However, Matthew's narrator describes that Jesus took "a few small fish" (ὀλίγα ἰχθύδια 15:34) along with the seven loaves of bread (15:36), then Matthew's Gospel simply drops the fish from the whole account of the Gospel.[113] Furthermore, the sequence of three verbs of Jesus' action, consisting of "εὐχαριστέω"[114] (give thanks) "κλάω" (breaking of bread), and "δίδωμι" (distribution) in v. 36 and the result that the crowds are satisfied (vv. 37–38) are mostly similar to the previous feeding narrative unit, representing similar meanings of the metaphor of bread.

As the first feeding narrative represents, Jesus' second feeding event shows its correspondence between Jesus' feeding and God's complete care for Israel again. Jesus' ministry and character evoke the reader's cognitive conception of the image of God in close covenantal relationship with Ancient Israel, which reflects the formation of Israel's communal identity and ideology and its formatting process in the history of Israel. When Jesus breaks the bread by his own hand, the breaking action itself as a metaphor in the second feeding scene also symbolically signifies *the end of hostility, making a covenant, and an actual formation of new community.* The reader who knows the metaphoric meaning of Jesus' first feeding ministry simply recognizes that Jesus invites all the crowds into communal solidarity in God's complete care and symbolically forms a communal identity and its visional community through breaking of bread. Furthermore, the crowds not only accept Jesus' invitation but also actively participate in Jesus' visional community. The metaphorical interpretation and theological significance of the second feeding narrative are basically the same as those of the first, so the detailed discourse of the second feeding does not need to be repeated here.

However, the most significant meaning of the repeated story of Jesus' second feeding is derived from the different features of the feeding stories. The most significant distinction is the constituency of the crowds: *the marginalized and the Gentile*. Whether the crowds are Gentiles or Jews is still debated. Nevertheless, the narrative flow and symbolic narrative features clearly support that the crowds in the second feeding narrative must contain many Gentiles. The narrative unit begins with the description of Jesus' location; Jesus now came "from there" (v. 29), which is the Gentile territory, the district of Tyre and Sidon (15:21–28), in which Jesus visited to meet the Canaanite woman, and then Jesus passed along the Sea of Galilee (v. 29f). As always happens in Matthew,[115] the large crowds followed Jesus (v. 30). So, the crowds are probably gathered at a certain place around the district of Tyre and Sidon and even the Sea of Galilee, which is around the border line between Gentile territories and Jewish territory.[116] In this respect and Jesus' itinerant route, the reader may assume that the crowds are mostly composed of the Gentiles, following Jesus' location.

Some narrative features implicitly support that the character of the crowds in the second feeding scene are Gentiles. The different number of loaves of bread and the baskets of leftovers; *Seven*, is very crucial for interpreting this narrative in terms of the components of the crowds. After showing Jesus' compassion to feed the crowds, Jesus asked the disciples, "how many loaves have you?" (v. 34).[117] Interestingly, in the first feeding narrative, Jesus did not ask anything, but just commanded, "you give them something to eat" (14:16). However, in the second feeding scene, Jesus actively asked and participated in the matter. The disciples answered, "Seven, and a few small fish." (v. 34). Furthermore, at the end of this narrative, the narrator places the number seven again on the baskets of leftovers. It describes that the disciples "took up seven baskets full of the broken pieces left over (v.37). It is obvious that Matthew's narrator intends to highlight the number of loaves, *seven*, signifying some special meaning, which can be a clue to the second feeding narrative.

Most scholars see that the number *seven* often represents a symbolic value as a "reference to the Gentiles."[118] The usage of the number seven for modifying breads and baskets of leftovers as a narrative strategy indirectly manifests the character of the crowds and the feeding event itself. If the five breads and twelve baskets each signify the Torah and the twelve tribes of Israel, the seven breads and baskets can be associated with the Gentiles.[119]

Furthermore, in this narrative unit, the Greek usage of the baskets shows its distinctive feature. While the narrator describes it δώδεκα κοφίνους πλήρεις (full of twelve baskets) in the first feeding narrative (14:20), the second feeding uses ἑπτὰ σπυρίδας for describing the leftovers (15:37). In the Gospel accounts, κοφίνος is always the word for the twelve baskets of leftovers (Matthew 14:20; Mark 6:43; Luke 9:17; John 16:13), which is "considered typical for the Jews,"[120] and σπυρίς[121] is used in reference for the seven baskets (Matthew 15:37; Mark 8:8), a typical term among the Greeks.[122] In this regard, the number of seven breads and baskets has a symbolical significance for presenting the character of the crowd and the feeding itself: *Gentile*. From this perspective, the reader can recognize that, while Jesus fed a Jewish crowd with the five breads and fully satisfied them with twelve baskets left over in the first feeding narrative (14:13–21). Here Jesus feeds the Gentile crowds including "the lame, the maimed, the blind, the mute" (15:30), which represent all the marginalized in Jesus' society, with seven breads and perfectly satisfied them with seven baskets left over, signifying all Gentile nations (15:29–30).

The distinct narrative features of the second feeding narrative intensify the metaphoric meaning of Jesus' prophetic fulfillment revealed in the first feeding scene. As was studied, Jesus' feeding and sharing bread with others symbolically connects to God's blessing and provision, acknowledging God's sovereign power and God's provision of a life-giving source. Based on these conceptions, the metaphor of bread, especially, the metaphor of the breaking of bread signifies *the end of hostility, making a new covenant, and the actual formation of a new community* in the second feeding narrative, as was in the previous narrative. However, here the object of the breaking of bread is extended from the Jews to the Gentiles. According to the metaphor of bread in the reader's conception, Matthew's narrative of second feeding metaphorically represents that all the Gentiles and the marginalized are invited to a community under God's complete care and God's sovereignty.[123] When Jesus breaks the seven breads, Matthew's Jesus proclaims the end of hostility in the relationship between the Jews and the Gentiles.

In addition, breaking the seven loaves of bread with the Gentile crowds, Matthew's Gospel signifies Jesus now makes a new covenant with them. Especially, in light of Jesus' breaking of bread happening on the mountain (15:30), as Donaldson argues upon the Sinai tradition of Jewish conception, the breaking of bread reminds the reader of *theophany* and signifies a "covenant-making ceremony."[124] Thus, Jesus' prophetic feeding action not only represents the revelation of God, but Jesus willingly binds himself to the crowds in a new covenantal relationship.

Furthermore, when Jesus breaks the bread, Matthew's narrator metaphorically represents that Jesus establishes a new community again, including the Gentiles. When Jesus breaks the seven breads with the Gentile crowds and all the people are fully satisfied with seven baskets left over, it signifies that all the crowds participate in Jesus' teaching and ideological claims.

Likewise in the first feeding as a family meal, when Jesus gives thanks (εὐχαριστέω) and breaks (κλάω) the bread (15:36), Jesus becomes a head of house, invites all crowds including the marginalized into a meal, and blesses them and solidifies them as a family under God's complete care. Accordingly, Matthew's narrator metaphorically represents God's metaphoric image as a provider and God's sovereign power in and through Jesus' compassionate action and prophetic action of breaking bread. Through the blessing and the breaking of bread, all the crowds, especially the Gentiles, at the meal are solidified as a single community under God's provision. From this perspective, while Jesus' first feeding concentrates on the restoration of Israel with the breaking of existing socio-religious boundaries, Jesus' second feeding extends the boundary of Jesus' visional community, opening it to all the Gentiles. In the second feeding narrative, Jesus' prophetic action of the breaking of bread not only means the breaking of socio-religious boundaries but also represents the expansion of the boundaries of the kingdom of heaven.

Eschatological Banquet: *New Israel*

One of the significant theological points of the second feeding event in light of the narrative feature of "the mountain" is that Jesus' feeding is identified with the eschatological messianic banquet.[125] Matthew's narrator clearly explains that the place where Jesus meets the crowd, is on the mountain (15:29), while the first feeding happens in a deserted place (14:13). This distinction is paid little attention by many scholars;[126] however, the mountain has a theological significance in Jewish tradition not only as a foundation of Israel's communal identity,[127] but also as a vehicle for eschatological hopes and ideals: *the messianic banquet.*

The banquet imagery is utilized as a metaphor of the vindication of God's people in Israel's scriptural traditions. Israel's conception of the eschatological messianic banquet derives from the so-called "Isaianic Apocalypses" (Isaiah 24–27), in which Israel envisions the final redemption of God's people in terms of the banquet on Mount Zion hosted by God.[128] Originally, Mount Zion has been recognized as Yahweh's chosen place as abode and the site of the throne of his rule and ultimately as the center of Yahweh's rule of the world (Psalms 47; 48; 99:1–5; 132:11–13)[129] in Hebrew scripture. In the eschatological vision, Israel prophetically envisions that Zion as Yahweh's dwelling place will be renewed and restored, and Yahweh will again gather his scattered people into a renewed fellowship on the mountain.[130] On the mountain "the Lord of hosts will make for all peoples a feast of fat things, a feast of wine on the lees," (Isaiah 25:6) and he invites all people, even to those "who have no money," and he says, "come, buy and eat! Come buy wine and milk without money and without price" (Isaiah 55:1). Furthermore, a widespread expectation that the messiah will invite the people to participate in the messianic banquet is found in the literature of the Second Temple period (e.g., 1QS 6:4–5; 1QSa 2:11–22; 2 Baruch 29:4–10; 4 Ezra 6:52; 1 Enoch 60:24; 62:1–16).

Claassens affirms, "Israel imagined their restored life with God as a banquet where the whole community eats together,"[131] especially on the mountain. So, the cognitive conception of the Jewish reader flashes into the reader's mind at the point of the fact that Jesus' second feeding is held on the mountain. The reader can map the structure of the metaphor of bread in the second feeding narrative in the light of Israel's eschatological vision. Thus, as Donaldson insists, the mountain of 15:29 functions as "an eschatological site."[132] When Jesus breaks the bread, it is not just sharing a meal or a compassionate provision of food but an eschatological messianic banquet in which Jesus symbolically re-gathers the scattered people into a renewed fellowship with a new covenant and restores Yahweh's rule of the world. At the same time, Jesus' breaking of the bread in the second feeding narrative in Matthew's Gospel metaphorically signifies the fulfillment of the expected eschatological vision in Jesus' ministry.

The most significant theological point is that the messianic banquets ultimately include the Gentile nations. Israel's prophetic traditions include the defeat of Gentile idolatry at Zion (Isaiah 44:6–20; Joel 3:9–21; Micah 4:11–13); at the same time these traditions clearly present the ultimate inclusion of Gentile nations as recipients of God's blessing in the eschatological age (e.g., Isaiah 24:23; 42:6; 49:6; 51:5; 56:6–8):

> "It is too light a thing that you should be my servant to raise up the tribes of Jacob and to restore the survivors of Israel; I will give you as a light to the nations, that my salvation may reach to the end of the earth." (Isaiah 49:6)

God will bring foreigners to his "holy mountain" to worship at the house of prayer (Isaiah 56:6–8); and the Gentile nations will participate in a banquet on "this mountain" (Isaiah 25:6–10) coming to worship Yahweh. So, it must not be surprising for the reader that Jesus in the prophetic tradition holds out the eschatological hope for the inclusion of Gentiles in the messianic banquet.

From this perspective, Matthew's second feeding narrative invites the reader to see the metaphor of bread, especially when Jesus breaks the seven breads, as the fulfillment of Israel's eschatological vision,[133] which particularly includes all the nations. All the elements of the narrative features–the gathering of the crowds on the mountain, which contains Gentiles (15:29), the healing of the lame, maimed, blind and many other sick people (15:30–31), and the feast of plentiful food (15:37, seven baskets leftover), which alludes to the messianic banquet–can be identified with the pattern of Israel's eschatological hope described with banquet imagery. The crowds have already participated in the messianic banquet, over which Jesus presides through the breaking of bread without any condition or boundaries. Thus when Jesus breaks the seven breads here, it metaphorically represents the messianic banquet, which fulfills not only the restoration of Israel but also the ultimate eschatological hope for reaching out to the end of the earth. Ultimately, the metaphor of bread and its breaking in Jesus' banquet shattered all the conditions and boundaries and established a new visional community.

The Role of the Second Feeding Narrative in the Context of Matthew's Gospel

Initial Step of the Second Phase of Jesus' Mission Beyond Israel

The second feeding has significant role in initiating the second phase of Jesus' ministry beyond the boundaries of Israel. Matthew's second feeding as the eschatological messianic banquet presents the ultimate objective of Jesus' mission: *including Gentiles in the kingdom*. The metaphorical discourse in the second feeding scene contradicts Jesus' previous mission instructions in 10:5–6 and 15:24; "only to the lost sheep of the house of Israel," and his actual ministry. As the fulfillment of Jesus' previous mission instructions, the first feeding narrative does not seem to be compatible with the second one, which opens the door to the Gentile. While the first feeding scene portraits the Jewish crowd as the restoration of Israel, the second feeding event objectifies the inclusion of the Gentile.

However, according to Matthew's narrative context and the development of plot, this contradictory repetitious story is utilized as a transitional part of the Gospel. Namely, Matthew's narrator naturally makes a bridge between two repeated stories with a transitional narrative unit, the Canaanite Woman (15:21–28).[134] After the encounter the Gentile woman and the affirmation of her faith (15:28), Matthew's narrator guides the reader's attention to the possible acceptance of Gentiles in Jesus' ministry. Then the reader actually encounters Jesus' prophetic fulfillment for expanding the boundaries of the Kingdom by offering an eschatological banquet for the Gentile crowds, which include all the marginalized in the second feeding scene (15:29–39). The second feeding functions to present the second phase of Jesus' ministry beyond Israel and its actual fulfillment.

As far as the inclusion of Gentiles is concerned, the narrator intimated to the reader about it in the previous story of the healing of a Centurion's servant (8:5–13). The reader imagines the ultimate objective of Jesus' mission, which is reaching out to all the nations. Of course, this narrative unit in 8:5–13 does not function to remove the barrier to the Gentile mission and to open the door of God's kingdom for the Gentiles in the Gospel of Matthew. In fact, Jesus has kept his mission instruction, prohibiting crossing over the border (10:5–6; only to the lost sheep of the house of Israel), and he has ministered to and addressed himself only to Israel until he meets the Canaanite woman in chapter 15. The narrative of the Centurion is the only exception, which associates a Gentile individual with Jesus' ministry, and this foreshadows the ultimate inclusion of Gentiles sharing in the banquet of God's kingdom.[135] At the end of this narrative unit, Jesus prophetically proclaims, "many will come from east and west and sit at table with Abraham, Isaac, and Jacob in the kingdom of heaven" (8:11). The reader imagines the Gentile pilgrims who come to Jerusalem to worship the God of Israel in Jewish prophetic literature (Isaiah 2:2–4; 25:6; Micah 4:1–4; Zechariah 2:11–12; 8:20–23) with the phrase, "many will come from east and west" and participate in the messianic banquet. Through Jesus' brief prophetic proclamation, Matthew's narrator foreshadows the ultimate objective of Jesus' ministry, which is the second phase of Jesus' ministry in the Gospel of Matthew.

However, some scholars, such as Allison, disagree that the phrase in Matthew 8:11[136] ("many will come from east and west") assumes Gentiles but rather argue that the phrase is related to the re-gathering of the Jewish Diaspora[137] and signifies hope for the restoration of Israel. Even in v. 11–12, the contradiction between "many" and "the sons of the kingdom" does not contrast Gentiles and Jews but rather the privileged Jews and the others. For this argument, Allison emphasizes that Gentiles are not explicitly named as the subjects of "many" in the phrase, at the same time he notes that the phrase "east and west" is not used for the eschatological pilgrimage of the Gentile in Jewish texts and Second Temple literature.[138] Rather, the reference of "east and west" may correspond to the Jewish Diaspora or the exiles (e.g., Isaiah 43:5; Zechariah 8:7; Baruch 4:37; 5:5; Psalm of Solomon 11:2; 1 Enoch 57:1) and directly refers to Egypt and Babylon, which are two centers of the Diaspora (e.g., Isaiah 27:13; Hosea 11:10–11; Zechariah 10:10).[139] In this regard, Allison clearly affirms that the phrase "many" will come from "east and west" must be identified with the scattered Jewish Diaspora.

In my opinion, Allison's argument seems plausible enough, if we concentrate on the logion and not on the context of the Gospel of Matthew. However, the phrase in 8:11–12 must be read as a part of the whole narrative of the healing of the Centurion's servant and within the whole context of the Gospel. Allison's argument is weakened by his scant attention to the narrative context. The narrator of Matthew obviously combines the phrase of the logion with the narrative of Centurion, which positively describes the faith of a Gentile, so that the phrase "east and west" cannot be isolated from the narrative context and its following perspective. It is quite reasonable that Matthew 8:5–12 positively presents the inclusion of Gentiles, connecting to the messianic banquet at the messianic era. Of course, the contrasting description in vv. 11–12, "the sons of the kingdom" does not simply refer to the Jews as a whole in contrast to Gentile. As Allison argues, they are some of the Jews, especially the wise or privileged, but not all the Jews.[140] However, "many" from "east and west" are convincingly identified with the Gentile in the context of the narrative. So the phrase in vv. 11–12 as Jesus' prophetic proclamation and the narrative unit in 8:5–12 briefly foreshadow the inclusion of Gentile in Jesus' ministry.

Thus, Jesus' prophetic proclamation in 8:11–12 connects to the theme of the eschatological banquet. The narrator utilizes the phrase to foreshadow the Gentiles participation of the banquet Jesus offered on the mountain later in the Gospel, which actually is the second feeding narrative (15:29–39). When the reader reads Jesus' breaking of seven breads with the Gentile crowds on the mountain, the reader not only flashes back to Jesus' proclamation in 8:11–12 but also realizes that Jesus initiates to fulfill the ultimate objective mission, which is extended from the first provision of bread. In this regard, the second feeding narrative serves to present the initial stage of Jesus' prophetic fulfillment of the second phase of Jesus' eschatological vision of inclusion of the Gentiles, which was foreshadowed in 8:11–12.

Toward the Great Commission

The second feeding narrative functions not only as the inauguration of the second phase of Jesus' mission but also as a basic motif for the rest of the discourse and Jesus' ministry in Matthew's Gospel. Right after the second feeding narrative, the narrator notes again that the bread is not just for human hunger, but is about teaching and ideology (16:12). The narrator reminds the reader of the metaphorical meaning and theological significance of the first and second narratives (16:9–11), when Jesus warns the disciples to "beware of the yeast of the Pharisees and Sadducees" (16:6, 11). Namely, Jesus' warning and hostile admonition against the Jewish religious leaders is justified and supported by the theological discourse in Jesus' feeding narratives. Later this hostile admonition connects to Matthew 23:1–36, in which Jesus denounces the Pharisees and Scribes again.

Based on the theological vision in the second feeding scene, as the second phase of Jesus' ministry, the narrator proclaims that Jesus will build his own community and invites the reader into Jesus' second teachings with a series of parables, which mostly touch upon the relationship between Jews and Gentiles in the kingdom of heaven and Jesus' ultimate eschatological vision.[141] In this manner, one can see that Jesus' ultimate vision in the second feeding covers the rest of Jesus' ministry and teaching until he dies on the cross, which actually is the second phase of Jesus' mission.

Furthermore, the theological significance in the second feeding narrative ultimately leads toward Jesus' Great Commission at the end of the Gospel (28:16–20). Based on the mountain motif, the second feeding is a messianic banquet, which this symbolically invites all the Gentiles and connects to Jesus' final commission on the mountain (28:16), reflecting Jesus' ultimate objective "to make disciples of all nations (Gentiles)" (28:16–20). Of course, there is no direct verbal link to the allusion of the metaphor bread or banquets motif between two scenes. However, in light of the eschatological motif of mountain, the second feeding narrative thematically supports Jesus' final instruction concerning the expansion of the boundaries of the Kingdom and the salvation of the Gentiles. Conversely, the narrator uses Jesus' final commission to synthesize and carry on Jesus' teaching, healing, prophetic actions, and all other ministries, even Jesus' ideology of the kingdom, in Matthew's Gospel.

Therefore, while the first feeding narrative corresponds to Jesus' first instruction in 10:5–6, the second feeding narrative stands for Jesus' final commission in 28:16–20. If the first feeding narrative functions as a prophetic fulfillment of Jesus' previous teaching and instruction from chapters 5–13, the second feeding narrative functions as a prefiguration of Jesus' last instruction, which indicates that the messianic banquet is at hand. Furthermore, the second feeding leads the reader into the second half of the Gospel in light of Jesus' ultimate messianic vision.

Matthean *Bread* and Identity In-between Formative Judaism and Roman Empire

Jesus' two feeding narratives and the bread metaphor in Matthew's Gospel clearly reveal the identity of Matthean community in the socio-religious contexts of the first century. In the first century, many groups and associations of Jesus-followers were integral parts of the Jewish community and not yet completely separated from formative Judaism. At the same time, those groups were struggling to maintain their identity under the colonial situation of the Roman Empire. In this section, I review Matthew's communal identity, revealed in the bread metaphor in the two feeding narratives, through the frame of the postcolonial concept, *the Third Space*.[142] Under the colonial context, Matthew posits its communal identity and ideological vision somewhere *in-between* the conventional understanding of formative Judaism and the new cultural power of the Roman Empire. Matthew does not get stuck into the indigenous religious-cultural heritage of conventional Judaism; at the same time Matthew denies the colonial cultural imposition and challenges the imperial ideology. Rather Matthew represents its own new identity and ideological vision beyond the two cultural entities in the *Third Space*.

Obviously various groups and communities within Jewish society maneuvered for power and strived to define the authoritative communal identity and to get a legitimacy of community. Based on the interpretation of the metaphor of bread in Matthew, one can conjecture Matthew's communal identity in the context of struggling between formative Judaism and Roman Empire. In this section, I examine Matthew's rhetorical claim of the metaphor of bread, representing Matthew's communal identity and its relevant context, while paying special attention to: 1) how Matthean community relates to other dominant parties, 2) how they define their communal identity and ideological vision and find legitimacy between the formative Judaism and Roman Empire.

Deviation from the Conventional Jewish Heritage

Matthew's two feeding narratives begin with Jesus' withdrawal from a certain place in which he would be in danger of persecution (14:13; 15:21; c.f., 4:21; 9:9, 27; 11:1; 12:9, 15; 13:53; 15:29; 19:15). His withdrawal is not just from a dangerous situation or place, but it also means to "withdraw from society"[143] where his ideology and teaching are not understood and accepted. This action of Jesus, entailing prophetic fulfillment, is a strategic starting point for making a new place for his community and seeking legitimacy. Jesus' two feedings and the bread metaphor reveal how Matthew's community relates with other groups in formative Judaism and differentiates from them by creating a new identity withdrawn from the dominant Judaism. Namely, the Matthean bread as metaphor implicitly integrates and represents a deviant character[144] and the vision of Matthew's community through the following features: a) *expansion of communal boundaries,* b) *legitimating of Matthean community as Ekklesia,* c) *and the different interpretation of Torah.*

Expansion of Communal Boundaries *(Inclusion of All Minorities and Gentiles)*

One of the most peculiar features in the narratives of the Gospel of Matthew, especially in the two feeding scenes (14:13–21; 15:29–39), is the expansion of the boundaries of the group of Jesus' followers. Thereby Matthew not only redefines the boundary of the Matthean community but also represents the expanded communal identity in light of the socio-religious, political, and ethnic perspectives. Through the metaphor of bread and Jesus' breaking action, the Gospel of Matthew not only exhibits the long awaited communal hope of the restoration of Israel, breaking socio-religious conventional boundaries in the first feeding narrative, but also clearly manifests Matthew's apocalyptic hope that ultimately includes the whole Gentiles into Jesus' community in the second feeding narrative.[145] The expanded communal identity of Matthew's community is not compatible with the religious ethnic boundary of the traditional dominant Judaism. Rather, Matthew intentionally alters and expands the socio-religious conception of the boundaries.

Jesus' two feeding narratives as prophetic fulfillments, while expressing an expansion of communal boundaries, are supported by previous narratives that foreshadow the inclusion of Gentiles and the marginalized. As far as the expansion of group boundaries is concerned, Matthew's Gospel indirectly intimates from the beginning of the Gospel that all the Gentiles and the marginalized would be included into Matthew's community.

The first clue is revealed in the scene of Jesus' birth, in which "Magi from the East" (μάγοι ἀπὸ ἀνατολῶν) appear (2:1–12). Although Matthew does not identify the Magi and it is difficult to get scholarly consensus on "from the East,"[146] most scholars see these mysterious Magi as "representatives of the best wisdom of the Gentile world."[147] In the Gospel account, Matthew's narrator also recounts that Magi do not know where the "king of Jews" is to be born (2:2), so that the reader can easily assume they are non-Jews.[148] The Gentile Magi who sincerely pay homage to Jesus as "king of the Jews" (2:2, 11) can be compared with Herod who claims to be "king of Jews" himself (2:8). Harrington argues that the Magi must be regarded as "models for Gentile believers" and prefigured representatives of Gentiles who have true belief in Jesus and are part of Matthew's community.[149] The appearance of the Magi in the scene of Jesus' birth as a literary strategy not only functions to foreshadow the expansion of the group boundaries but also reflects the communal identity of the Matthean group.

Second, in Jesus' healing narrative of a Centurion's servant (8:5–12), Matthew's narrator provides another clue that is to be developed later by Jesus' prophetic fulfillment of the inclusion of the whole Gentile into Matthew's community. Jesus' praise of Centurion's faith and his healing activity seem to present Matthew's basic visional premise that non-Jews can be admitted to the people of God. Of course, no one can generalize that the narrative of the Centurion's faith signifies the acceptance of the whole Gentiles. In a sense, this is probably an example of a proselyte in the first century; but not for presenting the complete openness toward Gentile mission. Matthew's Jesus does not change his narrow-strict mission instruction (10:5–6) until he meets the Canaanite woman (15:21–28). For the reader, this may be one of the good examples of a proselyte and a general apocalyptic view of Judaism in the first century.[150]

However, with the Magi's appearance in Jesus' birth story and the faith of the Centurion, the feeding narratives function to foreshadow the ultimate inclusion of all Gentiles into Jesus' community later in the Gospel of Matthew and "the successful evangelization of the nations (28:16–20).[151] The foreshadowing intimations of Gentile inclusion are supported by Jesus' following address: "I will tell you, many will come from east and west and sit at table with Abraham, Isaac, and Jacob in the kingdom of heaven" (8:11). Here, as was observed, "many from east and west" clearly indicate the Gentiles according to the narrative context of Matthew chapter 8. The apocalyptic vision of the inclusion of the non-Jews coming to worship the God of Israel is a common feature in prophetic literature.[152] Thus, Matthew's account of the Centurion's servant envisions the ultimate fulfillment of the prophetic inclusive vision and foreshadows its prophetic fulfillment of the inclusion of the Gentiles in Jesus' ministry.

One of the interesting points is that Matthew's prophetic vision in the narrative of the Centurion's servant is quite subversive. While unspecified people from east and west will participate in the banquet of God's kingdom (8:11), "the sons of the kingdom will be thrown into the outer darkness" (8:12). This vision is not just about the inclusion of the Gentiles but also contains the exclusion of the one who does not have an appropriate right. Of course, "the sons of the kingdom" does not mean all Jews or actual heirs of God's kingdom but natural or rightful heirs of the kingdom.[153] This phrase also indicates some Jewish representatives who do not have appropriate belief in Jesus and follow Jesus' teaching. Matthew clearly affirms that the natural or rightful heirs of God's kingdom are not the actual heirs of the kingdom. Jewish traditional theology of elitism and ethnic boundaries do not function at all in the prophetic vision of the kingdom of God. This Matthew's prophetic vision re-appears in Jesus' parable teaching in 21:33–46, in which Jesus affirms that the kingdom of God will be taken away from the natural heirs to "a nation" (21:45). Therefore, one sees that Matthew's prophetic subversive vision weakens Jewish traditional religious ethnic boundaries and redefines their communal identity, which is not limited by Jewish traditional religious-ethnic boundaries.

Furthermore, Matthew's account connects the inclusive prophetic vision to the messianic banquet of God's kingdom.[154] The inclusion of all Gentiles is fulfilled and signified by sharing a life-giving source in the messianic banquet provided by God, to which Jesus' first and second feeding correspond. In this way, the reader recognizes that Matthew's prophetic vision, foreshadowed by the Magi and the account of the Centurion's servant, is fulfilled by Jesus' two miraculous feedings. In the first feeding narrative, Matthew's narrator metaphorically expresses the actual formation of new community, signifying the restoration of Israel, through the breaking of bread. Then, through the second feeding as an apocalyptic messianic banquet, Matthew ends hostilities, forms a new covenant and expands communal boundaries to include all Gentiles through the breaking of bread. Jesus' feeding scenes in Matthew not only represent the fulfillment of Matthew's ultimate prophetic vision but also reflect Matthew's actual communal identity in light of the socio-religious-ethnic perspectives. Thus, being a member of God's kingdom and Matthew's communal identity are no longer confined or ruled by the Jewish concept of closeness and any other biased ethnic boundaries.

Legitimating of Matthean Community: *Ekklesia* vs. *Their Synagogue*

Now it is clear that the metaphor of bread and Jesus' feeding activities in Matthew function as a metaphoric expressional source of the formation of new community and a theological premise for the expansion of the communal boundaries. In this perspective, all Jesus' previous teachings, discourses, and prophetic vision in Matthew ultimately concentrate on and support Jesus' two feeding scenes and his formation of community. All Matthew's discourses and narratives indirectly or directly reflect the reality of Matthew's community and their identity; thereby one can conjecture how Matthew's group seeks to legitimate their communal identity among first-century formative Judaism. In this process, differentiation from others in a negative contrasting way normally contributes to the negotiation of boundaries between "us" and "them," especially for the process of gaining legitimacy for the community.[155] It is quite important to recognize that Matthew draws sharp distinctions between Jesus' group of people and the Jewish leaders.

In fact, Matthew draws sharp distinct boundaries[156] from the Jewish leadership in order to legitimate the community's self-understanding as Jesus' believers and justify it communal identity under Jesus' authority.[157] In order to do this, Matthew's narrator seeks specifically to de-legitimize the traditional and dominating leadership group of the Jewish Community.[158] For instance, in Jesus' birth account, one can clearly find the comparison between the Magi who sincerely pay homage to Jesus as "king of the Jews" (2:2, 11) and Herod who claims to be "king of Jews" himself (2:8); and the comparison between Gentiles/the marginalized who have faith in Jesus and the religious leaders who do not recognize the identity of Jesus but plot to kill Jesus (e.g., 2:7–12). Through the contrastive descriptions, Matthew not only de-legitimizes the Jewish conventional hegemonic identity as the chosen people in God's kingdom, but also legitimates Matthew's prophetic vision and its identity. In this regard, Matthew's narrator keeps presenting appropriate comparisons between the positive characters among Jesus followers and the negative counter characters among the Jewish leaders.

Furthermore, Matthew's Gospel engages in lively and serious controversy with Jesus against Jewish religious leaders and describes potential tensional conflicts, danger, and clear distinctions between Jesus' group and Pharisees and the Scribes. All potential dangers from the conflicts with Jewish religious leaders, entailing Jesus' withdrawal (ἀναχώρεω),[159] are followed by Jesus' prophetic fulfillments in Matthew's Gospel,[160] through which Matthew draws a sharp distinction between Jesus' discourse and that of Jewish leadership. In many cases, Matthew's Jesus indirectly attacks the legitimacy of the Jewish religious leaders and their authority through Jesus' own teaching and healing and prophetic fulfillment that present counter narratives and delegitimize the ideology of Jewish leaders. For instance, just before the second feeding scene, Jesus has a debate with the Pharisees and scribes on Jewish tradition and the dietary/purity law, which is a key demarcation between Jews and Gentiles (15:1–20). Then Matthew's narrator presents Jesus' withdrawal from there (ἀνεχώρησεν ἐκεῖθεν v. 21) coming into Gentile territory, the district of Tyre and Sidon. Even though Jesus flees from the potential conflict and danger, the itinerant move of Matthew's Jesus is quite intentional. Then, Jesus feeds and breaks bread with the crowds that include the Gentiles and the marginalized (15:29–39). Jesus' itinerant moves to the Gentile world and his feeding literally function to respond to the previous debate with the Pharisees and Scribes on the purity and demarcation of Jews, and it also functions to attack and delegitimize the ideology of the Jewish leaders. Through this work, the Matthean community seeks its own legitimacy of the formation of community and their communal identity.

Right after Jesus feeds the four thousand (15:29–39), Matthew's narrator finally delivers the news that Jesus concretely builds his community, called ἐκκλησία,[161] that will challenge the Jewish conventional association *Synagogue*, and Jesus proclaims, "the powers of death shall not prevail against it" (16:18).

In the narrative context, ἐκκλησία must be identified with the community Jesus forms, which is identified with Matthew's community in the first century. Namely, Jesus' disciples, followers and the crowds, including the Gentiles, especially those with whom Jesus feeds and breaks bread are the constituents of the ἐκκλησία, which denotes the identities of Matthew's community. Many scholars see the term ἐκκλησία in the light of the Christian meaning of church derived from Pauline letters and subsequent Christian literature. However, beyond the Christianized concept[162] of the church, the ἐκκλησία is also a common Greek word for representing an assembly and an association of people. Davies and Allison argue that the term in Matthew possibly derives from the LXX (e.g., Deut. 31:30), where it is used with meaning of 'assembly,' 'convocation,' 'congregation,'[163] which corresponds to Jewish synagogue. In this manner, Saldarini argues that the usage of this term in Matthew "must be determined from immediate literary and social context and not by usage in other Christian literature."[164] If Matthew's narrator used this term in light of the LXX's usage or the common Greek usage for the contemporary reader, the ἐκκλησία cannot be understood as a Christianized concept of church, but rather it represents the assembly or voluntary association of Jesus-followers and Matthew's community in relation to the Jewish context in the first century.

From this perspective, the ἐκκλησία in Matthew, according to Matthew's narrative plot and context, is primarily used to legitimize Matthew's community in the social context of the first century, especially among formative Judaism, rather than representing the Christianized concept of church. At the same time, Matthew's use of the ἐκκλησία functions not only to differentiate its identity from the Jewish traditional conception of the assembly but also to delegitimize the counter part of Jewish leader's group or Jewish assembly, Synagogue. In this regard, Saldarini argues:

> "Matthew probably used the word *ekklesia* to denote his group in order to differentiate himself from his opponents in the Jewish community. Since the leaders who rejected Matthew presided over assemblies designated in Greek as synagogue, he was reluctant to use that word."[165]

Of course, the avoidance of the term synagogue does not mean that *ekklesia* denies Matthew's Jewish identity. Rather this designation as a counterclaim differentiates from the ideology of Jewish leaders and their institutionalized assembly and seeks to delegitimize the teaching and discourse of synagogue.

Matthew intentionally refers to synagogues with the second/third person, plural, genitive pronoun six times: *"their synagogue* (ταῖς συναγωγαῖς αὐτῶν)" or "*in your synagogue* (ἐν ταῖς συναγωγαῖς ὑμῶν, e.g., 23:34)."[166] The use of the second/third person pronoun "their/your" signifies an estrangement from the entity of the first person pronoun "our," through which Matthew's narrator exhibits that there are distinctions between Jesus' community and the traditional Jewish assembly, synagogue.[167] However, as Saldarini argues, this does not mean "a lack of relationship or absolute separation."[168] The phrase "their synagogue" appears at the beginning stage of Jesus' ministry in Galilee: "teaching in *their synagogues* and preaching the gospel of the kingdom and healing every disease and every infirmity among people" (4:23). This shows that Jesus has a relationship with the traditional Jewish assembly from the beginning of his ministry, teaching and preaching in their assembly. At the same time, Matthew's narrator differentiates Jesus himself from the Jewish traditional assembly of synagogue and presents Jesus' own teaching and interpretation of the Law (chapter 5–7), and healing ministry (chapter 8–10). Then Matthew metaphorically reveals that Jesus forms a new community with his followers through the breaking of bread twice, one for the Jewish beyond and the other for Gentiles (chapter 14–15), in which Jesus later called "ἐκκλησία" projecting Matthew's community (chapter 16). The most important point is that the formation of Jesus' community in Matthew is revealed by distancing away its discourses, teaching, prophetic vision from those of the Jewish traditional assembly, especially Jewish leadership group.

From this perspective, one knows that all these Matthean accounts with the description of conflicts, debates, comparison, alternation, and the bread metaphor presents the formation of Jesus' community, which clearly projects on the context of Matthean community in the first century. Having a good relationship with Jewish roots, Matthew keeps presenting the differentiation from certain parts of Judaism, especially the conventional Jewish leadership group of formative Judaism. Through differentiation, Matthew seeks to legitimize the establishment of Matthean community and a new identity and delegitimize the counterpart of the Matthean group in the age of formative Judaism.

Different Interpretations of Torah

The foundation of the community of Jesus-followers and its ideology in Matthew are based on Jesus' teaching and ministry, especially his own interpretation of the Jewish Torah, which is a distinctive feature of Matthew's Gospel. At the beginning of Jesus' own ministry, Matthew describes that Jesus teaches and preaches about the gospel of the kingdom to his followers everywhere,[169] even in the synagogue (4:17, 23). Jesus' teaching discourses mostly comes from the Sermon on the Mount (5:1–7:28), mission discourse (9:35–10:42), and several conflict narratives on the

Jewish traditions, which mostly present Jesus as an accurate and true interpreter of the law;[170] thereby it is exhibited the foundational ideology of the community Jesus forms in Matthew. In Matthew's Gospel, all Jesus' teaching discourses are not just relevant to his innovative understanding of the kingdom of heaven and Jewish traditional Torah, but also represent Jesus' ideological discourses for the alternative visional community. When Matthew describes that Jesus forms a community through the breaking of bread, it shows that the group of Jesus' follower is established and legitimized by those teachings. As was observed, the acceptance of broken bread metaphorically symbolizes not only the acceptance of Jesus' authority but also participation in Jesus' ideology of the kingdom of heaven. When Jesus breaks the bread and shares the bread, Jesus' teaching establishes a binding agreement, acceptance, and covenant among the crowds. For the crowds, the breaking of bread is participation in the common sense and ideology, especially Jesus' teaching in the narrative context. Jesus' own interpretation of the Torah and his teachings are very important to represent and legitimize the identity of Matthean community.

Most of all, the perspective of Matthew's Jesus on Torah and its own interpretations show an important link to Matthew's Jewish relations and how the Matthean community legitimizes their own identity. Overman argues that Jesus' interpretation of the law serves as the means of discrediting the group of opponents and of vindicating Matthew's position.[171] In the Sermon on the Mount in 5:17–19, Matthew's narrator clearly states that Jesus has not come to "abolish" or "destroy" of the law or the prophets but to "fulfill" them, even "one stroke of a letter." No matter what the phrase "Jesus fulfills" means,[172] these verses show that Matthew's community keeps the validity of the Torah and retains its adherence to the Jewish law.[173] According to v. 17, μὴ νομίσητε ("do not think"), there might be a perception among the formative Jewish groups that the Matthean community does not follow the law.[174] So, Matthew defends against this accusation and legitimates their perspective on the law.

Ulrich Luz insists 5:17–19, especially v. 20 as the key statement of the theme for the antitheses (5:21–48) functions to frame all of Jesus' other radical teachings and interpretation of the law within the Jewish background.[175] Daniel Harrington also affirms that Jesus' proclamation in 5:17–20, which projects Matthew's perspective on the law and Judaism, serves as "a further reminder of the organic relation" between Judaism and the Matthean community;[176] thereby Matthew's narrator clearly presents that all Jesus' teaching and the ideology of the Matthean community take seriously their Jewish root and its heritage and legitimize the identity of the Matthean community standing in continuity with the Judaism.

Aaron M. Gale argues that Matthew is applying the rabbinic teachings of their time with its own perspectives, describing Jesus as an authoritative interpreter of the Torah.[177]

Matthew's narrator frequently uses fulfillment citations as an application of a prophecy from the Hebrew Bible (e.g., 1:22–23; 2:15, 17–18, 23; 3:3; 4:14; etc.). Thereby Matthew claims that a certain event in the life and ministry of Jesus took place as a "promise-fulfillment" according to Jewish prophecy.[178] As Overman argues, the fulfillment citations are not just mere references revealing Jesus' authority but function to make overt the connection between the life and ministry of Jesus and the traditions of Jewish history and heritage.[179] Through the fulfillment citations, Matthew seeks the appropriate legitimacy and defense of its community among the traditions of formative Judaism. Overman states:

> "Matthew claims that the beliefs of his community are not new or misguided but rather established and traditional. They have their ground in the very promises and traditions of the history of Israel. Matthew has tried to traditionalize the beliefs of his new movement through the use of fulfillment citations. His use of Scripture in this way would defend the beliefs and behavior of his community to members who might have started to doubt the legitimacy of the group's peculiar interpretations and actions."[180]

The fulfillment citations also function as a reading frame, through which the readers unconsciously see all Jesus' teaching and activities in light of the fulfillment of the prophecy of Jewish tradition, whether the narrator clearly states the citations of the Hebrew Bible or not in each event in the Gospel. The narratives of Jesus' feeding and metaphorical action of breaking bread can be read as the fulfillment of the prophecy of Jewish tradition, representing the ultimate formation of community in God's kingdom and envisioning the messianic banquet for the restoration of Israel. In this way, Matthew confirms that the beliefs and life of Matthew's community firmly stand in the same tradition and prophecy in Judaism.

At the same time, Matthew presents its own perspective on Jewish heritage from the conventional understanding of formative Judaism. Matthew's narrator presents conflicts over the interpretation of the law between Jesus' perspective and the traditional understanding of Torah dominated by Jewish leader's group. Although Matthew's Gospel shows the affirmation of Jewish law with the ultimate fulfillment of all elements of the law (5:17–19), Matthew presents different understandings and interpretations of the law that must be fulfilled and embodied in the Matthean community. As Saldarini argues, Matthew's interpretation of the law is a special program or strategy to legitimize Matthew's community and its identity against the group of Jewish leaders who dominated the mainline Jewish discourse and rejected the other minorities.[181] In fact, Saldarini states:

> "In first-century Judaism, interpretation of the law was a political act in which the control of society was at stake. Disagreements among groups involved substantial conflicts over public laws and norms. Combatants over the interpretation of Scripture or the correct implementation of biblical law sought to delegitimize their opponents and establish their own views as the correct way for the Jewish community to think and act."[182]

Matthew's narrator describes Jesus as a teacher and a new authoritative leader, sent by God with authority and exhibits Matthew's alteration of self-understanding as well as their own interpretation of the law, which differed from that of Jesus' opponent groups, Jewish religious leaders.

Jesus' new teaching on the Mount and Matthew 5:17–20 is followed by the so-called six antitheses, which means "contrasts" or "oppositions."[183] As was in vv. 18 and 20 with the form of "I tell you (ἐγὼ γὰρ ὑμῖν)," Matthew's narrator keeps the same form of "ἐγὼ δὲ λέγω ὑμῖν" six times for presenting Jesus' own, which is a new interpretation of the law and tradition. Matthew exhibits six dyadic-schematic phrases, in which a part of the dyadic phrase contrasts the other.[184] "Ἠκούσατε ὅτι ἐρρέθη" (you have heard that it was said) as one set firstly presents the traditional perspective on the Torah, then ἐγὼ δὲ λέγω ὑμῖν ὅτι (but I tell you that…) as a point of contrast offers Jesus' own interpretation,[185] which is Matthew's new perspective of Jewish tradition. Concerning murder, adultery, divorce, oaths, retaliation, and enemies, Matthew presents Jesus' agreement with the traditional instruction of the law, at the same time, he "urges his followers to go deeper or to the root of the commandment."[186] Here the six antitheses and its dyadic-schematic form reaffirm Matthew's organic relation to Judaism in light of keeping the validity of Torah and Matthew's explicit alteration from the traditional perspective. Thereby Matthew's narrator draws sharp contrasts between Matthean ideology and the traditional Judaism. Then, Jesus' other teachings and instructions follow, which primarily focus on the ordering of relationships and behavior within the community. Matthew 5:17–20 and Jesus' alternative interpretational perspective can be a fundamental frame of Jesus' other instructions.

In addition, the conflict stories reveal Matthew's defense of his community and ideology with the description of Jesus as an accurate and true interpreter of the law, projecting Matthew's ideological root of Judaism and its alteration of perspectives. Among several conflict stories, three narrative units present Matthew's clear point of view on Jewish tradition and law: Sabbath laws (12:1–14), Purity and Dietary laws (15:1–20), and the Love commandment (22:34–40). In the dispute over Sabbath observance against the Pharisees (12:1–14), Matthew quotes a passage from Hosea 6:6 that is used previously in Matthew 9:13; "I desire mercy, and not sacrifice ("Ελεος θέλω καὶ οὐ θυσίαν). The interesting point is that Matthew's Jesus says, "if you had known what this means… you would not have condemned the guiltless" (12:7), just prior to the quotation. This means that the problem is not the disciple's violation of the Sabbath law by plucking grain for their hunger but a misunderstanding by the Pharisees about the law and its application. Obviously, Jesus does not deny or abolish the validity of the Jewish heritage of the Sabbath observance as some kind of legalism but emphasizes appropriate interpretation of the law and its application.[187] In this regard, Overman argues that Matthew's Jesus presents his own alternative perspective in which the law and its application are primarily understood as the demand of compassion.[188] Compassion and mercy as a new paradigm must be a primary value that guides the interpretation and its application of the law.[189] Compassion and mercy justify Jesus' ministry, especially dining with tax collectors and sinners (9:9–13) in which Matthew quotes Hosea 6:6 first (v. 13), and these primary values also motivate Jesus' feeding the crowd and forming his community (14:14; 15:32).

The paradigm of Jesus' interpretation of the law also appears in the dispute about purity and dietary law in 15:1–20. The Pharisees and scribes accuse that the disciples eat with unwashed hands, so that they break the appropriate law of purity (15:1–2). Jesus responds with two imperatives "hear and understand" ('Ακούετε καὶ. συνίετε·) in v. 10. These imperative verbs indirectly present that there are some misunderstandings of the purity law that need to be corrected and heard. Then, Jesus says, "not what goes into the mouth defiles a man, but what comes out of the mouth defiles a man" (v. 11). This means that to eat with unwashed hands does not violate the tradition and the law, but the real transgression derives from a result of what is inside, coming out of the mouth. Namely, the formal legalism based on human prejudice cannot keep the purity, so that one must check what is inside and the heart, which can render a person impure. That does not just refer to a word coming out of mouth but all kinds of disobedience to God's commandments: "evil thoughts, murder, adultery, fornication, theft, false witness, slander" (15:19). Matthew's Jesus rather accuses the Pharisees and scribes of transgressing God's commandment for the sake of keeping their tradition (15:3).

Matthew's answer seems to mitigate the more radical answer of Gospel of Mark: "all foods are clean." (Mark 7:19);[190] thereby one can see that Matthew does not deny or abolish the validity of purity and dietary law but rather presents an appropriate understanding of the concept of purity and defilement.[191] In Matthew, the purity issues connect to contact with and incorporation of Gentiles and Jewish sinners.[192] So, the interpretation of the purity law (15:1–20) leads Jesus coming into the district of Tyre and Sidon and encountering the Canaanite woman who has a demon-possessed daughter (15:21–28). Further, Jesus heals and feeds the crowds including the Gentiles in foreign territory (15:29–39). In this regard, Saldarini affirms that "yet significant contact is made, and the boundaries that purity rules define and defend have been breached, even though no law has been broken."[193]

With regard to Matthew's relation to Judaism, Matthew does not deny or abolish the validity of the law and Jewish traditional heritage, but subordinates them to a higher value, which is Jesus' alternative interpretation of the law, overriding the conception of Jesus' opponent group. In Matthew's Gospel, Jesus' altered interpretation of the law presents a foundation for Matthew's community and its basic ideology, which keep the validity of the Torah and Jewish heritage, at the same time it differentiates from that of the dominant group, the Pharisees and scribes. In this way, while Matthew delegitimizes their opponent groups through Jesus' new interpretation of the law, Matthew seeks to legitimize the foundation of the community and to establish an appropriate self-understanding for the community to think and act.

Resistance to the Roman Imperial Ideology

Matthew's community obviously struggled to determine appropriate relations with its surrounding civic communities, the Jewish community as well as the Roman society. The life and contexts of the Matthean community cannot be separated from that of other civic communities under the Roman colonial situation. How did they negotiate the claims of Rome's ideology? What were their attitudes and practices toward the imperial orders and festivals? Were there certain socio-political strategies against Roman Imperialism? Obviously the Gospel of Matthew and its relevant community formed under the influence of the Roman Imperialism, so that the texts naturally reveals Matthew's attitude toward Roman Imperialism and leave some traces of the colonial influence.

Especially, Matthew indirectly exhibits resistance against the Roman Imperial ideology in the texts. As was in James C. Scott's conceptions,[194] Matthew's community as a subordinate group creates its Gospel as a "hidden transcript" that indirectly or metaphorically represents a critique of power and challenges the dominant imperial theology and ideology. In this view, as Warren Carter observes, the resistance of Matthew's community against the Roman Empire can be violent and nonviolent, hidden and open, directly confrontational or more concerned with the distinctive practices and alternative theological-ideological perspectives.[195] Beyond the miraculous events, Matthew's two feeding narratives and the metaphor of bread present the critical attitudes and resistance of Matthew's community toward the Roman imperial ideology.

Provision of God over the Empire

Matthean bread as metaphor represents the abundant provision of God by means of Jesus, evoking the provision of manna in the wilderness, while presenting Matthew's communal identity as an alternative emerging power and kingdom, and resisting the Roman Imperial ideology. The Roman Empire claimed that Rome was chosen and sanctioned by the gods, especially Jupiter, to rule over the world without end and to manifest the gods' blessings and abundance.[196] Based on this, Rome also claimed the emperor as the agent of the gods' sovereignty, and his sanctioned authority would bring well-being, blessings of peace, fertility, harmony, security, safety and the like to the world.[197] Under Roman imperialism, inhabitants must have submitted to and cooperated with this imperial ideology, as the means of participating in the will of gods and its blessing, for the appropriate ways of living to survive. Even the elites and leaders of Empire "represented and institutionalized imperial power in traditional indigenous religious forms."[198] Namely, the survival, welfare, and general life of people were inseparable from religious credits and legitimacy, which also was inseparable from politics in representing an ideological vision and structuring the power relations of society. In the first century, the establishment of Roman peace and the representation of societal well-being, the so called *Pax Romana*, clearly show how Rome institutionalized their ruling ideology with networks of power: the political, economic, military, and religious. The Roman propaganda, the *Pax Romana*, is advocated by the major premise that the gods sanctioned all blessings to Roman rule and claimed to have special relationships with the emperors.[199]

However, Matthew's Gospel with the bread metaphor thoroughly negates the Roman imperial ideology and exposes it as false claims; instead Matthew presents an alternate sovereign power for blessing and societal well-being through the bread Jesus breaks and the metaphoric conception of God's provision. When Jesus feeds thousands of people (14:13–21; 15:29–39) through the small amount of bread and fish, the *hidden transcript* of Matthew's ideology subverts that of the Roman Empire. The blessings and abundance of provision do not come through the agent of gods, the emperor, but through Jesus who has compassionate heart for the crowds. Originally, Matthew's narrator signifies that the resources of provision come from God, not the gods like Jupiter. In the two feeding stories, Jesus recognizes only God as the gracious benefactor and the only source of blessing, when Jesus looks up to heaven to give thanks to God for the miraculous provision. The well-being and blessing of peace and fertility, which were supposed to be brought by the Roman emperor, were brought by Jesus and sanctioned by God.

The provision also miraculously overflowed. With only small amount of food, thousands of people were satisfied and twelve baskets and seven baskets were left. While lots of inhabitants, especially the peasant group, have suffered a lack of food under the Roman Empire,[200] the people were provided abundant food and satisfied by the provision of Jesus. In this regard, Matthew's Gospel demonstrates Jesus' lordship over life-giving resources,[201] in which the authority of the emperor of Rome and its ideology are delegitimized. Although Matthew seems to be assimilated and mimicking the imperial theology, God's empire and Jesus' authoritative lordship are highlighted and legitimized, while criticizing the false image of the Roman Empire.

Furthermore, the metaphor of bread and Jesus' feeding scenes in Matthew evoke the experience of liberation from Egypt and the memory of God's provision in the wilderness. Matthew exhibits the liberating power of God and represents Jesus as engaged in a liberation and renewal of Israel from the Roman Empire. Matthew's narrator describes the background of two feeding scenes as "the deserted place" and the time was late (14:15; 15:33). This reminds the reader of Israel's experience at Sinai and the liberating journey from Egypt. Moreover, the bread itself in the wilderness background evokes the reader's memories of Moses, especially the unleavened bread at the Passover meal. Actually, throughout the history of Israel, people have commemorated the liberation of Israel from Egypt by keeping the Passover meal with the unleavened bread. Through the bread in the wilderness context, Matthew evokes the reader's cognitive knowledge about the time when Israel was liberated from Egypt. Furthermore, Jesus' feeding and bread as metaphor correspond to God's provision of manna and quail in the liberating journey through the wilderness. During the liberating journey of Israel, God was the only authority and provider of life-giving source who had led the Israelites out of the Egypt toward the Promised Land.

In this way, Matthew indirectly represents the hope of the new liberation of Israel from the Roman Empire. As God's agent Moses had led the Israelites out of the slavery of Egypt, now Jesus will renew the future of Israel and liberate Israel from the Roman Empire. In this respect, Jesus' feeding and the bread in Matthew is not just a miraculous event that shows the supernatural power of Jesus. Rather the bread as metaphor in Matthew reminds the reader of the memory of liberation and God' providence for the fate of Israel and evokes hope among the readers and hearers that a new exodus will be held and is under way in Jesus' mission.

From this perspective, the Matthean bread as metaphor exhibits Matthew's ideological hope and communal identity that ultimately aim to liberate them from the Roman Empire and challenges imperial dominance by presenting Jesus' alternative kingdom ruled by God. Furthermore, the Matthean community clearly denies the Roman Imperial ideology and its sovereignty and indirectly expresses their resistance against the imperial hegemony of Rome, while representing God's sovereign power.

Meals as Resistance to the Roman Empire

In Gospel accounts, the motifs of banquet and meal are frequently presented in Jesus' parabolic teachings and his ministerial actions. As Dennis Smith argues, these types of meal or banquet motifs in texts are usually presented as a "parabolic action," by means of which Jesus proclaims or the gospel narrator wants to emphasize a particular message.[202] Namely, the meals or banquets of Jesus in the texts clearly function as "literary events"[203] beyond the historical perspective. Especially, when one sees the motif of meal or its relevant elements of the text as a metaphor, another layer of the meaning as hidden transcript, in which the Gospel would intend to proclaim, can be found. In this perspective, Matthew's feeding scenes as a representation of customary meals can be interpreted in light of the messianic banquet and other Greco-Roman banquet traditions that bind social ideology and identity. Matthew's anti-imperialistic visions and resistance are revealed here.

Messianic Banquet of Zion. Many scholars see Matthew's two feeding scenes as Israel's messianic banquet at which the Messiah is deemed to be present and the victorious restoration of Israel is fulfilled. The scene of messianic banquet in the Gospel accounts functions to reveal a political manifesto or ideological vision of community. Many scholars refer to "the messianic banquet" as an earlier Israelite version of political idealization, while projecting on the social significance of the meal.[204]

The banquet imagery is utilized as a metaphor of the vindication of God's people in Israel's scriptural traditions. Especially, Israel's conception of the eschatological messianic banquet derives from the so-called "Isaianic Apocalypses" (Isaiah 24–27), in which Israel envisioned the final redemption of God's people in terms of the banquet on Mount Zion hosted by God.[205] The motif of the divine banquet and its pattern derive from the creation myths in the Ancient Near

East, in which the gods assemble people to celebrate victory with a great banquet when a battle has been won.[206] The myth of the festive banquet culturally can be regarded as "the primary social institution for celebrating victory and deliverance."[207] So, Jesus' feeding as a messianic banquet signifies the ultimate liberation and victory over the bondage of the Roman Empire.

Furthermore, Mount Zion has been recognized as Yahweh's chosen place of dwelling and the site of the throne of his rule and ultimately as the center of Yahweh's rule of the world (Psalms 47; 48; 99:1–5; 132:11–13)[208] in the Old Testament. At the same time, as an eschatological vision, Israel prophetically envisions that Zion as Yahweh's dwelling place will be renewed and restored, and Yahweh will gather his scattered people into a renewed fellowship on the mountain again.[209] On the mountain "the Lord of the hosts will make for all peoples a feast of fat things, a feast of wine on the lees," (Isaiah 25:6) and he invites all people, even those "who has no money," and he says, "come, buy and eat! Come buy wine and milk without money and without price." (Isaiah 55:1). Here God's provision of food plays a central role for describing Israel's eschatological vision in the form of banquet.[210]

From this perspective, the reader recognizes the meaning of the metaphor of bread and Jesus' feedings in light of Israel's eschatological vision, which can symbolically delegitimize the ideological vision of Roman Empire. As Donaldson argues, the mountain of 15:29 and "the deserted place" in which the crowds assembled function as "an eschatological site."[211] Through this place, Matthew exhibits the prophetic fulfillment of Israel's apocalyptic hope by Jesus' feeding and proclaims that God chose this place as abode and the site of the throne of his sovereignty and God restored the kingdom. At this point, Matthew clearly opposed Rome's imperial domination and its ideological premise that the gods had chosen Rome; and its emperor is agent of the gods' rule.[212] Thus, Jesus' breaking of bread and feedings function as a hidden transcript in Matthew for attacking the Roman Imperial ideology.

When Jesus breaks the bread, it is not just sharing a meal or a compassionate provision of food but also an eschatological messianic banquet that reveals Matthew's ideological vision that Jesus symbolically re-gathers the scattered people into a renewed fellowship with a new relationship and restores God's rule of the world. Matthew's vision thoroughly challenges the imperial ideological vision. God's restoration power and the establishment of the kingdom are already celebrated by the festive messianic banquet, which evokes the ultimate victory of God's kingdom over any other imperial power. Therefore, one can see that Jesus' feeding with the bread in Matthew reveals the Matthean community's ideological correspondence to Israel's apocalyptic vision of God's final restoration, in which God will reveal God's presence by hosting a festival to celebrate the victory over chaos and the enemy: the Roman Empire.

Association Meal Gathering for Social Bonding. The common meal or banquet in the Gospel accounts exhibits the political stance of the community. Communities celebrate meals together, and those meals become significant moments for the formation of communal identity.[213] At the same time, the scene of a communal banquet in the text functions to provide an ideological vision and idealizes model for the life, and a socio-religious communal identity. The function of social bonding in Jesus' feeding and meals would be a threatening force to the Roman Empire.

Dennis Smith argues that the feature of Jesus' banquet and meal in the Gospel accounts has been constructed throughout with reference to the Greco-Roman banquet tradition and ideology.[214] Formal meals in the Mediterranean culture of the Hellenistic and Roman period, including the early Christian meal, take on a homogenous form,[215] which presents social conventions, values, ethical foundation, and ideological vision. The formal Hellenistic meals have some common characteristic features including the reclining of all participants, while eating and drinking together in the evening; two divisions of the supper (*deipnon*) of eating; and an extended time of drinking and conversation (*symposion*).[216] Besides these common typological features of form, the most important characteristic point is that the meal itself functions as the social values of *koinonia*, friendship, and group solidarity. Hal Taussig, following Klinghardt's observation,[217] argues that the Hellenistic meals provide social structure and processes for identity formation and articulation of meaning of social value; and through the meals people envision the ideal society and a concrete utopia for community.[218] Dennis Smith also emphasizes the social dynamics of the meal in the Greco-Roman banquet custom, which affects social boundaries, social bonding, social stratification, and even the identification of social values.[219] One particular banquet with a similar form and socio-political purposes in the Greco-Roman culture functions as "a single social institution,"[220] bonding people with a common value and identity.

As Hellenistic meals and banquets functioned in Greco-Roman culture, in Matthew Jesus' feeding as a banquet functions to represent social bonding, social dynamics, and a new communal value of solidarity. Matthew's description of Jesus' breaking of bread and people's sitting on the ground presents a specific indication for the community meal gathering,[221] Jesus' blessing of the bread and distribution of food function as signals of the primary *deipnon* activity in a formal meal. As Smith states, although Jesus' feedings are described as outdoors events, "when Jesus hosts the miraculous meals outdoors, they become reclining banquets as well."[222] In this regard, Matthew presents the meals of Jesus' feeding as a formal banquet of the social institution of Jesus' community. When Jesus breaks the bread, it metaphorically represents the making of a new covenant and formation of new community. The crowds are identified as those who follow Jesus and accept the provision of Jesus. The object of following is not just Jesus but his teaching and vision of kingdom. The acceptance of provision does not just mean the bread but Jesus' prophetic vision and ideology in Matthew. Sharing bread with people is a sign of their membership in the group. The banquet and the sharing of bread in Matthew function as a social bonding, defining social boundaries and identity. That is the reason that Jesus warns the disciples to avoid the "yeast of the Pharisees and Sadducees" (16:6).

Hal Taussig argues that Hellenistic meals can be connected to the cultural emergence of associations in the Hellenistic era, which can be recognized as political entity. He sees "the semiprivate nature of the meals" constituted a major component of the social bonding for the associations of people.[223] Furthermore, from the socio-political perspective, he argues that the Hellenistic meal itself functions as "a replacement for the tribal, extended familial and national assemblies."[224] The meal and the feature of association can be regarded and used as the expression of resistance to the dominant group ideology and imperialism in the Roman Imperial context. The character of associations of people becomes a political gathering if the meal gathering and the association function as social bonding and a replacement of a certain group identity. So, the imperial governments carefully monitored associations' meal gatherings with suspicious eyes on the possibility of the gatherings for sedition or planning for sedition.[225] Wendy Cotter's observation presents substantial evidence for the Roman Empire's restriction of voluntary associations, concerning possible sedition or rebellion.[226]

Of course, although there were possibilities of sedition or antagonistic tension against the Imperial power, not all associations in general were subversive groups.[227] However, Matthew's Jesus' feeding banquet and its association led by Jesus, as a subversive group, thoroughly challenges the Roman Empire and its ideology. Jesus' feeding banquets as an association of people affirms God's provision of life-giving source, by evoking God's liberation power and Israel's liberating experience in the wilderness of Sinai. This affirmation of Jesus' association challenges the Roman Imperial theology that the Emperor is sanctioned by gods to rule over the world without end and manifest the god's blessings and abundance. As Hellenistic meals in general functioned to express utopian hope, Jesus' association as a messianic banquet envisions a renewed Israelite community with a new relationship and restores God's rule over the world; here the Roman imperial ideological vision must be challenged by the celebrating a banquet for the ultimate victory of God's kingdom.

Furthermore, Jesus' association holds up the values of social equality and inclusivism against the social hierarchical stratification valued by the imperial ideology. In Jesus' meal association, Matthew not only affirms the inclusion of women and children (14:21; 15:38) but also opens the door to all the marginalized (15:30) and the Gentiles (15:21–39); thereby all recline at the meals and envision a counter-imperial hope, and form a new communal identity.

Hal Taussig affirms that the meal and its association can be understood as "behavior emblematic of ideal society."[228] Regarding the meal association as a social practice, he states:

> The meals enacted the new social alternatives so vividly that the meal participants experienced themselves as actually a part of a new social order. Both as group and as individuals, many of those at the meals felt as if they were living in a different world. The ingestion of the food and all its communal dynamics internalized the social values and vision. It is this obviously simultaneous fantasy and transformation inside of the meal participants that made the meals themselves spiritual and enhanced them as social experiments.[229]

Jesus' feeding scenes in Matthew's Gospel are a form of voluntary association and manifest not only God's life-giving and liberation power but also Jesus as God's agent for bringing of peace. They rhetorically function as representations of a counter-society against the Roman Empire and the formation of new common identity. Consequently, Jesus' feeding narratives in Matthew reveal a *hidden script* of Matthew's resistance to the Roman Empire.

Establishment of the Alternative Kingdom and Ideology

The metaphor of bread and Jesus' feedings signify Matthew's alternative vision of community that challenges the Roman imperial power and structure. The feeding scenes with three verbs, εὐλογέω, κλάω, and δίδωμι, function as a meal hosted by Jesus; thereby Jesus' breaking of bread notifies the commencement of the common meal as a communal entity in solidarity.[230] At the same time, the metaphor of the breaking of bread not only signified the launching of new community, but it also actualized the formation of community. Through the act of breaking of bread, Matthew's narrator presents that Jesus promulgates the end of hostility among the crowds and ultimately establishes a new community with the crowds twice in feeding scenes. Furthermore, the Matthean Jesus binds the crowds as a communal entity in solidarity with his teachings and ideological vision of the kingdom of God. When the crowds share the bread broken by Jesus' hand, the crowds tacitly accept the power and authority of Jesus, at the same time they accept the direct rule of God and depend on the sovereignty of God, as did the ancient Israelite.

Matthew's formation of alternative community stands in the metaphor of bread and God who provides, which is used as a source of the formation of communal identity for the Ancient Israelite at the liberation from the bondage of the Egyptian Empire. Jesus' miraculous feeding scenes in Matthew are a symbolic proclamation of the formation of alternative community, corresponding to that of ancient Israel's exodus, which must be crucial and threatening to the Roman Empire. In Jewish tradition, the bread as a conceptual metaphor represents a fundamental source of Israel's identity in Ancient Israel's experience, based on God's complete care, provision of food, liberating power from slavery, and God's covenant with Israel, which all are closely linked to the bread. Based on the cognitive conceptual analogy, Matthew evokes the liberating power of God and God's sovereignty over the world, which forms an alternative community and identity under the direct rule and complete care of God. The recovery of Israel's identity with the memory of the original Exodus evokes a yearning for a new Exodus from the bondage of the Roman Empire.[231]

The most distinctive forms of protest against the Roman Imperial rule and against other imperial powers in Ancient Israel was Israel's prophetic tradition and messianic-apocalyptic vision. The fundamental pattern of prophetic and apocalyptic vision shows the liberation or restoration of the Israelite, which "entails God's defeat or judgment of Israel's foreign or domestic rulers."[232] The prophetic vision originates in Israelite heritage of liberation whom many imperial powers conquered; so the prophetic hope and vision of the restoration of Israel reflects back to the stories of Abraham, Elijah, Moses, Joshua, and others whose commitments become embodied in the ministry of Jesus. Moreover, Israel's prophetic tradition not only reveals hope of the restoration of Israel as an independent kingdom and alternative society under the God's rule, but it also presents the embodiment of the Israelite people's exclusive loyalty to God's ruling power and the principle of political-economic justice under God's providence.[233] Jesus' feedings as a fulfillment of prophetic vision proclaim Israel's independence as an alternative society and represent Matthew's strong resistance against the Roman Empire and its ruling authority.

Furthermore, Jesus' establishment of an alternative community challenges the Roman imperial ideology and denies their ruling authority and even their political-economic justice. Jesus' community under the rule of God in Matthew presents an alternative system driven by "compassion, sufficiency and shared resources," while Matthew attacks the injustice of the sinful imperial system, in which the elites dominate most life-giving resources with presenting immorality and death rather than compassion.[234] In Jesus' feedings, compassion is revealed as the motivation of Jesus' action, which corresponds to Matthew 9:36, describing the people as "sheep without a shepherd." Here Matthew indirectly denies the authority of the leadership under the Roman Imperial ideology and condemns the absence of authoritative leadership among the people.

In addition, as Carter argues, by evoking the *shepherds/leader* and Ezekiel 34, Jesus' compassionate feeding condemns the injustice of the leaders of dominating power, feeding themselves but depriving others of food (Ezekiel 34:2, 8).[235] This condemnation attacks to the Roman imperial system, in which the ruling class exercised social and economic power by dominating all social agendas and ideology. Thereby the empire is sustained by the hierarchical structure for the elites' status quo, exploiting the right and human dignity of the marginalized. However, Jesus presents alternative leadership under God's complete care in expressing compassion in both tasks of healing and supplying food and forms a new community, including women and children (14:21; 15:38) and even the most marginalized: "the lame, the maimed, the blind, the dumb and many others" (15:30). Jesus' feeding as a common meal and banquet stand in contrast to the banquet of the client king, Herod, representing the Imperial order and ideology. The client kings and other native ruling elites were integral parts of the established Roman imperial order at Jesus' time. Therefore, criticism of the domestic rulers under the Roman order may actually be regarded as a direct attack on the Roman Imperial order. Matthew presents Herod's banquet as full of the immorality and death of the elite's status quo, but Jesus' meal includes all the marginalized and promotes "their well-being with healing the sick and supplying adequate food, and anticipates God's different future, God's new creation and empire."[236] Matthew attacks the false ideological system under the imperial rule and presents an alternative community under God's compassionate sovereignty and Jesus' lordship.

Matthew as Voluntary Association in the Third Space

Voluntary Association

Philip Harland argues that it is from the framework of unofficial voluntary associations in the Greco-Roman world that one can get better understand the social dimensions of Judean gatherings and Christian congregations, including issues of identity.[237] Private and voluntary associations[238] were essential phenomena of the

Hellenistic period, mediating social-cultural dynamics. The term "association" is used to describe social bonding and groupings in ancient time, in which people shared characteristics, identity, and purpose in common.[239] The associations would also be recognized as an analogous group that has particularity and distinction by the outsider of group. The term "voluntary," as Wilson states, is designed to distinguish the members of associations from institutions such as the state, city or family where membership was determined by birth,[240] rather referring to groups that people opt to join by their own decision. The voluntary association is a group or social bonding of men and/or women autonomously organized on the basis of freely chosen membership for a common purpose or identity, which was separated from official associations of government. As Harland observed, social networks such as *household/family, the neighborhood, the workplace, religious temple/faith, and geographical origin/ethnic identity* framed social relations and played a role in the formation of membership of a particular association in the Greco-Roman world.[241]

In this regard, one may conjecture that Judean gatherings or Christian groups as voluntary associations were probably framed by the religious faith or ethnic identity. Saldarini insists that Matthew's group would have been understood as a private, voluntary association in Greco-Roman society.[242] Matthew's feeding scenes exhibit the features of association, reflecting the character of the Matthean community. All the crowds fed by Jesus are the voluntary followers of Jesus, including the twelve disciples. From the beginning of Jesus' ministry, Matthew's narrator recounts that "great crowds followed him from Galilee and the Decapolis and Jerusalem and Judea and from beyond the Jordan" (4:25), and they were taught by Jesus (5:3–7:29), being witness to Jesus' healing and compassionate ministry (8–9). Of course, the crowds, in Matthew's Gospel, are a shifting, unreliable, and unfixed group.[243] The components of the crowds are variable according to the narrative flow, and this indicates that people in various contexts voluntarily participate in the group.

The only commonality of social bonding of the crowds as a voluntary association is their decision to follow Jesus and his teachings. Through Jesus' feeding scenes with the metaphor of bread, Matthew proclaims Jesus as God's agent of the life-giving source and exhibits the actual formation of new community. The bread as metaphor evokes the cognitive conception of Israel and forms the communal identity of the crowds as an association based on the wilderness experience of ancient Israel. Furthermore, *eating/sharing* bread metaphorically presents that the crowds accept Jesus' teachings and participate in Jesus' ideological vision of the kingdom. So, when Jesus breaks the bread and the crowds share it, the feeding scenes present the self-understanding of Matthew's community as a voluntary association of the followers of Jesus.

In addition, Matthew's use of the term, *ekklesia*, reveals the feature of association in Greco-Roman world. In Matthew' account (16:18; 18:17), the references to *ekklesia* clearly refer to the assembly of Jesus-followers, sanctioned by the authority of Jesus (16:18), and the gathered as an assembly that seems to be institutionalized (18:17). The Greek term *ekklesia* was primarily political and judicial rather than religious and normally refers to an assembly of citizens duly assembled by the herald.[244] In the biblical tradition, especially in the Septuagint typically corresponding to Hebrew term *qahal*, *ekklesia* means an assembly or the act of assembling with some significant religious meaning. In Matthew' Gospel, *ekklesia* presents the assembly of Jesus-followers that voluntarily gathered with common faith in Jesus and shows an intimate relationship of members and their disciplinary power (18:17). *Ekklesia* as the designation of Matthew's assembly corresponds to the Jewish synagogue, which can be categorized as a religious-ethnic association.[245] Matthew's *ekklesia* functions to distinguish them from the Jewish synagogue and to designate them as similar in structure to a voluntary association.[246]

Accordingly, Matthew's *ekklesia* clearly shows the features of a voluntary association, autonomously summoned by faith in Jesus and his teaching. Dennis Duling argues that the Matthean *ekklesia* can be described "as a fictive kinship group or fictive brotherhood association,"[247] which assembled as a type of voluntary association. Saldarini also observes that, although association cannot define the Matthean community precisely, *ekklesia* denotes several types of assembly of believers-in-Jesus, especially as a household assembly of Jews who believe in Jesus, which corresponds to the Jewish synagogue. Therefore, the Matthean *ekklesia* can be categorized as a voluntary association in light of the social context of the Hellenistic and Greco-Roman world.[248]

Communal Identity in the *Third Space*

According to the social context under the colonial dominance of Rome, the cultural identity of Matthew's voluntary association can be reviewed by the postcolonial concept of the *Third Space*. It is in the third space that Matthew's community places and represents their new communal identity, which "constitute the discursive condition of enunciation"[249] beyond the colonial cultural imposition. Homi Bhabha has developed the concept of "third space" from literary and cultural theory to describe the construction of culture and identity within the social context of colonial antagonism. Homi Bhabha affirms that there can be no cultural singularity or pureness to cultural enunciation because all cultures are mobilized. When two cultural entities encounter, "these two places be mobilized through a third space,"[250] which represents both the general conditions of indigenous identity and the specific applications to the contexts. In this process of relation, the act of interpretation and understanding unconsciously produces the recognition of "an ambivalence" on the cultural systems and inherent originality, which reproduces new meaning and cultural identity in the third space, challenging the validity and authenticity of any essentialist cultural identity. Bhabha calls it as "ambivalent space of enunciation"[251] and affirms:

> The intervention of the Third Space, which makes the structure of meaning and reference an ambivalent process, destroys this mirror of representation in which cultural knowledge is continuously revealed as an integrated, open, expanding code.[252]

While the originality of Jewish culture has encountered Roman Imperialism, Matthew's community and its characteristic voluntary association reproduce a new structure of meaning and cultural identity and enunciate their communal identity and ideological vision in the third space, in-between the parent Jewish culture and the Roman Imperialism.

Matthew's community keeps presenting its communal identity and ideological vision throughout the Gospel narratives in order to legitimize the group identity and its value of existence within the broader social context. Matthew's community, like other Christian groups, is a cultural minority alongside Judean gatherings in the formative Judaism in the first century; and Matthew's association is recognized as a minority due to their rejection of sacrifice to the Roman gods. In-between two cultural entities, Matthew's community as a voluntary association is constructed in the contradictory and ambivalent space of enunciation, which deconstructs the primordial fixity of Jewish identity and the colonial cultural imposition. The associations of cultural minorities in the Greco-Roman world had some processes of negotiation, which entail both differentiating from others and assimilating socio-cultural origins.[253] Comparison with other groups within a larger society and categorizing "the other" in a negative way can be a central process of identity formation for "internal group self-definition and the negotiation of boundaries between 'us' and 'them.'" [254] In this manner, the Gospel of Matthew develops its whole narratives to legitimize the self-understanding of the Matthean community; Matthew defines and expresses the identity of association and its ideological vision that is different from that of formative Judaism and of the Roman Empire. Rather Matthew places their communal identity *in-between* somewhere, *the third Space*.

In fact, one can see that how Matthew assimilates and differentiates from formative Judaism, especially the group of religious leaders and the majority of Judaism, and how they maintain their socio-religious identity under the Imperial domination. Most of all, Matthew's community preserves the origin of communal identity based on its Jewish heritage and its prophetic vision.[255] At the same time, they distinguish themselves from the conventional perspective of formative Judaism through the expression of the expansion of group boundaries, designating them *ekklesia*, and their different interpretation of Torah. When Jesus breaks the bread and feeds the crowds in the first feeding scene, most of the crowds were Jews, the children/the lost sheep of house of Israel (10:6; 15:24). However, in the second feeding, the door of the feeding as a messianic banquet widely opens to the Gentiles. Furthermore, the crowds at both feedings include all the marginalized (14:14; 15:30), including even women and children (14:21; 15:38). Two feeding scenes and the metaphor of bread clearly reflect how Matthew envisions the ultimate expansion of their group boundaries beyond the conventional concept of boundary of Judaism. Furthermore its ideological visions are based on Jesus' own teachings, which present a different interpretation of the Torah from that of formative Judaism. Designating its association group as *ekklesia*, Matthew as the counter-part of the Jewish synagogue presents an alternative community the prophetic fulfillment. In this perspective, as Saldarini argues, Matthew's group can be characterized as an active deviant association and sect within Judaism,[256] still bound within Jewish community.

At the same time, Matthew does not take the colonial cultural imposition of the Roman Empire, while mimicking imperial theology for the representation of Jesus' identity and alternative community; but it rather resists their imperial ideology and represents an alternative identity and ideological vision. The bread metaphor in Matthew, representing the abundant provision of God and Jesus' lordship over life-giving resources, challenges the Roman imperial ideology and political theology which claimed that Rome was chosen, blessed, and sanctioned by the gods. The metaphor of bread and the vision of the messianic banquet envision the ultimate victory of God's kingdom/empire ruling over the other imperial power. Matthew ultimately binds voluntary followers of Jesus as a communal entity in solidarity with Jesus' teaching and new ideological vision of the kingdom of God and envisions the alternative community beyond the injustice of dominating power and the Roman imperialism. Matthew clearly denies the colonial cultural imposition or cultural fixity in the representation of identity as the colonized. Instead Matthew negotiates and reproduces their cultural identity in the third space and represents the alternative vision of communal identity.

The third space is a mode of articulation, not merely a way of describing reflective, but an articulating productive, interruptive, interrogative, enunciative, and subversive space for new possibility[257] and new forms of cultural meaning and vision beyond the socio-cultural, religious, and political boundaries. In this regard, Matthew's community and its character as a voluntary association in the third space, in-between the conventional identity of formative Judaism and Roman Imperialism, presents quite well their deviant communal identity from formative Judaism and ideological vision against the Roman Empire.

The Metaphor of Bread toward All Nations

New Covenant and Ideology in Hybridity

The narrative of the Canaanite woman functions literarily to exhibit the radical transition from Jesus' narrow mission strategy (10:5–6, especially: "Go nowhere among Gentile") to the Great Commission to make disciples of all the nations (28:19). The metaphor of bread (ἄρτος) that Jesus allows the woman to eat connects the first feeding narrative and the second feeding scene, which initiates the first step of the second phase of Matthew's mission program beyond Jew. Ultimately the narrative plot leads up to Jesus' Great Commission at the end of the Gospel (28:16–20). Furthermore, Matthew officially legitimizes and corroborates Matthew's communal identity and ideological vision through presenting the metaphor of bread again at Jesus' Last Supper. Through the Passover context, Matthew keeps evoking Israel's wilderness experience in the exodus and shaping the frame of the hermeneutical lens to retrospect Jesus' ministry and teachings. The identification of Jesus with the bread and the cup makes the reader review what has already been presented in the bread metaphor and its relevant meanings. At the same time the identification and the bread metaphor explicitly legitimize Matthew's communal identity and ideological vision and promulgate an alternative vision of the kingdom of God.

In light of the transition of mission strategy and new covenant, Matthew presents the expansion of the communal identity and its socio-religious, even political boundaries; and affirms the new ideological vision as an alternative covenantal community. In this perspective, one can see how Matthew relates with other dominant parties and how they define their communal identity and ideology and find legitimacy between formative Judaism and the Roman Empire.

In this chapter, I investigate narrative features and the literary motif of the metaphor of bread in the narrative of the Canaanite woman (15:21–28) and Jesus' Last Supper (26:26–29); and I re-interpret these narratives within the context of Matthew's Gospel as a whole in light of the metaphor of bread, while paying special attention to the role of each narrative unit as a special narrative apparatus within the whole Gospel: *transition and concluding climax*. Then, I examine the rhetorical claim of Matthean bread, presenting Matthew's communal identity and ideological vision.

The *Bread* and the Canaanite Woman: *"Even the Dogs Eat the Crumbs!"*

The narrative of the Canaanite woman is located between two feeding narratives in a sandwich structure, which enriches the meaning of the bread metaphor and its narrative role. This section concentrates on the role of the metaphor of bread in the narrative of the Canaanite woman in shaping the plot of Gospel of Matthew: *Transition* and *Prophetic fulfillment*. It also pays attention to significant narrative features and the meaning of the breaking/sharing of the bread.

Significant Features of the Narrative

Jesus Comes into the District of Tyre and Sidon

Matthew's account of the Canaanite woman (15:21–28) begins with the description of Jesus' itinerant route and location with a special verb ἀναχώρεω. After the debate with the Pharisees and Scribes on the dietary/purity laws (15:1–20), Jesus comes out "from there and withdrew to the district of Tyre and Sidon" (ἐξελθὼν ἐκεῖθεν ὁ Ἰησοῦς ἀνεχώρησεν εἰς τὰ μέρη Τύρου καὶ Σιδῶνος, v. 21). As was stated in previous chapter, the narrator uses ἐκεῖθεν (from there) and ἀνεχώρησεν (withdrew) again as a special pattern in Jesus' itinerancy for presenting Jesus' prophetic fulfillment.[1] The reader can recognize Jesus' itinerant route and location as a significant backdrop of Jesus' ministry and expect Jesus' prophetic action, as happened in Matthew 14:13–21.[2]

Especially, verse 21 starts with a positive conjunction καὶ, connecting to the previous account of Jesus' debate on the tradition of the elders and Jewish dietary law (15:1–20). The Jewish tradition of ritual purity and dietary law functions as a demarcation between Jews and Gentiles. The disciples are accused of eating with unwashed hands (15:2), which ultimately defiles the food and even the person. Although there is much debate on Jewish ritual purity in Jesus' time, the ritual purification itself is ultimately concerned with "marking out the holiness of God over against the lack of holiness which constantly threatens to contaminate human," and functions to sustain the socio-religious identity of Jewish community,[3] differentiating it from Gentiles and others. Harrington sees Jesus' debate on ritual purity and its Jewish tradition as ultimately concerned with what qualifies one for or disqualifies one from participating in the communal life of Jews.[4] In this narrative, Jesus withdraws (ἀνεχώρησεν) to the Gentile territory, "from there" – the place of the debate on the demarcation between Jews and Gentiles, so the reader can expect Jesus' prophetic action to be performed in Gentile territory, corresponding to the debate on ritual purity in Jewish tradition and participation in Jewish communal life.

This time, Jesus' withdrawal signifies the shift of the stage of Jesus' ministry from Jewish territory to the Gentile world. Matthew's narrator leads the reader's attention to two old cities named Tyre and Sidon, in which Matthew adds "καὶ Σιδῶνος" to Markan origin, τὰ ὅρια Τύρου (Mark 7:24). In the narrator's redaction, Matthew's account makes the reference to the old cities as the stereotyped pairing to conform to the usage of the Old Testament, and pairing these Gentile cities Tyre and Sidon may signify the whole Gentile world.[5] Tyre and Sidon as ancient "twin Phoenician cities" are considered the most ancient and the most prominent of the Canaanite/Phoenician coastal cities, which had never been recognized as a part of the land of the Ancient Israel.[6] In Old Testament tradition, prophets regularly condemn Tyre and Sidon as typical heathen cities,[7] often in the context of destruction–like Sodom and Gomorrah;[8] and they are traditionally recognized as the pagan region to the northwest of Jewish territory.[9] Even in Matthew 11:21, the narrator describes them as the object of judgment. In this regard, it is evident to the reader that the region of Tyre and Sidon is not an appropriate place for Jesus' ministry, representing the whole places of Gentile territory. However, the narrator clearly draws the reader's attention to the shift of Jesus' location to the district of Tyre and Sidon in v. 21.

Some scholars argue that Jesus does not cross over the borders of Gentile territory and meets the Canaanite woman in Jewish territory.[10] The reason for this perspective is the usage of the preposition εἰς which can be translated "toward," "up to," or "in direction of," so that it is not certain that Jesus actually enters the Gentile world.[11] Furthermore, the narrator states that the Canaanite woman "came out from that region" (γυνὴ Χαναναία ἀπὸ τῶν ὁρίων ἐκείνων ἐξελθοῦσα) to see Jesus, so that the encounter may occur on Jewish territory or on the border of Jewish territory. According to Amy-Jill Levine, the fact that the woman accepts the temporal priority of the Jews and she calls Jesus "son of David," implies that the woman encounters Jesus in Jewish territory.[12] Furthermore, Jesus' mission instructions in 10:5–6 support the idea that Jesus' itinerant route should be confined to Jewish land.

However, this perspective is not quite convincing to me. This interpretation would be literally reasonable and can be one of the possible ways of understanding the passage because the description of Jesus' itinerancy in verse. 21 is ambiguous as to the location of Jesus. However, no one can obviously be sure that there are clear borders or boundaries of Jewish territory in Jesus' time. So one cannot clearly predicate whether Jesus crosses the boundaries and enters into that region through the description in v. 21. Rather, according to the narrative plot and literary expression, one must accept that Jesus enters a part of the Gentile region, as other literal expression did with the typical itinerant term, "from there" and "withdrawal."

Furthermore, as Gundry insists, Matthew's narrator changes Mark's ambiguous expression, εἰς τὰ ὅρια Τύρου (Mark 7:24) to εἰς τὰ μέρη Τύρου καὶ Σιδῶνος, in order to make clear that Jesus' location is in Gentile territory.[13] Mark's term ὅρια presents a "marker of division between two areas, boundary,"[14] so it can be translated as "into the border of Tyre." In this regard, Jesus' location in Mark is quite ambiguous as to whether he is in or out; however, Matthew's narrator avoids the possible ambiguity with the replacement of ὅρια with μέρη, which can be translated as "district" or "part,"[15] presenting Jesus' location as a part of "Tyre and Sidon." Through Matthew's description εἰς τὰ μέρη Τύρου καὶ Σιδῶνος, the reader understands that Jesus is already located in a part of the region of Tyre and Sidon.

Some scholars argue that the woman's coming out of the region to see Jesus indicates that Jesus' location is still not in the district of Tyre and Sidon; however, Matthew's expression of the Canaanite woman's coming forth from that region or border in verse 22 (γυνὴ Χαναναία ἀπὸ τῶν ὁρίων ἐκείνων ἐξελθοῦσα) does not seem to present the woman's geographical location, but rather expresses the woman's socio-ethnic origin and her willingness to see Jesus. Verse 22 is not a clue to Jesus' location in Jewish territory, but rather the description of the woman's hastened moving toward Jesus, and her Gentile origin highlights Jesus' ministry to Gentiles.

From this perspective, the narrator clearly places Jesus' location in a part of Gentile territory at the beginning of the narrative of the Canaanite woman. One of the important points of this narrative is that this shift of Jesus' location and the expectation of Jesus' prophetic fulfillment cued by the special pattern of the term ἀναχώρεω, correspond to the previous debate on the demarcation between Jew and Gentile in 15:1–23. It also contrasts to Jesus' mission instruction in 10:5–6, so the district of Tyre and Sidon is very significant in this narrative unit.

Dialogue Between Jesus and the Woman

The most distinctive feature of Matthew's narrative of the Canaanite woman is a dialogic structure.[16] The narrative unit itself can be seemingly categorized as a miracle story that shows Jesus' miraculous healing of a demon-possessed daughter from a distance. However, the focus of the narrative is not on Jesus' healing activity but on the controversial conversation between the Canaanite woman and Jesus.[17] Although Matthew's narrator retells the narrative of Mark 7:24–30, the narrator adds some conversational components for unfolding the story dynamically. In the case of Mark's account, the narrator simply explains the situation that a woman comes and falls down at Jesus' feet begging Jesus to heal her demon-possessed daughter (Mark 7:25–26). Jesus rejects the woman's request one time (7:27), and the woman speaks to Jesus one time (7:28). Then, the problem is simply resolved by Jesus' affirmative saying (7:29). The scene itself is not dialogic but descriptive for emphasizing Jesus' miraculous healing itself.

In the case of Matthew's account, however, not only does the reader clearly hear the woman's own voice but also the woman has more direct speech with Jesus (15:22, 25, 27).[18] Luz clearly argues that vv. 22–25 have been completely rewritten by Matthew.[19] The scene itself is driven by the controversial dialogue between Jesus and the Canaanite woman, not by the narrator's descriptive account. In Matthew's account, Jesus' healing moment is weakened[20] by the dynamic conversation, but rather Jesus' healing action ultimately functions as the final answer in the controversial dialogue. In this regard, Hagner affirms that the healing miracle becomes "primarily a framework and vehicle for the teaching"[21] and ultimate discourse of Matthew.

The dialogic part of this narrative is composed of "four dyadic units,"[22] in which each unit describes the request of the Canaanite woman or the disciples and Jesus' response. The Canaanite woman speaks to Jesus three times (vv. 22, 25, 27); the disciples request once (v. 23b); and Jesus responds all four times including his tacit ignorance (vv. 23a, 24, 26, 28). Interestingly, as Davies and Allison explain well, Matthew's narrator clearly structures each dyadic dialogue with Jesus' repetitious response, beginning with "ὁ δε□ἀπεκρίνομαι" (vv. 23a, 24, 26). Only the last verbal response changes to to,te for presenting Jesus' final acceptance of the woman's request:[23]

> The first dyadic unit: The woman's request (v. 22)
>   – Jesus' first response (v. 23a: ὁ δε….ἀπεκρίνομαι)
> The second dyadic unit: The disciples' request (v. 23b)
>   – Jesus' second response (v. 24: ὁ δε….ἀπεκρίνομαι)
> The third dyadic unit: The woman's request (v. 25: ἡ δε…λέγω)
>   – Jesus' third response (v. 26: ὁ δε….ἀπεκρίνομαι)
> The fourth dyadic unit: The woman's request (v. 27: ἡ δε…εἶπον aorist of λέγω)
>   – Jesus' fourth response (v. 28: τότε….ἀπεκρίνομαι)

Jesus' sequence of three negative responses and the woman's tenacious requests raise the tensional dialogue to the climax. At the same time, this narrative structure draws the reader's attention to the content of the conversation, weakening their concerns with Jesus' miraculous activity. Jesus' final response, beginning with the exchanged word τότε, leads the reader into Jesus' eventual acceptance of the woman's request, leaving a strong impact on the reader's mind and giving the reader an ultimate answer to the controversial dialogue, and even to the previous debate in 15:1–20. In this regard, one needs to keep in mind that the distinctive feature of Matthew's narrative of the Canaanite woman is dialogic conversation between Jesus and the woman, not Jesus' miraculous healing.

The Dogs and the Canaanite

The dialogic tension in the narrative of the Canaanite woman comes to a climax with Jesus' answer to woman's third request (v. 26). When the woman kneels down at Jesus' feet, saying Κύριε, βοήθει μοι, Jesus answers that "it is not right to take the children's bread and throw it to the dogs." The tension is at its highest pitch by the woman's fourth request with her wise answer (v. 27): "yet even the dogs eat the crumbs." At the climax, for the reader, the most attentive point is the metaphoric usage of the term, κυνάριον (dog) by Jesus' mouth. Although the term κυνάριον could be a stumbling block for the reader, one easily recognizes that the metaphoric mockery with the κυνάριον modifies to the Canaanite woman as a representative of all the Gentiles, rejecting her request strictly. Namely, the reader can identify the children with Israel; and the dogs represent Gentiles.[24]

At this point, the reader must be reminded of the negative connotation of 'dogs' in Matthew 7:6: "Do not give what is holy to dogs (κυσὶν); and do not throw your pearls before swine (χοίρων), or they will trample them under foot and turn and maul you." The dogs are metaphorically the same as swine or outcasts. (c.f. 8:31–32). For the reader, the Canaanite woman is identified with the dogs in 7:6 that cannot get the pearls or even recognize the value of the pearls. Fiorenza indicates that 'dogs' and 'swine' are regarded as figurative characterizations of pagans, with whom early Jewish Christians avoid sharing the gospel of the kingdom and table-fellowship with Gentiles.[25] Even in the Old Testament, dogs are described as a common metaphor for outcasts with swine harlots (e.g., Psalm 59:6–8; Isaiah 56:10–11; Job 30:1).[26] Some bad connotations derive also from dogs.[27] Of course, not all descriptions of the dogs have bad connotations and they should be considered in the contexts of the Scripture,[28] however, in many cases in the scriptures, the term dog has a bad connotation, especially metaphorically representing the other outside from Jew. Many scholars agree that Jews commonly used "dogs" as a derogatory epithet for indicating Gentiles or a person outside the Jewish faith,[29] so the reader can easily recognize the κυνάριον is used as a mocking expression designating the Canaanite woman.

The term κυνάριον itself only occurs in Jesus' metaphoric saying in Matthew 15:26 and in Mark 7:27 in the New Testament. In many cases, dogs appear as κυων. The term κυνάριον, probably referring to a pet, house-dog, or lap-dog, is the diminutive form of κύων, which normally presents "the annoying and despised eastern dog of the street."[30] Some scholars argue that the diminutive form does not necessarily contain a slurring reference to Gentiles.[31] However, according to the narrative plot, the narrator does not seem to have any concerns about how to soften Jesus' words by using the diminutive form of κύων, or how to weaken the meaning of derogatory epithet "dogs." But rather the narrator seems to try to make clear the circumstance of Jesus' metaphoric mockery, in which the dog is under the meal table and could not be allowed to sit with the children and get the food on the table (15:26). The usage of κυνάριον is more appropriate than κύων in this narrative because the scene is metaphorically described around the meal table inside a house. However it does not weaken the meaning of the dogs as a derogatory epithet. In this respect, the diminutive form κυνάριον does not affect to weaken its nuance of a slurring reference to Gentiles. It just shows that Jesus is adopting a Jewish common derogatory epithet for the metaphoric indicating Gentiles.

Used as a derogatory epithet to Gentiles, the term κυνάριον combines with the woman's ethnic origin, Χαναναῖος (Canaanite) in this narrative. Matthew's narrator adds "Sidon" to Markan geographical setting of this narrative and changes the woman's ethnic origins from "Syrophoenician" (Mark 7:26) to "Canaanite" (15:22). Most scholars agree that the term, "Canaanite" identifies the outsiders or

Israel's enemies in the Old Testament.[32] Lemche observes the history of Canaan and the Canaanites in the Old Testament, primarily analyzing the Pentateuch and the Deuteronomistic history. In this work he identifies the Canaanite as a characteristic description, revealing 'ideological prototype' especially as a principal enemy of the Israelites:[33]

> The Canaanites and their land had no independent history of their own; they were only included in the historical narratives in order to further the intentions of the narrators. The biblical Canaanites thus had no historical role to play, and the Old Testament historical literature cannot be used as information about historical Canaanites, simply because the Canaanites of the Old Testament are not historical persons but actors in a 'play' in which the Israelites have got the better, or the hero's part.[34]

The Canaanite of the Old Testament represents the stereotypical hostile as the opponent of the Israelites, who is not compatible with Jewish community; even Ancient Israelites were prohibited from having relationship with Canaanites or inter-marrying with them.[35]

Matthew's change of the woman's origins to Canaanite clearly represents and underscores the being of the other from Judaism, whether by race, religion or trade. Namely, the Canaanite woman is representative character of the outsider, who maybe deserve to be called dog, κυνάριον, and who must be excluded from the object group of Jesus' ministry according to Jesus' previous mission instruction (10:5–6). In this regard, Jesus' derogatory epithet κυνάριον and the woman's ethnic Χαναναία are very significant narrative features, through which the narrator brings the tensional discourse of Gentile mission into a common table in Matthew's vision.

The Metaphor of Bread and the Canaanite Woman

It Is All about the Bread: *Debate on the Metaphor of Bread*

The narrative unit of the Canaanite woman presents tensional dialogues between Jesus and the woman, composed of four dyadic dialogues through which the narrator leads the reader's attention to the metaphor of bread. The dialogue is seemingly concerned about whether Jesus heals the demon-possessed daughter, as Jesus heals the servant of the centurion in 8:5–13; however, the dialogue in tension is metonymically expressed with the feeding metaphor and the bread, so that the reader naturally has concerns about the metaphoric conversation about the bread. At the climax of the conversation, Jesus suddenly brings out the issues of feeding with the bread metaphor in v. 26: "it is not right to take the children's bread (τὸν ἄρτον τῶν τέκνων) and throw it to the dogs." Then the woman appropriately understands and responds to Jesus: "even the dogs eat the crumbs" (v. 27). According to this dialogue, as Gail O'Day argues, one can recognize that the narrative of the Canaanite woman is "a richly layered and densely textured text," which cannot simply be read for what it seems to be saying on a single line.[36] At the surface level of the narrative, the theme is Jesus' healing; on a deeper level, the narrator metaphorically brings in the theme of feeding and the breaking of bread.

In the main dialogue, the Canaanite woman shouts firstly to beg for Jesus' mercy and the healing of her daughter with the title "Son of David" (υἱὸς Δαυίδ v. 22); however, Jesus refuses to hear her petition "at all" and simply ignores her request (v. 23a). In the first dyadic unit, the reader simply knows the story as it concerns Jesus' healing ministry. Theissen argues that the cry for help normally appears as a standard feature in miracle stories,[37] and the title "υἱὸς Δαυίδ" as a messianic title must allude to Jesus as healer for Matthew's reader because the usage of υἱὸς/υἱέ Δαυίδ is common in therapeutic contexts (9:27; 12:23; 15:22; 20:30–31).[38] Therefore, the reader naturally expects Jesus' response as a healer in this account; however, Jesus does not even answer her.

The narrator then leads the reader into the second dyadic dialogue: the disciples say to Jesus, "send her away" (ἀπόλυσον αὐτήν" v. 23b). The meaning of disciples' request, ἀπόλυσον αὐτήν is ambiguous as to whether they want Jesus to grant her request or they simply want to get rid of her annoyance from there, avoiding contact with a Gentile.[39] The narrator clearly describes that even disciples recognize the woman's request is about Jesus' healing action. The matter of the reader's concern is only whether Jesus accepts her request for healing her daughter or not. Jesus answers, "I was sent only to the lost sheep of the house of Israel" (v. 24). Jesus' answer seems to completely exclude the Gentile from the benefits of Jesus' healing ministry. Even this answer is not spoken to the woman, but to the disciples. The woman's petition is totally ignored by Jesus. Interestingly, Jesus' refusal to answer reminds the reader of Jesus' strict instruction of mission to only the Jews in Matthew 10:5–6, so the reader may imagine a negative result in this story.

In the third dyadic dialogue unit, the woman kneels down and says, "Lord, help me" (Κύριε, βοήθει μοι; v.25). Then, Jesus answers, "it is not right to take the children's bread (τὸν ἄρτον τῶν τέκνων) and throw it to the dogs," βαλεῖν τοῖς κυναρίοις (v. 26), and leads the dialogue to its climax. It seems that there is no way that the woman will obtain Jesus' mercy to heal her demon-possessed daughter. The most significant point of this narrative unit is that Jesus suddenly leads the dialogue into the theme of feeding with the metaphoric term, bread (ἄρτος)[40] in his refusal. While, on the surface of the narrative, the woman obviously begs for Jesus' mercy for healing, the narrator metonymically describes Jesus' negative answer using the metaphor of feeding and of the bread. In this way, Matthew naturally brings the bread metaphor into the dialogue with the Canaanite woman and invites the reader into the discourse of the metaphor of bread and feeding. In the very next dyadic unit, the Canaanite woman responds to Jesus' bread discourse: "yet even the dogs eat the crumbs that fall from their masters' table" (v. 27). The woman's response to Jesus appropriately touches upon the bread metaphor, and the woman clearly affirms that even dogs may eat the bread under the masters' table.

At this point, the reader recognizes that the main theme of this narrative is not only Jesus' healing ministry but also the bread and feeding, especially feeding the Gentiles. The key interest of the reader now becomes whether the Canaanite woman can get the bread from Jesus or not. As far as the bread is concerned, the reader also recalls the bread Jesus provided for the crowds in the previous chapter (14:13–21) and the bread in Jesus' temptation narrative (4:1–11), evoking the reader's cognitive conception of the bread and breaking/sharing of the bread. As studied in the previous chapter, in neither narrative does the bread function for the satisfaction of human hunger; rather the bread as a metaphor in Israel's cognitive concepts signifies God's complete care, provision, and life-giving source, which is a fundamental source of Israel's identity. The tensional dialogues in this narrative evokes the reader's cognitive conception and reminds the reader of the previous discourse around the metaphor of bread in Matthew, so that the reader can appropriately map the structure of the meaning of the bread for the children (τῶν τέκνων) and even for the dogs (τοῖς κυναρίοις).

Dogs Eat the Broken Bread

The tensional conversation between Jesus and the Canaanite woman reaches its climax with the bread metaphor and Jesus' strict refusal: "It is not right to take the children's bread and throw it to the dogs," Οὐκ ἔστιν καλὸν λαβεῖν τὸν ἄρτον τῶν τέκνων καὶ βαλεῖν τοῖς κυναρίοις (v. 26). The narrator not only brings the bread metaphor into the main dialogue but also uses the Canaanite woman as a representative for all Gentiles, referring to her with the derogatory term, dogs. Now the main concern with the metaphor of bread is whether Jesus allows her to eat the bread he provides on the level of narrative; this concern also reveals whether the Gentiles can participate in the meal table with the children of Israel on the level of metaphoric meaning. The reader simply understands that Jesus' metaphorical rebuff in v. 26 is a clear affirmation that he is not going to grant her special favor because she is outside of Jesus' national kinship community. At the same time, the reader recognizes that Jesus will not allow the Gentiles into the messianic banquet reserving a life-giving source only for the Jews.

The climax of the tensional conversation is hit by Jesus' strong rejection of the acceptance of Gentiles into the boundaries of his mission. The premise of this metaphoric refusal is preceded by previous verses, "I was sent only to the lost sheep of the house of Israel" (v. 24), which is based on Jesus' mission instruction, presenting an Israel-oriented mission in10:5–6. What Jesus' instruction actually prohibits is going εἰς ὁδὸν ἐθνῶν and εἰς πόλιν Σαμαριτῶν (10:5), but it only accepts to coming for τὰ πρόβατα τὰ ἀπολωλότα οἴκου Ἰσραήλ (10:6). In this regard, granting the woman's request in Gentile territory does not simply mean Jesus' merciful healing act but an abnormal feature of ministry, which breaks his mission instructions and the socio-religious boundaries in Jewish culture. In this narrative, however, Jesus clearly re-affirms his instructions and refuses to grant her request. Jesus is described as a single-minded person who has consistent belief, and his focus is firmly focused on the people of Israel (cf. v. 24). In addition, the Matthean omission of the Markan phrase: "Let the children first be fed; Ἄφες πρῶτον χορτασθῆναι τὰ τέκνα" in 7:27, seems to make Matthew's Jesus more strict. While the Gospel of Mark presents the priority of Israel to the Gentiles, in which there seems to be secondary possible room for the Gentiles to come later, Jesus' rebuff in Matthew seems to deny any possibility for the Gentiles at all in Jesus' ministry.

The situation is totally changed, however, by the woman's wise answer in the fourth dyadic conversation in v. 27. With the adverb ναί, the woman agrees with Jesus' statement first, and the narrator leads another round of tensional dyadic conversation with ἡ δὲ εἶπεν.[41] The woman's answer, ναὶ κύριε(reveals clear boundaries between Gentiles and Jews again, in which she recognizes and accepts her status outside the boundary, and the woman's recognition of Jesus' obligation in that regard. At the same time, she keeps asking Jesus and arguing: "even the dogs eat the crumbs (τῶν ψιχίων) that fall from their master's table" (v. 27). Basically, the Canaanite woman knows what Jesus is talking about exactly, especially about the bread metaphor, so she asks for even the crumbs of the bread. These crumbs of bread are the broken bread on the meal table and a superfluous piece of bread possibly fallen from the master's table.

The woman seems to argue with Jesus about the superfluous life-giving source God provides that would not diminish Israel's privileges. For the reader, the crumbs (τῶν ψιχίων) allude to the baskets of leftovers from Jesus' first feedings (14:13–21),[42] which can symbolically be available for the Canaanite woman, represented as dogs. She tries to persuade Jesus that there is superfluous life-giving source leftover in God's provision, and her wise answer reminds Jesus of the overflowing source of God's salvific authority over the world.

Matthew's redactional change of Markan description, τῶν παιδίων in 7:28 to "from the master's table; ἀπὸ τῆς τραπέζης τῶν κυρίων αὐτῶν" presents that the bread is provided by the master and the children are fed by the master. Davies and Allison insist that here "the woman raises the possibility of being fed even now, at the same time as the children are fed."[43] At this point, for the Jewish reader, the τὸν ἄρτον τῶν τέκνων and its relevant metaphoric theme are very significant for the communal identity and have various socio-religious meanings in the reader's cognitive conception.[44] At the same time, the reader recalls the bread Jesus provides for all of the crowds in the previous chapter (14:13–21) and the bread in Jesus' temptation narrative (4:1–11), evoking the reader's cognitive conception of the bread.

Accordingly, the metaphor of bread, that is the crumb of bread (15:27), in Jesus' negation as a source domain of metaphorical conception, functions to denote the source of Israel's communal identity, which can only be shared within the community and demarcates the boundary of socio-religious and ethnic identity. The source of communal identity and its relevant conceptual knowledge function as a target domain of the bread metaphor. Therefore, when bread is shared with the other, the metaphor of bread signifies the acceptance of the other into community, the breaking of any socio-religious boundaries, and the actual formation of community under the same table.

Jesus finally accepts her request and says, "Let it be done for you as you wish" (v. 28). The narrator signals the end of the tensional dialogue with the replacement of the ὁ δὲ ἀποκριθεὶς with the τότε ἀποκριθεὶς. Then, Jesus proclaims that he will now act according to what the Canaanite woman wishes, which is actually her persuading suggestion. It is a great moment that Jesus not only accepts the woman's request to heal her demonized daughter, but also the dogs are to be fed by their lords, as the children are fed. Namely, this is the very moment when Jesus decides to share the bread for the children of Israel (τὸν ἄρτον τῶν τέκνων) with the dogs, the Gentiles.

When Jesus accepts the Canaanite woman and the dogs get the crumbs of bread, the objects of sharing of bread and Jesus' feeding are extended to the Gentiles as well as the children of Israel. Namely, the narrative of the Canaanite woman metaphorically demonstrates that all Gentiles and other marginalized living outside of the boundaries are also to be fed by God and invited to community under God's complete care with the children of Israel. Furthermore, Matthew's narrator metaphorically represents that now Jesus overcomes the socio-religious boundaries that existed before and establishes a new covenant and community with the Gentiles. Jesus becomes the head of the house and the master of the table, invites the dogs–Gentiles to a meal, *breaking/sharing* the bread, even though it is crumbs. Thereby Matthew's Jesus symbolically proclaims the end of hostilities between Jews and Gentiles, blesses all beings around the table, and solidifies them as a familial community under God's complete care and provision. Therefore, through the Jesus' metaphoric dialogue and prophetic decision of sharing of bread, Matthew proclaims that the dogs and all the Gentiles are included and solidified as a single community under God's provision. This is the very moment when Jesus accepts the Gentiles into communal identity and when Jesus' mission is turned and extended to the Gentiles. And this is the very moment of the fulfillment of prophesy that the reader expected because of the term ἀναχώρεω.

Prophetic Fulfillment

Matthew's familiar form of phrase, ἐκεῖθεν and ἀναχώρεω, drives the narrative of the Canaanite woman into the main theme, in which the reader recognizes the acceptance of the Gentile woman's request as a proceeding prophetic fulfillment. All of the narrative features, such as Jesus' previous debate on purity, his withdrawals, his itinerant move, and the sharing of bread with the Canaanite woman, turn out to be prophetic fulfillment. In the previous narrative (15:1–20), the scene comes with Jesus' debate with the Pharisees and Scribes on Jewish tradition especially the dietary/purity laws,[45] which represents the demarcation of the identity of Jew from the Gentiles. In the debate, Jesus severely criticizes the Pharisees and Scribes, calling them "hypocrites" and "blind guides" (vv. 7, 14). Then the narrator delivers a tensional atmosphere of the debate through the disciples' voice: "do you know that the Pharisees were offended…?" (v. 12). Perceiving the potential danger and hostility, Jesus withdraws from there and enters the district of Tyre and Sidon, Gentile territory. Now the reader expects to see the proceeding prophetic action.

Jesus' itinerant route symbolically takes him from the *'clean/pure'* Jewish territory toward the *'unclean/impure'* Gentile territory where he encounters the Canaanite woman. Using the motif of ἀναχώρεω, entailing Jesus' prophetic fulfillment, the narrator leads the reader's attention from the debate on the demarcation of the identity of Jews in terms of tradition and dietary/purity laws[46] to the prophetic answer about the boundary of Jewish identity and its prophetic fulfillment. As was in previous debate, Jesus challenges that tradition is not always identified with "the word of God" (15:3–6), Jesus prophetically accepts the Canaanite woman, the representative of dogs, for having bread and participating at his table with the children of Israel. With the affirmation of the woman's faith, Matthew prophetically breaks the traditional boundaries between Jew and Gentile and redefines the identity of the children of God.

A most attentive point of this prophetic fulfillment is the significant role of the Canaanite woman contrasted to the passive character of Jesus. As Gail O'Day affirms, the Canaanite woman as a protagonist initiates all the actions and conversations, which not only change Jesus' mission statement and Israel's history of salvation[47] but also offer great motivation and possibility for Jesus' prophetic fulfillment. Gail O'Day argues that the woman's resilience of faith and her daring words correspond with the petitioning cries for deliverance in Israel's lament psalms.[48] She observes that, as lament psalmists boldly address, complain, petition, and present motivations to God with reasons for why God should change and should act, the Canaanite woman bravely approaches, addresses, debates, and presents the motivation to Jesus with reasons not only to heal her demon-possessed daughter,[49] but also to feed the dogs. As lament psalmists remind God of God's faithfulness to God's promises, the Canaanite woman reminds Jesus of "the fullness and vitality of the promise" through her faith, so that Jesus can step forward to new possibilities and fulfill that promise.[50] By means of this, the Canaanite woman seems to co-operate with Jesus for fulfilling prophetic proclamation for moving toward the Gentiles.

The Canaanite woman and her significant role in prophetic fulfillment correspond to the five women, including Mary in Matthew's genealogy, who are actively involved in the fulfillment of God's providence in the history of Israel. The genealogy in Matthew has a monotonous literary formula presenting Jesus' genealogy from Abraham: A (a man) ἐγέννησεν B (a man) referring to male activity. This consistent formula is unexpectedly interrupted by four women of the Old Testament: Tamar, Rahab, Ruth, and the wife of Uriah, Bathsheba, eventually connecting to Mary.

Tamar:	1:3 Ἰούδας δὲ ἐγέννησεν τὸν Φάρες καὶ τὸν Ζάρα	ἐκ τῆς Θαμάρ
Rahab:	1:5 Σαλμὼν δὲ ἐγέννησεν τὸν Βόες	ἐκ τῆς Ῥαχάβ
Ruth :	Βόες δὲ ἐγέννησεν τὸν Ἰωβὴδ	ἐκ τῆς Ῥούθ
Bathsheba:	1:6 Δαυὶδ δὲ ἐγέννησεν τὸν Σολομῶνα	ἐκ τῆς τοῦ Οὐρίου

— Mary 1:16 Ἰακὼβ δὲ ἐγέννησεν τὸν Ἰωσὴφ τὸν ἄνδρα Μαρίας, ἐξ ἧς ἐγεννήθη Ἰησοῦς ὁ λεγόμενος Χριστός.

The ethnic origin of two women, Tamar and Rahab, is Canaanite,[51] corresponding to that of the Canaanite woman.[52] Daniel Harrington states, "Canaanite" is an ancient designation of the pagan inhabitants; even woman's names are barely used in Jewish genealogy in the first century,[53] so it is possible that Matthew's narrator seems to use this term anachronistically. However, Matthew intentionally uses "Canaanite" as a narrative strategy, which not only corresponds to the backdrop of the narrative in Gentile territory, Tyre and Sidon, but also reminds the reader of the character of women in Matthew' genealogy. The role of the Canaanite woman can be identified with that of the four women in Matthew's genealogy in light of the prophetic action in the salvation history of Israel. In this respect, the main discourse of the Canaanite woman can be hinted by the character of women in the Genealogy.

These unexpected and irregular appearances of four women are very questionable[54] and have led to scholarly debates for a long time. Why did Matthew include the names of four women in a patriarchal genealogy prior to Mary? What is the role of these women in Matthew's narrative as a whole? Some scholars concentrate on the women's sinful character, saying that Matthew highlights Jesus' role as the forgiving savior and advocates for Mary's virgin pregnancy.[55] Others regard the women as foreigners; thereby Matthew foreshadows the acceptance of the Gentiles.[56] Most scholarly debates and observance are valuable to see the Gospel of Matthew. However, the most convincing interpretation, for me, takes into account the coherent commonality of these women's characters including the case of Mary.

As Raymond Brown suggested, the common feature among these women is that they "showed initiative or played an important role in God's plan and so came to be considered the instrument of God's providence."[57] No matter what these women's socio-political religious status is, such as prostitute or Gentile, each one is part of the salvation history of Israel and has a certain unexpected role in fulfilling God's providence, which can be called "divine irregularity,"[58] or "detours of God's way."[59] Interestingly, each woman is wise and bold enough to see God's hidden plan, overcoming human obstacles in furthering God's providence in the history of Israel. From this perspective, Wim J. C. Weren argues that all the women contribute boldly protecting to the development of Israel's history by their position within their family, clan, or nation in accordance with legal provision and wisely responding to the situation by taking the hidden possibilities for surviving; thereby the women contributed to the development of Israel's history.[60] And she states that:

> "the new situations which the women face reveals hidden possibilities enabling them to contribute to the development of the house of Israel. Israel's history would have been cut short prematurely, or would have been completely different, had these women not

mapped out alternative paths to the future. Some of the women cleverly take advantage of ambiguities and lacunas in the legal order, and they meet support as well as resistance from male persons who surround them."[61]

Tamar, the Canaanite, continues God's providence by initiating a scandalous union with her father-in-law, Judah (Genesis 38). Tamar creatively uses the possibilities offered by the levirate law and manages to continue the familial line.[62] Another Canaanite woman, Rahab takes a risk by giving two spies shelter, which makes it possible for Israel to come into the Promised Land.[63] In exchange for this protection, she obtains the two spies' willingness to spare her and her family (Joshua 2, 6). Ruth also chooses an uncertain life with her mother-in-law Naomi in Bethlehem, in which they must be outsiders in the social order. However, Ruth succeeds in enticing Boaz to step into building the house of Israel (Ruth 1–4). The case of Bathsheba is not clear because she is a victim of David's adultery; but her resilient attitude and wisdom have a significant role in the turbulent period of the succession, persuading David to appoint Solomon as his successor[64] (2 Samuel 11–12; 1 Kings 1–2). Finally, Mary courageously accepts her virgin pregnancy, which is an unacceptable occurrence in the customary law, and gives birth to the baby Jesus (Matthew 2).

From this perspective, what the five women had done in the history of Israel were a prophetic fulfillment that has shown God's providence and plans throughout the history of Israel. Namely, all the women are used as instruments of God's prophetic provision. Furthermore, the character of the women in Matthew's genealogy corresponds to that of the Canaanite woman. Acting boldly the five women have done, the Canaanite woman boldly approaches Jesus and wisely debates Jesus' narrow mission instruction and the bread metaphor in a public arena. Her persevering faith and wisdom change Jesus' mind to accept the Gentile, participating in the meal table and having bread as a family with the children of Israel. Thus, the faith of the Canaanite woman as a prophetic action continues and expands the divine irregularity of God's providence initiated by the five women in Matthew's genealogy.

The Breaking of Bread: *Breaking Boundaries*

The metaphor of bread, which Jesus shares with the dogs, signifies the breaking of boundaries. The breaking incident in this text is not just confined to the religious-ethnic boundary between Jew and Gentile,[65] but it extends to multivalent dimension of boundaries formed by human prejudice. As the narrative of the Canaanite woman is "a richly layered and densely textured text,"[66] the boundary breaking in this text cannot simply be understood on the surface issue, but it should be read through multivalent lenses. During the last decades, the narrative of the Canaanite woman has been concretely analyzed by many feminist scholars with multi-lenses, highlighting the diverse ways of reading and challenging many other socio-political boundaries and human prejudices.[67]

Jesus' encounter with the Canaanite woman presents that a number of the religious-ethnic boundaries are overcome by sharing the bread. Despite Jesus' narrow/strict mission instruction in 10:5–6, the narrative of the Canaanite woman clearly begins with Jesus himself crossing over the boundary of his own instruction, entering into the district of Tyre and Sidon (15:21). Obviously, Matthew's narrator uses Jesus' itinerant route to highlight the existence of the religious-ethnic boundary between Jew and Gentile. Furthermore, through Jesus' strong refusals using the contrastive designations, dogs and children (15:23, 24, 26), the reader recognizes a clear boundary between the children of Israel and the other ethnic group. Interestingly, although Jesus is described as a single-narrow minded person who strongly refuses to grant the woman's request even after he has crossed the border between Jew and Gentile, he brings the discourse of the metaphor bread into the main dialogue with the Canaanite woman (15:26). Later, with Jesus' celebration of the woman's great faith and wisdom, the children's bread is shared with the dogs, whereby Matthew's narrator proclaims Gentiles access to healing, the life-giving source and salvation beyond the religious-ethnic boundary.

This is the first moment that Matthew's Gospel breaks Jesus' previous narrow-minded mission instruction. At the same time, through the breaking/sharing of bread, Matthew's Jesus breaks the religious-ethnic boundary between Jews and Gentiles and opens the door for all Gentiles to access Jesus' community.

Second, the breaking/sharing of bread in the narrative of the Canaanite woman overcomes the boundary of gender relation. In recent years, many feminist scholars have reinterpreted this narrative, more concerned with gender relation than with the ethnic relation. Obviously, the first century Mediterranean world is a very patriarchal and androcentric society, in which the woman's stereotypical social location is inferior to men and the woman's activity is limited to the private domestic sphere.[68] In this narrative, however, most feminist scholars, including Gail O'Day, Elaine Wainwright, and Frances Taylor Gench, concentrate on and highlight the Canaanite woman's active character, role, and wisdom, which break the bonds of gender-stereotyping and bias in the ancient world.[69] The Canaanite woman's character in Matthew's account is more active than its parallel in Mark 7:24–30.[70] She is described as an active debater who not only initiates conversation and speaks directly to Jesus in a public area[71] but also holds fast to her own views eventually persuading Jesus, while the male characters, Jesus and his disciples, are depicted as passive and debasing in attitude that signify the fixed gender boundary and social bias to female.

The woman changes the whole situation, even Jesus' strict mind, and achieves what she, as a social minority in a patriarchal society, wishes despite the gender boundary. Matthew's description of the Canaanite woman, especially her role as a debater against a male in the public arena, is "an indicator of a significant gender question" for the reader.[72] While men dominate the public arena in all matters of social life, the role of woman must be limited to the private, domestic sphere in the first century Mediterranean world. So the woman's bold debates with Jesus in the public arena and her success must be regarded as subversive and as having rhetoric power for the first century readers who are bombarded by the anderocentric worldview.

Furthermore, she addresses Jesus with Christological titles such as "Lord" and "son of David" (15:22, 25, 27). According to Wainwright, these terms are representative of the liturgical and theological terms developed by the Matthean community, reflecting on the person and work of Jesus.[73] Wainwright sees that the words given to the Canaanite woman and narrative features present the gender issues beside the ethnic question; in light of the fact that the Canaanite woman knows liturgical language and uses Christological titles.[74] In the context of the Matthean community, the early church may have struggled with women's participation in liturgical and theological life of the community. In this context, the Canaanite women's liturgical wording in a public place strikes the heart of socio-religious boundaries, not only the ethnic boundary but also the issue of gender. Matthew's Canaanite woman boldly participates in the liturgical and theological life of a community, dominated by androcentrism. Wainwright argues that the Canaanite woman is catalyst for all Gentiles and women who are eager to be freed from restrictive and oppressive socio-religious bondages. Consequently, the crumb of bread that the Canaanite woman obtains signifies the breaking of the gender boundary.

Third, as the ethnic and gender boundaries are integral to the narrative of the Canaanite woman, so are the socio-political and class boundaries, which the breaking/sharing of bread metaphorically shatters. Since feminist perspective pervades all sectors of biblical interpretation, postcolonial feminist readers add gender analysis to other possible boundaries formed by imperialism/colonialism in national and international relations. Postcolonial feminist readers are concerned with how gender oppression functions with other forms of oppression such as class, race, ethnicity, age, sexual orientation, and economic, political, cultural boundaries.[75]

The readers can find that the woman is subject to the multiple forms of oppression and boundaries that are integrated in the narrative of the Canaanite woman.

According to Musa Dube's reading of this narrative, Jesus can be categorized as an "imperializing character," a colonizing traveler, whose divinity, class, race, and gender endow him with privilege and authority.[76] Jesus leaves his own land geographically, travels to a foreign land, the district of Tyre and Sidon (15: 21–22), and encounters the Canaanite woman, through which the reader imagines the historical power relation[77] and anticipates the great commission at the end of Matthew's Gospel (28:18–20). Conversely, the Canaanite woman and her daughter are described as foreigners and "Canaanite" other, who can be invaded, conquered, annihilated, in light of the promised foundation myth.[78] In this perspective, the woman's desperation for surviving and Jesus' strict denial and negative insulting response clearly reveal multifold forms of boundaries and oppressions. Especially, in comparison to the narrative of the Centurion (8:5–13), in which Jesus quickly and positively responds to a foreigner's need, the character of Jesus in front of the Canaanite other intensifies the socio-political, class, imperial/colonial boundaries formed by the power relation.

Matthew's narrative of the Canaanite woman, however, breaks multiple forms of boundaries through the woman's wise answer and the sharing of the bread, which indicate that the foreign others are not to be subjugated but rather are to join the children's table as family. Musa Dube reads Matthew's narrative of the Canaanite woman as a "possession type-scene," embracing imperialistic values and strategies as well as the marginalized image and inferior status of the foreign other that reinforce the oppression of the woman.[79] In her reading, the woman is portrayed as accepting her inferior socio-political status, assigned as a dog and as agreeing to stay under the table to survive. She does not overcome the boundaries but highlights the multifold forms of boundary. For me, however, although Matthew's Gospel obviously highlights the multifold forms of boundary such as socio-political, race, class and the like, Matthew clearly shows all boundaries are broken by the metaphor of bread and its breaking and sharing.

From this perspective, the bread in the narrative of the Canaanite woman not only highlights multiple forms of boundary such as gender, race, class, socio-political, and socio-religious, that exist in our lives, but also shatters all forms of boundary, signifying the termination of any hostility, segregation, discrimination, or exclusivism formed by human prejudice and greed. This is the central moment that Jesus changes his narrow tradition-based mind and opens the door for all Gentiles; thereby the reader anticipates the great commission at the end of this Gospel (28:18–20).

The Role of the Canaanite Woman in the Context of Matthew's Gospel

The narrative of the Canaanite woman is located at the center of the Gospel as a whole, which literarily functions to exhibit a plot transition from Jewish-centered ministry to its expansion toward the Gentiles. The bread that Jesus allows the woman to eat connects the first feeding narrative and the second one, while revealing the transitional point of the plot of Gospel, in which the meaning of bread metaphor is enriched by the sandwich structure at the center of Matthew 14–15. As was studied, the first feeding narrative functions to present Jesus' breaking of bread as a prophetic action, confined by a strong concentration on the restoration of Israel and the particular socio-religious ethnic group, Jew. In the second feeding narrative, however, Matthew expands the boundary of Jesus' ministry to the inclusion of Gentiles and all the marginalized. Even the narrative ultimately leads the reader's attention to connect Jesus' great commission at the end of Gospel (28:16–20).

In fact, Matthew's Gospel shows a contradictory narrative flow in light of the object of Jesus' ministry. The Gospel begins with the identification of Israel as the people whom Jesus has come to save (1:21), and even through half of the Gospel, Israel is the only object of Jesus' mission (10:5–6; 15:24). In the second half of the Gospel, however, Jesus again feeds the crowds including Gentiles and all the marginalized, denounces Jewish leaders, and presents the ultimate eschatological vision using some parables: the parable of the lost sheep (18:10–14), the parable of the unforgiving servant (18:23–35), the parable of the laborers in the vineyard (20:1–16), the parable of the wicked tenant (21:33–44), and the parable of the wedding banquet (22:1–14). These two contradictory phases of Jesus' ministry are literarily connected by the Canaanite woman who actively engages in dialogue with Jesus and changed Jesus' mind.

From this perspective, the bread in the narrative of the Canaanite woman functions as the center of the gospel and as a transitional bridge between two different phases of Jesus' mission. The expansion of Jesus' ministry and community is foreshadowed by the previous accounts of the wise men at Jesus' birth (2:7–12) and the faith of the Centurion (8:5–13). The Canaanite woman initiates actual transition as a prophetic action in the unexpected manner, signified by the five women included in Matthew's genealogy. This transition is not limited to the inclusion of the Gentile but also represents the breaking of multiple forms of hostility, segregation, and exclusivism, which are formed by socio-religious boundaries, ethnic barriers and human prejudices in the first century. Thereby Matthew re-defines the boundaries of community in light of the metaphoric bread Jesus breaks and shares; and the narrator leads the reader into Jesus' second phase of ministry beyond the Israel-centered mission, through which Matthew presents their own communal identity and ideological vision. Following structure demonstrates the way of reading the Gospel of Matthew[80] as a whole in this book, showing the transitional function of the Canaanite woman:

Introduction : *Presenting Main Character Jesus and Reflecting Matthew's Vision*
Chapters. 1–4: The Birth of Jesus and the Beginning of Jesus' Ministry

A Section: *Deviant Jewish Communal Vision and its Mission for the House of Israel*
5–7: Jesus' Teachings and Discourse, demands upon Israel
8–10: Jesus' Ministries through words and deeds/healings of others
11–13: Israel's negative response and Jesus' defense

[Sandwich Structure]

14:13–21: *The First Feeding of the Jewish Crowds*:
Establishment of Alternative Jewish Community

B Section: *Transition: 15:21–28:*
The Canaanite Woman (Opens the door for the Gentiles)

15:29–39: *The Second Feeding of the Crowds including Gentiles*:
Expands the Boundaries of the Community

C Section: *Journey to Jerusalem, Reaching out to the Nations*
Chapters 15–17: Establishment of new alternative Community of God, the *Ekklesia*
18–20: Instruction to the *Ekklesia*
1–25: Jesus' teaching of the final vision

Conclusion: *The Confirmation of Matthew's Identity and Ultimate Ideological Vision*
26–28: Jesus' Death and Resurrection
26:17–35: The Confirmation of Matthew's Communal Vision
28:16–20: Ideological Manifesto (the Great Commission)

The Bread in Jesus' Last Supper: "This is my Body!" (26:26–29)

The bread in Jesus' last supper is the last appearance of bread in Matthew's Gospel. With the identification of Jesus with the *broken bread* and cup, Matthew corroborates the meaning of the metaphor of bread and the breaking of bread, legitimizing the formation of Matthean community, identity, and their ideological vision. This section examines Jesus' meals in the context of the Passover and

Jesus' own interpretation of the bread and cup: *This is my body*. It also focuses on the concepts of the bread in previous narratives and the role of Jesus' last supper in the context of Matthew's Gospel.

The Metaphor of Bread and Jesus' Last Supper

Narrative Context of Passover

The scene of Jesus' last supper meal (26:26–35) is set during the Jewish festival of Passover in Matthew's Gospel, mostly following the account in the Gospel of Mark (14:12–26). In Matthew's account, the narrator set the background of the scene in the Passover, which leads the reader into the climax with the plot to kill Jesus (26:1–5). The narrative begins with the story of Jesus' passion and death, connecting with the context of the Passover. Jesus commands his disciples to "go into the city" for the preparation of the Passover (26:18); the preparation is not for making the Passover meal but finding the place to have the Passover meal. Jerusalem at Passover is fully crowded with many people so that one evening the sacrificial meal can be eaten anywhere in Jerusalem.[81] The disciples are command-ed to find an appropriate place for having the Passover meal that Jesus already set. It seems that Jesus hosts the Passover meals, not waiting for the invitation from another: "I will keep the Passover at your house with my disciples." The reader naturally connects the Passover meal to Jesus' last supper, especially since the narrator kindly explains that Jesus' command is given "on the first day of Un-leavened Bread" (26:17), which is an alternate name for the Passover.

Whether Jesus' last supper was a Passover celebration is an awkward question in Matthew's context.[82] In light of the features of the traditional Passover celebra-tion, Jesus' supper has few connections to the Passover tradition. Basically, the essential feature of Passover is the meal shared by the household, but Jesus' gath-ering is not a family or kinship base. According to real practices that are explained in Exodus 12 and 13,[83] there are three divisions of rituals of practice: the Passover sacrifice, the feast of Unleavened Bread, and the consecration of the first-born. The Passover meal regarding food must contain eating the roasted lamb and the unleavened bread, and the bitter herbs, which are prescribed in the Hebrew Scrip-ture. Even in Jesus' time, when the Passover has become more ritualized and kept by people as a pilgrimage festival in Jerusalem. For Jews in Jesus' time, the sacrifice of the Passover lamb at the Temple and the eating of roasted lamb, the unleavened bread, and the bitter herbs are the center of the Passover celebration.[84] In this regard, Matthew's account of Jesus' last meal fails to give a complete account of what a Passover should be.

Matthew's narrator, however, strives to make a close connection between Jesus' last supper and the Passover meal. The narrator sets the background of Jesus' meal gathering at the time of Passover and the narrative context shows that Jesus is preparing to keep Passover with his disciples (26:18): "I will keep the Passover at your house with my disciples," so the reader naturally assumes the gathering at the table is just for keeping the Passover meal. The narrator describes the time of Jesus' meal gathering as beginning in the evening, which reminds the reader that the Passover meal normally is eaten after sunset or far into the night.[85] Then, Jesus and the twelve disciples recline at the table of the supper, and according to rabbinic sources, it is a ritual duty to recline at the table during the Passover meal as a symbol of freedom.[86] Also in Matthew's description, it is presumed that the Passover meal is already in progress before the breaking of the bread (26:26: "while they were eating"). This means that the several features of the Passover meal that Matthew's account misses have already passed before Jesus' breaking of bread. According to Hellenistic custom, wine becomes important and necessary to the Passover meal,[87] as Jesus shares the cup of wine with his disciples. Jesus concludes the Passover meal with "a hymn," which is probably the Hallel in the rabbinical literature (26:30).[88]

From these analogies, one can assume that the narrator intends to place Jesus' last supper in the context of the Passover meal. According to the narrative context, Matthew does not need to present all the features and orders of the Passover in Jesus' last meal gathering; also the narrator does not seem to have been concerned with whether Jesus keeps the Passover correctly or not. Rather, Matthew intends to present Jesus' bonding with his disciples at the meal, eating the bread and drinking wine together, and the interpretation of the bread and wine in the context of the Passover meal or as the Passover meal. Of course, the early Christian Eucharist probably influences the description of Jesus' last supper in Matthew, causing the diminishing of the references to the Passover.[89] At this point, Jesus' last supper in Matthew can be regarded as a Passover meal, diminished in its description by Matthew; at the same time Jesus' last supper was just a regular meal at the Passover time. However, the most important point is that Jesus' last supper is closely associated with the Passover and its narrative meaning and rhetorical claim should be understood within the theological theme of the Passover.

Representation of New Communal Identity

Placing Jesus' last meal *in/as* the context of Passover, Matthew re-presents the communal identity of the Matthean community in light of the origin of Jewish identity formed at the Exodus and redefines Jesus' teachings and ministry of the Gospel in the frame of the theology of Passover. [90] Reflecting on the common experience, theological conceptions, and the relevant identity of the Passover, the readers read Jesus' last supper and his interpretation of the bread and wine. Here the reader can link all previous discourses of the bread metaphor to Jesus' last supper.

The unleavened bread in the Passover meal celebrates the season of God's deliverance at the departure from Egypt, remembering the urgent situation of exodus.[91] The unleavened bread (*matzah*) has become a symbol of salvation and of God's presence, past and future, among the Israelites.[92] At the same time, the feast of unleavened bread in Jewish culture and history functions to mark the beginning of the harvest season and recognizes the dependence of humans on God for fertility. When the first Passover is instituted by God's commandment, the book of Exodus clearly states, "this month shall mark for you the beginning of months; it shall be the first month of the year for you" (Exodus 12:2). This means that the month containing Passover must be "the head of months of year," which discern a "qualitative distinction"[93] that clearly exhibits the line of demarcation between two qualitatively different entities by the terms of "before" and "after." The month with Passover must be a moment of New Year (season) or New Beginning. Therefore, the Passover with the lack of leaven is attributed to the haste with which Israel left Egypt toward the new freed life, but it also retains its metaphoric reference to beginning of new life.[94] From this new life and new relationship with God, Israel establishes a new communal identity.[95]

Accordingly, Jesus' last meal gathering at the Passover season, especially during the feast of unleavened bread, metaphorically signifies the beginning of new life, new season, and new community, formed by Jesus. As Israel formed their communal identity with the Passover, Matthew presents the beginning of new life and community and redefines its communal identity at Jesus' last supper.

The Metaphor of Bread and Jesus

This Is My Body: τοῦτό ἐστιν τὸ σῶμά μου

As far as the bread is concerned in Matthew, the climax appears at Jesus' last supper. Especially, Matthew's version of the last supper is enriched by its link to the two feeding narratives and to the Canaanite woman through the bread metaphor. While the disciples are having the Passover meal (26:26f), the narrator clearly describes Jesus' actions: "Jesus took bread, and blessed, and broke it, and gave it to the disciples" (λαβὼν ὁ Ἰησοῦς ἄρτον καὶ εὐλογήσας ἔκλασεν καὶ δοὺς τοῖς μαθηταῖς). The reader easily recognizes that the description of Jesus' action is parallel to the two feeding narratives (14:13–21; 15:29–39). Particularly, the three verbs, εὐλογέω κλάω and δίδωμι– blessing, breaking, and giving – remind the reader of the moment when Jesus feeds the crowds and the very moment when Jesus breaks the bread. The three verbs εὐλογέω κλάω and δίδωμι with the bread ἄρτος bring up the metaphoric image of God's provision and the structure of metaphor of the bread in two feeding scenes: such as *the end of hostility, making a covenant, actual formation of community, participation in common ideology beyond the socio-religious boundaries*; through which the reader implicitly makes a frame for reading Jesus' last supper. The Passover context enriches the reader's cognitive conceptions of the bread, corresponding to Israel's wilderness experience at the exodus and its relevant metaphoric meanings for representing the formation of new communal identity.

Matthew's narrator reaches the climax at Jesus' interpretation of the bread. After the breaking of bread, Jesus says, "take, eat; this is my body – λάβετε φάγετε, τοῦτό ἐστιν τὸ σῶμά μου" (v. 26). In the metaphoric description "τοῦτό ἐστιν τὸ σῶμά μου," the demonstrative pronoun τοῦτο contextually modifies the bread ἄρτος that Jesus takes and breaks in this verse, even though the gender does not grammatically match each other.[96] The broken bread ,τοῦτο) is connected with τὸ σῶμά μου that is Jesus' body through the verb of identification, ἐστιν. Namely, the bread τοῦτο/ἄρτος as a source domain of the metaphor directly identifies with τὸ σῶμά μου Jesus' body that is a target domain. Matthew clearly identifies Jesus' body with the bread that is broken by Jesus' own hand. The description is not a figurative expression but a metaphor of identification; and all cognitive conceptions and social memory of the bread can be applied to and identified with Jesus' body. Obviously, Matthew is not identifying Jesus' physical body with the element of the bread. As Allison insists, σῶμα, can mean simply 'self' like the Aramaic words *gûp* and *bisrā,* signifying "the person" as whole being, not a part of a person or body.[97] In this regard, 'this is my body' may originally have meant 'this is myself' or 'this is my whole being.' The 'self' or 'whole being' means one's whole personality, which includes soul, mind and ideology.[98]

Consequently, the metaphoric description, "this is my body" means: all discourses and metaphors of the bread identify with all Jesus' teachings, healings, and ministry. Reversely all Jesus' teachings and ideology identically correspond to the meaning of bread given by God in two feeding narratives and the narrative of Canaanite woman. In such a way, based on the metaphoric expression, "this is my body," the reader can map the structure of the metaphor of bread: Jesus can be a life-giving source, as the bread *is/was*; Jesus signifies God's complete care; Jesus and his teachings are the source of the breaking of boundaries; and Jesus' ideological vision are the foundation of new community, as the meaning of the bread metaphor found in two feeding scenes and in the narrative of Canaanite woman. In previous narratives, Jesus is described as the agent of God who provides the life-giving source. Now, Jesus becomes the life-giving source itself, the bread provided by God. In other words, Matthew's Jesus identifies himself with what he has taught and done in the Gospel of Matthew and metaphorically proclaims that those teachings and ideological visions are the true life-giving source provided by God. The reader can retrospect Jesus' defending words at the first temptation in 4:4: "one does not live by bread alone, but by every word that comes from the mouth of God." Matthew's Jesus, a whole being identifies with the word of God, which is the true life-giving source given by God.

The symbolic action of the breaking of bread here signifies Jesus' broken body on the cross.[99] The reader who already knows of Jesus' death on the cross can easily recognize this identification when Jesus breaks the bread and proclaims, "this is my body." In this regard, Jesus' broken body on the cross can be redefined by the meaning of the bread metaphor in Matthew; at the same time Jesus' sacrificial death supports as a basic source for the legitimacy of the discourse and ideology around the metaphor of bread with the significance of the act of breaking, distributing and eating together.[100] Jesus' broken body—Jesus' sacrificial death—metaphorically not only identifies with the socio-religious meaning of the breaking of bread in Matthew's Gospel, but it also functions to legitimize the identity of Matthean community. Jesus' identification with the bread manifests that Jesus' whole being, including all his teachings and ministries, as life-giving source becomes basic source of Matthew's communal identity.

Matthew's Jesus invites all disciples to participate in the world of the bread metaphor. Jesus urges disciples to "take" and "eat" the bread (λάβετε φάγετε v. 26). Although Matthew mostly follows the Markan version of the last supper, the Matthean narrator adds another imperative, "eat" to Mark's "take." The imperative "take" in Mark implicitly contains the point of eating, however Matthew completes his urging invitation by adding a secondary imperative "eat," which emphasizes the metaphoric meaning of the action of eating and sharing food. In Matthew's previous accounts, when the crowds share the food and eat the bread, broken and distributed by Jesus, the act of eating the bread signifies the acceptance of Jesus' authority and teachings and the participation in Jesus' community. When the Canaanite woman metaphorically eats the broken bread fallen from the table, she is completely accepted into Jesus' banquet. The bread that Jesus identifies with himself implicitly indicates all teachings and ideology of Jesus, just as the food God provides is identified with God's word in the Old Testament and the food embodies his wisdom in the wisdom literature (Proverbs 9:1–6; 10:11; 13:14; 14:27; 16:22; 24:13–14; Psalms 36:9; 42:1–3, 23; Isaiah 12:3; Jeremiah 17:13).[101]

Jesus' invitation to eat the bread metaphorically represents participation in the common sense of value and ideology, instructed by Matthew's Jesus. Since all of Jesus' ministry and teachings are achieved and accomplished by Jesus' sacrificial death, the eating of the bread urges disciples to participate in Jesus' meaningful death[102] and to continue the fruits of Jesus' death.

All the meanings of the metaphor of bread in Matthew's last supper are enriched by the context of Passover. Basically, as the feast of Passover commemorates God's complete care and liberating act at the exodus, leading the Israelites into new freed life, Matthew reframes God's liberating works in Jesus' ministry in light of the bread metaphor, establishing a new communal life. As the Passover commemorates God's life-giving provision and God's life-saving action in the wilderness, Matthew merges them in a new way of life-giving provision in Jesus' ministry and sacrificial death. According to Joachim Jeremias' observation, the old Aramaic Passover or the question/answer session in the standard Jewish Passover[103] says, "this is the bread of affliction, which our fathers had to eat when they came out of Egypt."[104] The affliction of those who eat the unleavened bread signifies the affliction of the ancient Israelites; but through participation in the Passover, people share in the redemption and new life freed from Egypt.

Now Matthew reframes it, however, presenting the bread as Jesus' self and his sacrificial death. Therefore, those who participate in the Passover and those who eat the bread presented by Jesus' impending affliction[105] now share in a new life in a new community with Jesus, as is represented by the bread metaphor. Like all religious rituals, Passover and its commemorating process form the communal identity of Israel: who we are and who we want to be.[106] In other words, Israel's self-awareness in light of the relationship with God, who liberated them from Egypt and made a concrete covenant, is basically formed by the exodus and Passover. Likewise, Matthew redefines the identity of its community within the frame of Passover and Jesus' ministry. Jesus becomes the basic source of Matthew's communal identity. Accordingly, Matthew reinterprets and reframes the Passover with Jesus' ministry at the last supper, especially through the metaphoric expression, "this is my body." At the same time, Matthew represents and legitimizes the communal identity of Matthew's community revealed by the bread metaphor.

Social Bonding in a New Covenant: *Forming New Identity*

The bread metaphor in Jesus' last supper represents Matthew's ultimate vision of social bond and the establishment of alternative community in a new covenantal relationship. The ultimate vision of social bonding in a new covenant is enriched by Jesus' interpretation of the cup at the last supper. The metaphoric meaning of Jesus' breaking of bread is intensified by Jesus' second command: drink the cup. After distributing the bread, Jesus takes a cup, and gives thanks and gives the cup to disciples, and commands them to drink of it (26:28). Then, Matthew's narrator explains the cup with another metaphoric expression, "this is my blood of the covenant. (τοῦτο γάρ ἐστιν τὸ αἷμά μου τῆς διαθήκης, v 28f)." In this expression, the demonstrative pronoun τοῦτο contextually modifies ποτήριον (the cup) that Jesus takes and commands them to drink; and through the verb of identification ἐστιν, Matthew identifies the cup with Jesus' blood, τὸ αἷμά μου.

In the narrative context, the blood signifies Jesus sacrificial death and his broken body, reminding one of the bloods of the lambs slaughtered at the exodus from Egypt.[107] Jesus' blood must be correlated with Jesus' passion and the broken body shedding blood on the cross; this correlation of blood and body metaphorically connects to the cup and the broken bread. Namely, the cup and bread as a source domain of the structure of the metaphor ultimately signify Jesus' broken body and his sacrificial death as target domain. In this relation of metaphor, two metaphoric expressions, "this is my body" in v. 26 and "this is my blood" in v. 28 are closely connected in light of the fact that each ultimately modifies to Jesus' whole being of self, including his teaching, ministry, even his death, which is the actual meaning of the bread metaphor. In addition, both expressions are very supportive to legitimize the meaning of the bread metaphor in Jesus' ministry in Matthew.

The bread and its metaphoric meaning and concepts are basic sources of Jesus' ultimate vision of social bonding; and the metaphor of the breaking of bread symbolically represents a new covenant in Jesus' community, which is enacted by Jesus beyond all socio-religious boundaries. At Jesus' last supper, Matthew firmly re-expresses the new covenant and affirms it by Jesus' sacrificial death, especially through sharing Jesus' blood (26:28). The description "my blood of the covenant" (τὸ αἷμά μου τῆς διαθήκης, v. 28) derives from Jesus' teachings, interpretation of the law, and all his ministries in Matthew's account, so the reader is reminded of Jesus' action of breaking of bread with the crowds in the two feeding scenes, which metaphorically signifies making a new covenant and forming a new community with the crowds beyond the boundaries.

Further, Matthew's Jesus clearly commands the disciples "drink of it," as was in verse 26, which is redacted from the Markan version. Like eating the broken bread together signifies participation in Jesus' ideology of bread, Matthew also commands the disciples to *drink/consume* the entire cup and urges them to willingly participate in the covenant enacted by Jesus' blood. In this regard, Matthew presents Jesus' sacrifice and the broken body/the bread as the basis of the new covenant of his community and legitimizes the communal identity.

Many scholars agree that 'the blood of the covenant' recalls Exodus 24:8,[108] where the covenant is ratified on Sinai while splashing blood on the people: "Moses took the blood and dashed it on the people, and said, see the blood of the covenant that the Lord has made with you in accordance with all these words." According to the context of Exodus 24, the blood is shared between the altar and the people, and the splashing action functions to bind God and the people together in a covenantal relationship.[109] Based on the commitments made on both sides of this covenant, God completely takes care of the life of the Israelites and their future fate and liberation; and the Israelites observe God's instruction and become people of God. Through this covenant, ancient Israel forms their communal identity and sustains the solidarity of community.

Alluding to Exodus 24:8, Matthew identifies Jesus' sacrificial death with 'the blood of covenant,' signifying Jesus' ratification of a new covenant. Especially, Jesus' firm command to "drink of it" and the image of sharing the cup reinforces the enactment of the new covenant. While there is no action of blood splashing, drinking of the cup of the blood metaphorically functions to bind Jesus and the people together in a new covenantal relationship. Thereby Matthew redefines Jesus' ministry and death, reemphasizes Jesus' new covenantal ideology revealed in the metaphor of bread, and legitimizes the communal identity of Matthew's community.

In addition, as Allison argues a typological relationship between the acts of Moses and Jesus, Jesus' proclamation of a new covenant can be understood as an expression of the beginning of the new season of covenant. As Moses made a sacrifice for the people so that Israelites could enter into a covenant with God, so does Jesus inaugurate a new covenant by sacrificing his own blood and his life.[110] Jesus' last supper, surrounded by the context of the Passover, enriches the meaning of the new communal life, just as the Israelites experienced freed new life at exodus. As ancient Israel made a covenant with God right after the Passover experience out of Egypt, Matthew metaphorically represents that Jesus makes a new covenant with the followers in his alternative community in the context of the Passover.

Breaking the Boundaries: *Heavenly Banquet*

Jesus' last supper firmly manifests the eschatological vision of new community, which ultimately shatters social conditions and boundaries and solidifies Jesus-followers as a new familial community. Especially, Matthew affirms this eschatological vision by Jesus' interpretation of the cup of blood in v. 28: "this is my blood of the covenant, which is poured out for many for the forgiveness of sins." In this phrase, the forgiveness of sins (εἰς ἄφεσιν ἁμαρτιῶν) is a redactional addition of Matthew (26:28), which cannot be found in other relevant texts presenting Jesus' last supper and Eucharist. As Jesus' sacrificial death confirms the enactment of a new covenant, now the covenant is closely associated with the forgiveness of sins (cf., Romans 11:26–7; Hebrews 10:16–19). The phrase, εἰς ἄφεσιν ἁμαρτιῶν reminds the reader of the interpretation of the name of Jesus in Matthew 1:21: "for he will save his people from their sins." At this point, one realizes that the covenant associated with 'the forgiveness of sins' has been already foreshadowed at Jesus' birth in Matthew's Gospel. Often times in Matthew, Jesus' healing acts are described as bestowing forgiveness of sins (9:2–5);[111] Jesus even instructs the disciples to forgive others "seventy times seven" (18:22), so it is not surprising that Matthew connects Jesus' ministry with the forgiveness of sins.

In Gospel accounts, "forgiveness ἄφεσις is a prerequisite for surviving the judgment and participating in the kingdom to come."[112] Forgiveness is especially associated with "repentance." Matthew's Jesus begins his ministry with the proclamation of God's kingdom that is to come and urges people to repent (4:17). Obviously, proper repentance involves a serious reorientation from the old to new being who is acceptable in God's kingdom, from which the forgiveness is received. The forgiveness closely involves repentance and signifies becoming an acceptable being, so the forgiveness of sins directly associates with acceptance in the kingdom and Jesus' community. When Jesus heals and feeds the sick and the marginalized, Jesus accepts them as his people and invites them into a new covenant (e.g., the tax collector 9:9–13). Matthew's Jesus clearly affirms, "I came not to call the righteous, but sinner," which means his acceptance and creation of a new relationship indicate the forgiveness of sins. From this perspective, the forgiveness of sins in Matthew signifies the acceptance of the other into God's kingdom, especially acceptance into Jesus' community. The forgiveness of sins is a basic premise and ideological source of Matthew's eschatological vision, which breaks the socio-religious prejudices and ethnic boundaries. When Jesus breaks bread with the Gentiles and when Jesus allows the Canaanite woman to have crumbs of bread, the forgiveness of sins is the basic premise of Jesus' fulfillment of prophecy.

According to this phrase, 'the forgiveness of sins' is fulfilled by Jesus' sacrificial death, especially by the sharing of the blood, which is metaphorically expressed by "poured out for many (τὸ περὶ πολλῶν ἐκχυννόμενον)" in Matthew. The term πολλῶν corresponds to 20:28: "ransom for many (λύτρον ἀντὶ πολλῶν), signifying Jesus' ultimate ministry. According to the context of Matthew, the people in the πολλῶν must be all people regardless of any socio-religious prejudices and boundaries. The meaning of the term, πολλῶν is manifested by reflecting on 8:11: "many will come from east and west and sit at table with Abraham, Isaac, and Jacob in the kingdom of heaven." As was observed before, "many from east and west" clearly indicates the Gentiles' inclusion according to the narrative context of Matthew chapter 8. Using a common feature in prophetic literature, Matthew presents its ultimate apocalyptic vision of the inclusion of non-Jews, by having them coming to worship the God of Israel.[113] Further, Matthew's account of the Centurion's servant envisions the ultimate fulfillment of the prophetic inclusive vision and foreshadows its prophetic fulfillment of the inclusion of the Gentiles in Jesus' ministry. In this respect, "many, πολλοὶ" in 8:11 foreshadows Jesus' prophetic ministry and represents Matthew's ultimate inclusive vision of community; and "many, πολλῶν" confirms the fulfillment of its vision and reaffirms Matthew's communal ideological vision through Jesus' sacrificial death and the blood of covenant.

Jesus' commandment in v. 28: "drink of it, all of you" is an official invitation to Jesus' community and new covenant. The context of Passover enriches Jesus' invitation to the new beginning of communal life of freedom, the new covenant, the new relationship with God who provides the bread, and the new communal identity and its solidarity beyond boundaries. This invitation is not just for the disciples but also for all readers. By the sharing of the blood, sins are metaphorically forgiven; those who share the cup of blood will be accepted and participate in Jesus' death so that they forgive and accept the other into the community, as they are accepted and forgiven.

From this perspective, Jesus' last supper represents the feature of messianic banquet that invites all people to share the food and drink. Allison argues that two feeding miracles in 14 and 15 anticipate Jesus' last supper, foreshadowing the messianic banquet in Matthew's world; the exodus from Egypt, the last supper, and the messianic banquet are not isolated but intricately associated.[114] In his view, the exodus has been typologically recapitulated at Jesus' last meal gathering, which envisions the return of the heavenly manna, newly provided by Jesus, the new covenantal relationship and ideology. Jesus' last supper, the exodus at Passover, and Jesus' feeding scenes as "superimposed images" reproduce a fundamental pattern of Jewish religious experience and apocalyptic imagination, which ultimately envisions the messianic banquet.[115] Consequently, Jesus' last supper itself envisions the messianic banquet and affirms the ultimate ideological vision of community, breaking social prejudice and boundaries formed by socio-religious convention.

The Role of Jesus' Last Supper in the Gospel of Matthew: Ideological Manifesto

In terms of literary structure, Jesus' last supper functions to review what has already been presented and occurred with the bread metaphor in Matthew's Gospel. At the same time, Matthew officially legitimizes and proclaims Matthew's communal identity and ideological vision through Jesus' identification with the bread. The narrative plot of Matthew as a whole is developed and enriched by some narrative strategies such as repetition, anticipation or foreshadowing, and retrospective review, in which the reader can map the structure of the narrative and the meaning of events and find the narrator's ideological perspective.[116] Through the Passover context, Matthew's narrator keeps evoking Israel's wilderness experience at exodus and shaping the frame of the hermeneutical lens to retrospect Jesus' ministry and teachings. Jesus' breaking of the bread and sharing of the cup allude to God's provision, Jesus' feedings, and the messianic banquet, and metaphorically underscore the formation of new communal entity and identity.

Especially, Jesus' identification with the bread leads the reader to reflect on what Jesus has done as the provider of the life-giving source in two feeding narratives and even other narratives of Jesus' meal table and healing stories. These retrospections connect the image of God who provides the food and God's complete care in the wilderness, signifying the formation of a new communal identity, new life, and new covenant. At the same time, Jesus' identification with the bread clearly affirms the role of Jesus as the one who is present with his community and who is the basic source of communal identity, covenant, and ideology. Furthermore, Jesus' identification with the cup of blood proclaims the legitimacy of Matthew's ultimate eschatological vision of community, making a new covenant beyond the boundaries, envisioned and already fulfilled by Jesus' sacrificial death.

Matthew's proclamations of "this is my body" and "this is my cup" firmly corroborate Jesus' last commissioning commandment and his promise, "I am with you always," (28:20) and reaffirm the prophetic fulfillment in Jesus' ministry and in his name "Emmanuel" (God with us, 1:23). Jesus' last supper literarily functions as a concluding confirmation of Jesus' ministry and the bread; at the same time it leads the reader to scan Matthew's Gospel as a whole from the beginning to the end. Furthermore, Jesus' last supper rhetorically functions as an ideological manifesto that proclaims the legitimacy of Matthew's community and their existential identity and ideology; thereby the reader redefines the death of Jesus and his teaching and ministry, presenting Matthew's communal identity and ideological vision.

Matthew's Communal Identity *in-between* Formative Judaism and Roman Empire

Matthew's communal identity, revealed by the metaphor of bread, can be reviewed using the frame of postcolonial conception, *Hybridity*, which is a core concept articulating the multiple and complex range of cultural struggles taking place when negotiating identity in the colonial context between the colonizer and the colonized. Under the colonial context, Matthean community as deviant Jews redefine their communal identity and ideology; specifically, Matthew alters the conventional socio-religious vision of Judaism and denies the new cultural imposition of Roman Empire, but rather hybridizes its indigenous cultural identity in *the third space, in-between* two cultural entities.

This section concentrates on Matthew's rhetorical claim of the metaphor of bread, representing Matthew's communal identity in the context of struggling between formative Judaism and the Roman Empire, while paying special attention to: 1) how they alter the cultural imposition of dominant parties, 2) how they reproduce and hybridize their communal identity and ideological vision through the metaphor of bread, and 3) how Matthean community finds legitimacy between formative Judaism and the Roman Empire.

Alteration from the Conventional Perspective of Judaism

Mission toward All Nations: πάντα τὰ ἔθνη

One of the interesting features of the Gospel of Matthew is the contradiction between Jesus' first mission instruction in 10:5–6 and later its expansion toward all nations (28:19–20). Obviously, Jesus instructs his disciples not to go among the Gentiles but only go to "the lost sheep of the house of Israel" (10:5–6); and he keeps this instruction himself until he meets the Canaanite woman. In Matthew's Gospel, Jesus' intentional entrance into the district of Tyre and Sidon and his encounter with the Canaanite woman as prophetic fulfillment (15:21–28) represent a transitional moment in the mission instruction. When Jesus metaphorically shares broken bread with the Canaanite woman, the metaphor of bread and its sharing signify the acceptance of Gentiles into Jesus' community as well as the abolishment of Jesus' previous mission-injunction to the Gentiles (10:5–6; 15:24). Then, Matthew's narrator clearly shows how Jesus embodies his change of mind and new mission instruction in his ministerial work: in the very next feeding scene (15:29–39), Jesus forms a new community, including the Gentiles and all the marginalized. In this regard, Jesus' second feeding is not just a provision of food but a prophetic transition to a new mission instruction and its fulfillment: *Inclusion of Gentile*. Jesus' second feeding ultimately projects his last commissioning statement, through which Matthew's narrator finalizes the mission instruction in Matthew 28:19–20.[117]

The contradiction of Matthew's mission discourse has been interpreted by the salvation history scheme for a long time, even until now.[118] For instance, Meier argues that Matthew's mission discourse in relation to 10:5–6 presents an "economy" of salvation: to the Jews first and then to the Gentiles. In Jesus' public ministry the gospel is to be preached only to Israel in the Promised Land under geographical limitation; then after Jesus' death and resurrection, this "economical" limitation is terminated by Jesus' commissioning order in 28:19–20.[119] Meier understands that the change reflects the historical order of salvation. The schematic perspective is normally divided into a three-stage salvation history: the pre-messianic stage in the history of Israel, Jesus' ministry to Israel, the church opening to Gentiles.[120] In this perspective, scholars see that Matthew's Gospel and its contradiction present the salvation history and dogmatize the order of salvation: Jew first and then Gentile.

Other scholars have interpreted this contradictory discourse of Matthew's mission in light of rejection and replacement. In this view, Israel has been rejected by God and has been replaced by a different entity that is the church. This perspective basically concentrates on Jesus' last commission for reading Matthew's Gospel, through which one can make a reading frame that the Jews have been rejected in favor of the Gentiles or the Jews no longer have special ongoing status in a new entity of church.[121] Although Matthew contains Jesus' strict limited mission instruction only to Israel, the gospel keeps reflecting God's rejection of Israel,[122] and it ultimately concludes with Jesus' last commission. For instance, Gaston insists that the ambiguity of Jesus' mission, especially the place of Israel, is to be comprehended at the end of Gospel, which presents the rejection of Israel and the calling of disciples from "all nations." He states, "Israel rejected her Messiah;

therefore God has rejected Israel."[123] Based on this perspective, Matthew's Gospel seems to be under anti-Judaism and alienates its identity from the Jewish heritage.

Neither interpretational frame is convincing; however, these scholarly works do have great value. It seems that Matthew does not have any concern with dogmatizing the order of salvation or alienation from the Jewish heritage. Matthew's inclusion of Gentiles is quite threatening and subversive to Israel, and it does not keep or recognize them as first: "the kingdom of God will be taken away from you and given to the people" (21:43). Also Matthew's account does not seem to divide the history by pre-messiah or post-resurrection, but rather the inclusion of Gentiles is already fulfilled in Jesus' ministry. Matthew's commissioning verses 28:19–20 must be understood as representing an extension of the mission field and Jesus' community from Israel to "all the nations," rather than the replacement of one entity with the other. In Matthew's Gospel, no one find clear description or evidence that God rejects Israel; and there is no reason to exclude Israel from Matthew's "all the nations" in 25:32 and 28:19.

Jesus' contradictory mission and its narrative plot rhetorically represent the communal identity of Matthew and its vision beyond the salvation history and anti-Judaism. Through Jesus' two contradictory mission instructions and the development of narrative plot from the Jewish-centered ministry of Jesus to the inclusion of Gentiles, Matthew defines their expanded communal identity and legitimizes their ideological vision in light of the relation to formative Judaism; and ultimately it shows how Matthew re-defines the boundary of the Matthean community beyond the conventional understanding of the socio-religious boundary of Judaism.

Mathew's community recognizes themselves as Jews who have fidelity to Jewish tradition and its heritage; at the same time, they are hostile to certain Jewish teachings and the larger group of Judaism and their leadership, so they differentiate themselves from the perspective of the larger Jewish groups and religious leaders, while keeping their Jewish heritage. Many scholars indeed see Matthew's community as a deviant group, sect, or deviant association, in which they call the group *ekklesia*.[124] As a deviant group, Matthew can be seen in tension between them and the dominant institution of formative Judaism, so the community not only hopes to convince the larger society to adopt its different behavior and outlook but also strives to seek the legitimacy of their communal identity and ideological vision.[125]

In the Gospel of Matthew, Jesus always obeys Jewish law and emphasizes the significance of the Torah and traditional teachings (5:17–18); and he concentrates his ministry on the "lost sheep of the house of Israel" (15:24; cf., 10:5–6). This clearly shows that Matthew understands the identity of the community in line with its Jewish origin and heritage; however, Matthew alters the ideology and communal vision from the dominant group of Judaism through the expansion of communal boundary. As was argued, all deviant alterations are supported by Jesus' own interpretation of Torah and prophetic ministry. In the middle of the Gospel, especially the narrative of the Canaanite woman challenges the conventional standards of Judaism, Jewish belief in the chosen people and elitism. Jesus is persuaded by the woman and changes his narrow mind to open the door of the messianic banquet to Gentiles (15:24–28); then Jesus breaks the bread with the Gentiles and the marginalized (15:29–39).

Matthew's Jesus even identifies himself with this deviant ideological and communal vision, which is metaphorically represented by the bread (26:26–27). Matthew presents a new mission instruction in 28:19–20 for "all nations" that is proclaimed by Jesus. In this regard, one realizes that the description of Jesus' different mission instructions and ministries reflects Matthew's deviant behavior, outlook, faith, and communal vision in formative Judaism. From this perspective, Matthew's contradictions of Jesus' mission rhetorically function to represent Matthew's communal identity as a deviant group and its context in the formative period of Judaism, rather than reflecting the salvation history. Furthermore, all the narrative plots and contradictory development that concludes with Jesus' identification with the bread legitimize Matthew's communal vision and ideology.

The Tensional Division between Jesus' Teaching and that of Jewish Leaders: *Beware of the Yeast of the Pharisees and Scribes*

Matthew's contradictory mission instructions and Jesus' ministry represent that Matthean community as a deviant group is not compatible with the ideology and teaching of the Jewish religious leaders and majority. Matthew keeps presenting hostile perspectives in the *bread (leaven)/teaching* of the elite groups of Judaism (16:5) which are the counterpart to Jesus' teaching and bread. Thereby Matthew presents the socio-religious context of Matthew's community and legitimizes their communal identity.

While presenting the continuation of Jewish heritage and teaching in Matthew's communal identity, Matthew's Jesus rejects the ideology and teaching of the Pharisees, scribes, chief priest and elders of the Jews, who are all members of the ruling classes. All Jesus' opponents are described as evil and hypocritical leaders who have misled the crowds, so Matthew's narrator describes the crowds as the sheep without a shepherd (10:6). The important point is that Matthew's hostile rejections are not "aimed at Judaism or the Jewish people as a whole, but rather at certain interpretations of Judaism," and a certain group of people, especially the group of Jewish leaders who reject Matthew's group and Jesus' teaching.[126] The objections of the Jewish leaders to Jesus are minimized, when compared to Jesus' hostile rejection of the Jewish leaders. Namely, the attitudes of the Jewish leader do not extend to vilification of Jesus, even though the scribes and Pharisees bring negative charges and questions. As Saldarini indicates, this point as a narrative technique of Matthew[127] presents that Jesus' teaching and its origin in Judaism are not problematic, but the real problem derives from the teaching of the Jewish leaders. Therefore, Matthew's rejections of the Jewish leaders seek to delegitimize the false authority of the community leader and to establish a new leadership for bringing the reformation of Judaism and claiming to be the genuine leader of Judaism.[128]

The bread, which includes accepting the Canaanite woman (15:21–28) and feeding the crowds including Gentiles (15:29–39), also entails Jesus' critical warning, "watch and beware of the leaven of the Pharisees and Sadducees" (Ὁρᾶτε καὶ. προσέχετε ἀπὸ τῆς ζύμης τῶν Φαρισαίων καὶ. Σαδδουκαίων) in Matthew 16:6. Here ζύμη (yeast) as a component of bread reminds the reader of bread that Jesus breaks and shares with the crowds in the previous chapter (14:13–21; 15:29–39) and the crumbs of the bread that the Canaanite woman shares (15:21–28). The narrator kindly explains that the ζύμη corresponds to the bread that the disciples experience, in vv. 9–11[129] and what the ζύμη means in 16:12: διδαχή (the teaching) of the Pharisees and Sadducees. The bread and the ζύμη do not signify bread or anything to satisfy human hunger, but they signify the ultimate life-giving source God provides, the teaching of Jesus and the ideology of Matthew's community. Through Jesus' bread, new community is established, including the Gentiles and the marginalized as a family and breaking the socio-religious boundaries and the traditional prejudices. Thus, the bread in Matthew signifies the ideological foundation and the basic premise for the formation of community and self-awareness.

Matthew's narrator clearly presents that Jesus' teaching is not compatible with the teaching of Jewish leaders. Specifically, the narrator uses ζύμη, which Harrington sees the leaven as a reference to "something with an inner vitality,"[130] rather than the bread. Davies and Allison see the common use of leaven symbolizing a corrupting influence, "an evil tendency which, although insignificant to start with, quickly multiplies to corrupt the whole."[131] In this regard, Matthew highlights the core values of the Pharisees and the Sadducees as a counterpart to Jesus' teaching, badly influencing the formative Judaism in Jesus' time. Here is clear tensional division between Jesus' teaching and that of the Jewish leaders.

At this point, the reader subconsciously remembers Jesus' previous teachings and interpretation of the law in several conflict stories and in the Sermon on the Mount (5–7). While Matthew's Jesus keeps the validity of the law and Jewish tradition, he subordinates them to a higher value that is Jesus' alternative interpretation of the law, overriding the teaching of the Jewish leaders. Now the reader clearly realizes that Matthew differentiates the basic instruction and ideology of the Matthean community from that of the Jewish religious leaders through the warning: Ὁρᾶτε και. προσέχετε ἀπὸ τῆς ζύμης τῶν Φαρισαίων και. Σαδ δουκαίων (16:5). Under the Roman imperial rule, the Jewish leaders and elites like the Pharisees and scribes invisibly ally themselves with the colonial power of Rome, so their teachings and interpretations of Torah must be connected to the benefit of the elites and status quo and this injustice is disguised and sanctioned as God's will.[132]

The tensional division between Jesus and the Jewish leadership in terms of the bread metaphor actually signifies Matthew's alteration and deviation of the ideology from the dominant Judaism in the first century. The clear opposition of Matthew seeks to legitimate its own self-communal identity in the social context of the formative Jewish societies, while delegitimizing the opponent groups, especially the Jewish elite classes. This perspective and attitude are highlighted in Matthew 23, which follows a series of disputes and the negative perspective on Jewish leadership in chapters 21–22 that lead to the climax of hostility.[133]

The object of Jesus' hostile criticism is obviously "the scribes and the Pharisees" (23:2), the representative of the Jewish leadership group, even though Jesus is speaking to the crowds and the disciples. Jesus firstly accuses them of sitting on "Moses' seat" without the appropriate acts or practice. According to Harrington, Moses' seat must be understood as a common metaphor for the teaching and ruling authority of the leadership group in the Jewish community.[134] The real object of Jesus' accusation can be presumed to concern the authority of the ruling classes. Jesus exhorts the crowd to "practice and observe whatever they say" (πάντα οὖν ὅσα ἐὰν εἴπωσιν ὑμῖν ποιήσατε καὶ τηρεῖτε, v. 3), but not to follow their way of life and attitudes. Here πάντα ὅσα ἐὰν εἴπωσιν in v. 3 obviously signifies the Jewish Torah and its heritage, which Jesus does not deny, but claims to fulfill throughout the Gospel. Matthew indirectly presents its position in relation to formative Judaism.[135] Namely, Matthew's Jesus does not attack or deny the fundamental legitimacy of Judaism and the Torah itself. Rather Jesus' criticism targets the authorities and their personal integrity as leaders of Jewish community, as well as the accuracy of their interpretation of Jewish law as teachers of community.[136]

Then Matthew presents the seven "woes," (vv. 23:13, 15, 16, 23, 25, 27, 29) condemning the scribes and Pharisees (23:13–31). All Jesus' previous teaching discourses (5–7), conflict stories and healing/feeding ministries become criteria for the criticism of the Jewish leaders. The first two woes (vv. 13–15) reflect Matthew's communal identity and its teaching and mission, contrasting it with that of the Jewish leadership. While the leader of the Jewish community prevents the members from accepting Matthew's teaching about Jesus, Matthew's *ekklesia* has the ability to open the kingdom of heaven (16:19). While Matthew's community broadly opens its door to the Gentile, breaking the bread and sharing with the other as family, the leader of the Jewish community maltreats even a single proselyte. In the third through the fifth woes (vv. 16–26), Matthew accuses the Jewish leader's perspective on the tithes and purity laws. All these elements are re-interpreted by Jesus' teachings and his ministry, keeping the validity of Jewish lawful traditions and heritage and rejecting the mechanisms and customs falsely established by the Jewish leaders. As appears in previous narrative and discourse in the Gospel, Matthew presents "justice, mercy, and faith" (v. 23) as central criteria for the interpretation of the law and instruction of the community life. In the last two woes (vv. 27–36), Matthew attacks the leader's personal ethics and integrity, charging them with lawlessness and murder. Adopting the form of prophetic denunciation using woe oracles,[137] Matthew's narrator clearly expresses the rejection of the leadership of the Jewish community.

Jesus' warning about the yeast of the Pharisees and the Sadducees (16:6) and his hostile accusation of the Pharisees and scribes in chapter 23 are not isolated features of the Gospel of Matthew but a co-related theme that is intermingled throughout the narratives and discourses of whole Gospel. While Jesus keeps affirming the validity of Jewish Torah and the heritage of Judaism, Matthew differentiates its own identity from the Jewish custom and mechanism established by the majority group and Jewish leaders who reject Jesus and his community. Matthew presents its values of Jewish origin and alternative identity through the reinterpretation of the law by Jesus and the hostile accusation of the opponent group and the Jewish leader. From this perspective, Matthew does not attack upon Israel or Judaism as a whole but attempts to provide a solution for the context of the Matthean community,[138] which is rejected by the majority group in formative Judaism.

Therefore, Matthew's alteration and deviance from the Pharisaic Judaism or the larger group of formative Judaism intends to weaken the legitimacy of the hegemony of the Jewish leader's group and to establish and legitimate the authority of his own group,[139] which has the genuine leader of Judaism.[140] Matthew, in this way, presents its identity as a new community, which defines itself by alteration and deviation from the majority group, elites, and religious leaders as well as from the conventional perspective of Judaism established by those leaders.

Jesus as a New Leader who Provides Life-Giving Source

Matthew seeks the legitimacy of its community, justifying the communal identity through the alteration and deviance from the tradition and custom of its opponents. Matthew's portrait of Jesus has a significant role for revealing the legitimacy of communal identity in the face of the larger group of formative Judaism. Despite defending the validity of Jewish Torah and the heritage of Judaism, Matthew clearly denies the dominant leadership and its ideology and emphasizes an alternative new leader of the community in Jesus whom the dominant Jewish leaders rejected. Matthew's portrait of Jesus and his teaching is a central deviant feature of Matthew's community.

Basically, Matthew describes Jesus as the Messiah who will "save his people from their sins" (1:21); especially Matthew mainly titles Jesus as "the Son of God."[141] From Jesus' birth narrative (1:18–2:22; "Out of Egypt have I called my son"), baptism (3:17; "this is my beloved son"), parables (21:33–46; 22:1–10), passion narratives (26:63; 27:40; 27:54), the confession of the disciples (14:33; 16:16),[142] and even Jesus' own understanding (11:25–27), Matthew consistently presents the identity of Jesus as the promised messiah, the Son of God. Jesus, the Son of God in Matthew, connecting the Davidic lineage, is the reigning figure in God's kingdom,[143] which establishes itself in the face of both Israel and the nations.

Matthew consistently emphasizes Jesus' thorough authority over the whole Jewish world and even over all the nations. Throughout the Gospel, Jesus' messianic identity as the son of God and its definitive authority are affirmed by Jesus' ministry of teaching, preaching, feeding, and healing, while Matthew attempts to seek the legitimacy of the community's leadership. Jesus' powerful healings evidently prove Jesus as a compassionate leader in chapter 8–9. Matthew's portrayal of Jesus as a teacher and as a new authoritative interpreter of the Torah (5–7 and other conflict narratives) is enough to appeal to the contemporary Jews that Jesus is a new authoritative leader who can supersede the current dominant leadership, the scribes and Pharisees. Especially portraying Jesus as a "new Moses,"[144] Matthew describes Jesus as an authoritative teacher, lawgiver, leader, and liberator. At the same time, Matthew emphasizes the Jewish heritage of Jesus and effectively legitimates Jesus' authority and Matthew's communal identity in the face of formative Judaism without breaking with the sacred tradition of Israel and dissociating from Judaism.

Matthew's portrayal of Jesus is intensified by the bread metaphor. First, Matthew exhibits Jesus' identity as an authoritative provider of life-giving source, corresponding to God who provides in the wilderness, and the founder of the community. In the two feeding stories (14:13–21; 15:29–39), Jesus feeds the crowds at the deserted place, through which the reader is reminded of the metaphor of God who feeds in the history of Israel; and Jesus is revealed as a provider of life-giving source, as is God. Between the two feeding scenes, Matthew reveals Jesus' identity as a provider of life-giving source through the dialogue between Jesus and the Canaanite woman (15:21–29). Although the dialogue concerns the healing of the demon-possessed daughter, Jesus talks about the bread, which is not to be offered to Gentiles, and the Canaanite woman is wisely eager to have the bread, even its crumbs. Beyond the motif of healing, Jesus is metaphorically revealed as a provider of life-giving source. In this respect, Matthew presents Jesus as the only appropriate leader through whom God's compassionate benefaction is present.

Second, Matthew presents Jesus' identity as the founder of the new community through the bread metaphor and feeding scenes. When Jesus breaks the bread in front of the crowds for the provision of food, it is not just a method of feeding, but it metaphorically signifies *the end of hostility, the establishment of new covenant,* and *the actual formation of a community.* Through the provision of life-giving source, Jesus actually forms a community with the Jewish crowd, signifying the restoration of a new Israel, and he expands the boundary of the community to the Gentiles through the sharing of God's benefaction with the Canaanite woman and other Gentile crowds. Matthew obviously presents Jesus as having "the keys of the kingdom of heaven" and the authority to "bind" and "loose" (16:19) in the world. Then, Jesus proclaims to build his own *"ekklesia"* (16:18), which can supersede the synagogue and the dominant group of Judaism. In this manner, Matthew exhibits Jesus as the only one through whom God restores Israel and forms a new Israel is formed.

Third, Matthew presents Jesus as the life-giving source itself for the community of God. At the last Supper meal (26:26–29), Jesus takes a loaf of bread and identifies with the bread, saying "Take, eat; this is my body" (v. 26). Obviously, Jesus is revealed as the provider of the bread, the life-giving source in Matthew like the metaphor of God who provides. Now, he himself becomes an entity of the provision, the bread. Matthew represents Jesus as the life-giving source that God provides. Jesus' identification with the bread leads the reader to recall what Jesus has done as the provider of the life-giving source and the founder of a new community in two feeding narratives (14:13–21; 15:29–39) and the narrative of the Canaanite woman (15:21–28). Also Jesus' body recalls the meaning of the bread metaphor that is the formational source of Matthew's communal identity and ideology. The metaphor of bread obviously represents a foundational source of Matthew's communal identity; and its *breaking/sharing* actions signify the formation of new community, new life, and new covenant, including the Gentiles. In addition, Jesus' identification with the bread clearly confirms that all Jesus' teachings and ideology must be identified with the bread; and the communal breaking/sharing of bread signifies the acceptance of Jesus' authority and teachings. From this perspective, God becomes a provider and Jesus is the source. Matthew proclaims that Jesus is the only appropriate life-giving source for the future fate of Judaism.

The portrait of Jesus in Matthew is the major source for legitimating the existence of the community. For the Matthean community, Jesus is the only life-giving source God provides for the formation of the community and their lives. Matthew's portrayal of Jesus and its discourse are the source of their alteration and deviance from the dominant ideology of Jewish leadership.

Resistance to the Roman Empire

Jesus as the Agent of God and the Only Life-Giving Source

Matthean bread in the narrative of the Canaanite woman (15:21–28) challenges the Roman imperial ideology and seeks to legitimate the community formed by Jesus. Jesus metaphorically allows the woman to have the bread, the life-giving source provided by God for the children of Israel; thereby Matthew metaphorically describes Jesus as the one who has the authority to mediate God's provision; at the same time, Jesus is described as the one through whom the true life-giving power is flowing. Namely, Jesus is described as the agent of God, who represents God's sovereignty over the life of the world and fulfills the will of God. Even in the two feeding narratives, Jesus reveals his role as the authoritative mediator or agent of God, who delivers God's compassionate will, blessing, and life-giving source. Matthew's presentation of Jesus as the agent of God contests the claims of imperial theology and ideology in which the empire/emperor is the agent of the gods' sovereignty, will, and blessing on earth. As Warren Carter argues, the portraits of Jesus challenge imperial claims that "the emperor embodies divine sovereignty and presence, and that the emperor as the agent of the gods, ensures societal well-being," through their alternative viewpoint and their presentation of a counter-character.[145]

While the Roman emperor is the agent chosen by the gods' will to manifest imperial ruling power, Jesus in Matthew is represented as God's agent to manifest God's sovereignty. Warren Carter observes three key titles of agency: Christ, King, and Son.[146] First, in the beginning of the Gospel, Matthew 1:1 introduces Jesus as "Christ," which means "the one who is commissioned" by God for a particular task, that is to save people from sin and to manifest God's presence (Emmanuel).[147] Second, Jesus is described as the long awaited agent as King of God's kingdom expected to enact and fulfill God's promise and will according to Israel's prophetic vision (Psalm 72, Isaiah 32:1–8, etc). Matthew's narrator designates Jesus as βασιλεύς "King/ Emperor" in the early chapters of the Gospel in Jesus' birth, which threatens to the client King Herod. Both Herod and Jesus are described as king (2:1–3, 9; c.f., 27:29). Third, Carter sees that the designation for Jesus as "son" (2:15) emphasizes that he is God's agent (3:17; 17:5, "beloved son"), who has a special relationship with God and is the recipient of God's love and will.[148] All these titles present Jesus as an agent, chosen to manifest God's sovereignty, presence, divine will, and blessing for human well-being; thereby Matthew challenges imperial claims and imperial theology while presenting an alternative empire and way of life.[149]

Besides these three key titles, Matthew ultimately presents Jesus as the true agent of God who mediates the life-giving source and enacts God's blessings in light of the bread metaphor. When Jesus looks up to heaven to give thanks to God for the food (14:19; 15:36), he breaks the bread and shares it with the crowds who are in need of life-giving source in the deserted place. Faced with the Canaanite woman who is desperate for the life-giving source, even for the crumbs, Jesus accepts her to participate in the banquet of the children of God (15:26–28). As God provides food to the Israelites in the wilderness, where the Israelite had God's provision as only relying on authoritative source for survival, Jesus as God's agent mediates God's will and provides the life-giving source for people, presenting God's blessing, presence, and sovereignty over the world.

In the ancient world, food and fertility are about power and are the main concerns of the people. The plentifulness of food, its production, distribution, and consumption reflects the well-being, status, and quality of life of the community. The abundant supply of food and its distribution are probably important tools to control inhabitants. According to Rome's imperial theology, the empire and the emperor as the agent chosen by gods must manifest god's will, blessings, and prosperity, presenting an abundant life-giving source. The Roman propaganda claims, "one of the gifts of the Roman Empire to its inhabitants was fertility and abundance."[150] This imperial claim must be a basic means of control over the inhabitants of the empire and the means of negotiation with the peasant group of people. Therefore, in order to preserve public order and Roman ideology, even to preserve honor, privilege, and power, Roman institutions and elites have to provide an adequate food for the people.[151] The provision of food for the populace, however, is so overwhelming, that half of the Roman inhabitants live in an agony of poverty and depend for their life on some powerful figures, personally and economically, while suffering indignity in order to preserve their lives.[152] Even the provision of food for the elite groups entails the Roman Empire's expropriation of resources from subject peoples.[153]

As the agent of gods, the emperor and other agents of empire fail to keep and to execute Roman ideology in the actual context of Rome. Under the Roman imperial theology and the agency of the emperor, people are exploited, personally and economically, and human dignity is impaired by the Roman agency and its hierarchical social structure. In this social context, the Matthew's portrait of Jesus as the agent of God who has authority over the provision of food challenges the Roman imperial ideology. Especially, when Jesus allows the Canaanite woman into the banquet of the children of God, it challenges the principles of Roman ideology and its social system, which subjects many populaces to indignity. Namely, the description of Jesus as the agent of God who provides the life-giving source and his work reaching out to the marginalized beyond socio-political boundaries must be subversive of the Roman Empire. Total sovereignty over life no longer belongs to Jupiter and the Roman emperor but to God, revealed through God's agent, Jesus.

When Matthew's Jesus identifies himself with the bread given by God (26:26), Matthew transforms Jesus, the agent of God who provides the life-giving source into the entity of God's provision, the true life-giving source. The metaphoric expression, 'this is my body,' means Jesus and all his teachings and ideological visions are the true life-giving source, which manifests God's sovereignty, presence, and blessing and human well-being. In other words, the works and teachings of Jesus are God's provision of life-giving source. When the Canaanite woman keeps asking Jesus to grant her a favor, despite Jesus' harsh mockeries, the woman is the only person who knows the life-giving power is flowing through Jesus. Matthew already presents Jesus as the only life-giving source and power that reach all the marginalized beyond the demonic structure of the false empire.

Furthermore, Matthew urges the reader to pursue the true life-giving source and invites people to participate in God's sovereignty: "Take, eat: this is my body." This phrase as Matthew's ideological manifesto and propaganda functions to challenge the Roman imperial theology and ideology. The community, established by the breaking of bread and formed by Jesus' teachings, is the true empire sanctioned by God. Eating the bread and participating in Jesus' meal signifies one's commitment to make something of the claim that God's life-giving provision comes true for Jesus-followers by including all Gentiles and the marginalized in the community beyond socio-religious, political boundaries formed by imperial ideology. In this way, Matthew's community represents its resistance to Roman imperial ideology, and as the alternative community in the context of first century subverts and fundamentally challenges the Roman Empire.

New Covenantal Community: *New Ideology*

The metaphor of bread and Jesus' identification with the bread in Matthew proclaim the enactment of new covenant and its ideological vision, which transcends the Roman imperial ideology. Especially in Jesus' last supper, the bread metaphor corroborates Matthew's ultimate vision of social bonding and alternative community in a new covenantal relationship through Jesus' identification with the bread. The ultimate vision of social bonding in the new covenant is manifested by Jesus' interpretation of the cup at the last supper. After distributing the bread, Jesus takes a cup, gives thanks, and gives the cup to his disciples, and commands them to drink of it (26:28). Then Matthew's narrator explains the cup using another metaphoric expression, "this is my blood of the covenant (τοῦτο γάρ ἐστιν τὸ αἷμά μου τῆς διαθήκης, v. 28f)." At this moment of Jesus' identification with the new covenant, all metaphoric meanings of bread, Jesus' teachings and prophetic ministries retroactively apply to the new covenant and its ideological vision.

Matthew's Jesus kindly explains that the core value of "the blood of the covenant" is aimed to "many for the forgiveness of sins." (26:28). The "forgiveness ἄφεσις is a prerequisite for surviving the judgment and participating in the kingdom to come"[154] and is associated with "repentance." Proper repentance involves a serious reorientation from the old to new being who is acceptable in God's kingdom, so forgiveness is closely involved in repentance and helps one change to be an acceptable being. Therefore, the forgiveness of sins is the core value of the new covenant in God's sovereign kingdom, and forgiveness is directly associated with the acceptance to the kingdom and Jesus' community, regardless of any socio-religious prejudice and boundaries.

Jesus' ministry involves practices of indiscriminate mercy and social inclusion of all minorities: seeking sinners not the righteous (9:9–13), healing many of the marginalized (chapter 8–9, 12:9–14, etc), feeding all crowds including women, children, and the diseased, even the Gentiles (14:13–21; 15:29–39), the Canaanite woman (15:21–28). Jesus' teachings also are concerned with the justice, love, and mercy (chapter 5–7), while criticizing the injustice, oppression, domination and economic greed of the elites, and their social prejudice for the status quo. Accordingly, Jesus' covenant in terms of "forgiveness" is not simply an isolated act or ideological vision for individual mercy, but part of a larger program of social transformation.[155] In Matthew's account, Jesus' two feeding scenes and the acceptance of the Canaanite woman as prophetic fulfillment present the ultimate new covenantal vision of community; and Matthew proclaims and confirms the enactment of the new covenant and its ideological vision.

The new covenant that Jesus enacts with the bread metaphor is subversive and challenging to the conventional way of life, which is manipulated by the social elites. In terms of "the forgiveness of sins" and Jesus' ideological vision, "the blood of the covenant" obviously refers to the transformation of social conventions or prejudices and "to different patterns of social, economic, and political interaction."[156] Therefore, Jesus' invitation into a new covenant signifies the liberation of people who are subjugated in social prejudice, conventional system, and hegemony. Carter argues that the term "blood" in 26:28 recalls the liberation of the people from Egypt;[157] and Carter states:

> The phrase "blood of the covenant" recalls God's covenant with the people at Sinai (Exod 24:8). The blood is poured out "for many" in anticipation of Jesus drinking it "with you" (plural) in the establishment of God's empire.[158]

In line with the meaning of the blood, the new covenant anticipates liberation from all socio-political bondage and envisions the new covenantal community as God's kingdom. Furthermore, the new covenant and its ideological vision pursue egalitarianism and common well-being in an alternative community, which actually terminates any hostility, antagonism, discrimination, exclusivism, and segregation formed by socio-religious boundaries, geographical barriers, and human prejudice.

The Roman Empire, however, is hierarchical with vast disparities of power, wealth, and even human dignity.[159] The life of the small ruling elite quite stable, but the majority of the non-elite struggle to find livable resources under the unequal and unsecured social system. The elite group pursues the emperor's favor in order to secure their privileged life and position; so they actively support the imperial ideology and strive to maintain the hierarchical system and social convention/ prejudice for the status quo. The ruling group manages the socio-economic system to display, protect, and improve their own power, wealth and status.[160] Clothing, housing, education, even quality and quantity of food are a "marker of status" and indicator of the division of elites from non-elites.[161] The social convention and imperial ideology are deeply embodied in these unequal socio-political-economic structures in the Roman Empire. This shows that Roman ideology and its propaganda about the life of well-being, fertility and abundance are actually not executed appropriately, and it reveals the injustice of the empire and the impairment of human dignity.

From this perspective, Matthew's "the blood of the covenant" represents the alternative ideological vision, not only pursuing egalitarianism, common well-being, and true liberation from all socio-political bondage, but also challenging the Roman imperial propaganda and ideology. Rodney Stark argues that the alternative vision of egalitarian community and its inclusive ideology were key aspects of the rise of Christianity as a dominant religious force, appealing to resistance to the empire.[162] The people who have struggled to survive under the Roman imperial hierarchical system are attracted by Matthew's ideological vision, so this alternative vision is quite challenging to the elite group of empire.

Consequently, Matthew's narratives and Jesus' identification with "the blood of the covenant" as hidden transcript offer an alternative or counter-ideology to negate the elite's dominant ideology and to assert the dignity and equality of people. As Passover signifies the New Year and new beginning, Matthew implicitly proclaims the new beginning of the season under the new covenant and new ideological vision. As the new season normally signifies the termination of the old one, Jesus' last supper as the Passover meal not only signifies the advent of the new season/ beginning of God's sovereignty with a new covenant, but it also quite challenges the Roman imperial ideology. In Matthew, Jesus invites all people into an alternative community, God's kingdom, and its alternative ideological vision without any limitations and boundaries. All people can share their own identity with each other and create harmony to be equal through the breaking of the bread.

Expansion of Boundaries

Jesus' acceptance of the Canaanite woman to get the broken bread symbolically promulgates the invalidation of the socio-religious-ethnic boundaries in Jesus' community, which can be a threatening discourse to Roman imperial ideology. The most challenging point to the Romans is that Jesus' mission reveals not only the expansion of God's ruling boundaries but also the territorial expansion of

God's kingdom: the movement out from Jerusalem to embrace all the nations.[163] Obviously, Jesus himself crosses over the borderline of Jewish territory, coming into the district of Tyre and Sidon (15:21). Jesus' movement is not just for travel or for sight-seeing but for fulfilling prophecy, especially the ultimate inclusion of Gentile nations as recipients of God's blessing as in the eschatological age in the Isaianic apocalyptic vision. (e.g., Isaiah 24:23; 42:6; 49:6; 51:5; 56:6–8). In this vision, God brings foreigners to his "holy mountain" to worship at the house of prayer (Isaiah 56:6–8); and the Gentile nations participate in a banquet on "this mountain" (Isaiah 25:6–10) coming to worship God's kingdom. Although the Gentile nations are included in God's restoration, ultimately the apocalyptic vision signifies the expansion of the domain of God's sovereignty, so Jesus' missionary transition in Matthew is not just inclusion but also the expansion of the sacred space, especially the territory of God's empire, which is no longer limited by the land of the Jews but expands to the whole world.

Furthermore, the vision of territorial expansion affirms Jesus' authority over the world: he is the only authoritative person who fulfills the ultimate vision of God's kingdom and carries this to all nations (28:20: "I am with you always to the end of the age"). Thereby Matthew delegitimizes the authority of the emperor and the imperial ideology and seeks to legitimate Jesus' community and its prophetic vision: the restoration of God's kingdom and sovereignty, ruling over the nations beyond the inner-circle boundary of the Jewish community.

From this perspective, Matthew's transition of missionary strategy challenges Roman imperialism. Rome's imperial ideology justifies their military and political domination of other people by socio-political-economic exploitation and pursues the territorial expansion and subjugation. Matthew's vision of the expansion of God's sovereignty and the expansion of Jesus' community toward "all nations" is provocative discourse as hidden transcript, challenging Roman imperialism and its dominant power. When Jesus allows the Canaanite woman to obtain the bread; when Jesus feeds the crowds including the Gentiles and the marginalized, making a new community, and when Jesus commands the disciples to baptize, to teach, and to make "all nations" disciples of Jesus, Matthew's Gospel exhibits their communal identity and ideological vision which denies the imperial ideology of Rome and strongly resists Roman imperial power and dominance.

Matthew's Community and Hybridity

In the previous chapter, I reviewed the identity of Matthew's community in light of the postcolonial conception, *the third space*. The third space is the place of articulation of cultural difference; and it is the indeterminate space in-between subject-positions, which produces new *hybrid* identity. Namely, the third space is the home of colonial *hybridity*, so Matthew's community and its identity under the colonial context can be reviewed and reframed by the postcolonial conception of hybridity.

Hybridity, an important concept in postcolonial theory, identifies with Matthew's alteration of Jewish heritage as a deviant group and cultural minority. Hybridity indeed helps to articulate the multiple and complex range of activities taking place in negotiating identity in the postcolonial context between the colonizer and the colonized. Robert Young argues that hybridity makes "difference into sameness, and sameness into difference, but in a way that makes the same no longer the same, the different no longer simply different."[164] Young argues that hybridity in "breaking and joining at the same time, in the same place" consists of "a bizarre binate operation, in which each impulse in qualified against the other, forcing a momentary form of dislocation and displacement."[165] In this sense, Homi Bhabha calls it a "third space" which neither subsumes the culture of the colonizer or colonized nor merely merges the two. Hybridity also does not imply a separate third culture but rather a process of continuous construction or formation and deconstruction of cultures by alteration-which is one of the good strategies to resist to colonizer.

Matthew's Gospel, especially the metaphor of bread clearly expresses not only anti-imperialism against the Roman imperial ideology but also an alternative prophetic vision that deconstructs Jewish conventional hegemonic beliefs and socio-religious boundaries. Most of all, Matthew de-legitimates the traditional value of the dominant group of Judaism and consistently legitimizes Matthew's own identity and ideological vision through alteration and deviance from dominant Judaism; as well as Matthew makes its ultimate identity as *the other*, even though Matthew does not deny the heritage of Jewish origin. When Jesus shares broken bread with the Canaanite woman (15:21–28), Matthew alters the conventional socio-religious boundaries of Jewish society to create new mission instruction.

Furthermore, while continuing to include Jewish heritage and teaching in Matthew's communal identity, Matthew's Jesus rejects and alters the ideology and teaching of the Pharisees, scribes, chief priest and elders of the Jews, who are all members of the ruling classes (16:5) and the group of competing opponents of Jesus. Matthew's ultimate identity and ideological vision derive from Jesus' own interpretation of the Torah and his teachings, through which Matthew alters the conventional vision and differentiates from the teaching of the dominant leadership of Judaism such as Pharisees and Scribes. In this sense, Matthew's alteration and deviance from the Pharisaic Judaism or another larger group of formative Judaism intends to weaken the legitimacy of the hegemony of the Jewish leader's group and to establish and legitimate the authority of his own group,[166] which has the genuine leader of Judaism.[167] Matthew, in this way, presents its altered vision of identity as a new community, which defines itself by denying the dominant Jewish leadership as well as altering the conventional perspective of Judaism enriched by those leaders.

Matthew ultimately presents Jesus' identity as an authoritative leader who can provide wisdom, alternative ideological vision, and the life-giving source, corresponding to God who provides in the wilderness and the founder of the community. Matthew also presents its character as hidden transcript, opposing to the Roman imperial theology and protesting against the flourishing cult and imperial ideological vision of Empire. Most of all, Matthew metaphorically describes Jesus as the one who has authority to mediate God's provision (14:13–21; 15:21–39); at the same time, Matthew presents Jesus' identity as the true life-giving source and authority (26:26). Thereby Matthew challenges and destructs the Roman imperial theology that presents the emperor as the agent chosen by god's will to manifest imperial ruling power and prosperous blessing. Beyond the imperial economic-political power and ideological vision, Matthew ultimately presents Jesus as the true agent of God who mediates the life-giving source and enacts God's blessings through the bread metaphor in hidden transcript. In the colonial context, Matthew's community as the colonized is probably assumed to be the adopted hegemonic power, mimicking imperial ideology; however Matthew clearly denies taking the colonial—cultural—ideological imposition but rather presents an alternative vision.

Furthermore, Matthew represents the ultimate vision of social bond and the alternate community in a new covenantal relationship in God's kingdom. The new covenantal vision that Jesus enacts in his ministry and the bread metaphor are subversive and challenging to the conventional way of life and hierarchical imperial order, which is manipulated by the social elites and imperial rulers. Matthew's new covenant anticipates the new liberation from all socio-political bondage and envisions egalitarianism and common well-being in an alternative community, which actually terminates any hostility, antagonism, discrimination, exclusivism, and segregation formed by the socio-religious boundaries, geographical barriers, and human prejudice, and so on. Thus, Matthew's ideological vision denies and alters that of the Roman Empire, which is very hierarchical with vast disparities of power, wealth, and even human dignity.[168]

With all of these alternative visions, Matthew exhibits the ultimate vision of God's kingdom and its expansion of communal boundary; all these alterations threaten the Roman imperial ideology. Matthew proclaims that the Gentiles can now access the life-giving source and salvation and participate in its social association under God's sovereignty beyond the socio-religious boundaries. Matthew denies the colonial imposition of identity and actively seeks to delegitimize the authority of the emperor and the imperial ideology; at the same time, Matthew's community reproduces its communal identity and seeks to legitimate its ideological vision: the restoration of God's kingdom and sovereignty, ruling over the nations beyond the Roman imperial hegemony.

From this perspective, Matthew's communal identity and cultural position were neither in formative Judaism nor in the Roman imperial ideology. Furthermore, Matthew's ideology and the discourse of the bread metaphor are not characterized by radical uniqueness but rather by creative alteration and inventiveness, which is revealed in re-working, negotiating, and re-appropriating Jewish heritage and Greco-Roman influences. With an appeal to a different interpretation of the Torah and the fulfillment of prophetic vision, Matthew creatively challenges the conventional identity of formative Judaism as well as the ideological discourse of Roman Empire. Accordingly, Matthew's community and identity can be understood as hybridity in their colonial situation. Namely, *in-between* the formative Judaism and the Roman Imperial ideology, Matthew constructs its own identity through "a process of alterity." Through a breaking and joining at the same time, in the same place, Matthew intentionally places its communal identity in the third space, subverting and deconstructing the hegemony and imperial ideology through the bread metaphor and its rhetorical claims in Hybridity.

5

Conclusion

I have presented the meaning of Matthean bread (ἄρτος) as a metaphor, which implicitly integrates the representation of the socio-religious context and the communal identity of Matthew into the Gospel of Matthew as a whole. Based on Jewish social memory, cognitive conception, and symbolic imagery of the bread, Matthean bread and the act of breaking of bread represent Matthew's communal identity and ideological vision that is newly reconstructed in-between formative Judaism and the Roman Empire. When Jesus breaks the bread, the metaphor of bread as a source of Matthew's rhetorical claim envisions an alternative community open to the nations beyond socio-religious boundaries, and reveals its ideological vision overcoming the hegemony of the dominant Jewish groups and Roman imperialism.

As indicated, the metaphor bread and the issue of food/meals are linked to the historical knowledge and Jewish cognitive concepts formed by previous understanding and common experience,[1] through which Jews establish a common sense of tradition and communal identity. In chapter 2, I studied the special experiences and conceptions on food, such as the bread in the wilderness, dietary laws, and festive meals, which lead the Israelites into a common sense of identity and religious imagination. Israel's ritualization of historical events and textual record on the bread and festive meals not only link to the formation of Israel's communal identity, but also preserve the Jewish indigenous identity and social memories throughout the generations. Thus, the issues of food/meals and their observation indeed functioned to bond people in solidarity in their sense of Jewish identity and to maintain the origin of Jewish heritage and communal boundary, even in first century Judaism.

From this perspective, one realizes that the issue of food/meals is not just a matter of nutrition, but an important source of historical knowledge, which forms social structure, national identity, and religious beliefs in Jewish cultural history. [2] In chapter 2, I also observed the historical knowledge, conception, and imagery of the bread in Jewish history and literature that would form a metaphoric conception and structure: 1) The bread is God's life-giving source, a sign of God's complete care, a sign of God's presence, and signifies God who provides; 2) The breaking of bread is sharing a meal, the end of hostility, making a covenant, an actual formation of community, blessing, a participating in an ideological claim; 3) Eating the meal/bread is learning God's word/knowledge, accepting God's wisdom/ideology, the acceptance of God's authority, participating in God's Sovereignty/Ideology.

In chapter 3 and 4, I interpreted Jesus' feeding scenes and meals, which especially include the term bread (ἄρτος) and its breaking action, in light of the metaphoric conception and Jewish understandings. The bread and its relevant narrative context evoke the reader's cognitive conception of the image of God's provision, the Passover meal, the Manna in ancient Israel's wilderness experience, and the socio-cultural understanding of the breaking of bread, while bringing this conceptual knowledge into the interpretation of Jesus' two feeding narratives (14:13–21; 15:29–39), the narrative of the Canaanite woman (15:21–28), and Jesus' last supper (26:26–29). When Jesus breaks the bread with the crowds, the Canaanite woman and the disciples, the bread is not just for human hunger; but rather the bread and Jesus' provision metaphorically represent the *establishment of a new community* and *making a new covenant* as an alternative Kingdom; and Matthean bread as metaphor envisions the messianic banquet for the restoration of Israel beyond socio-religious ethnic boundaries.

By this study one can find that the Gospel of Matthew deconstructs multiple boundaries of religion, ethnicity, ideology, gender, class and so forth, and reconstructs the community's own identity and ideological vision through the bread Jesus provide. Especially, when Jesus identifies himself with the bread, which is broken and given to the other, Matthew corroborates the Matthean ideological vision, which overcomes boundaries and hegemonies by reaching out to the nations (Gentiles). Matthew's community, as a voluntary association of deviant

Jews, does not get stuck in the indigenous religious-cultural heritage of conventional Judaism, but redefines their communal boundary and vision. At the same time, Matthew denies the colonial cultural imposition and imperial ideology and reconstructs a new identity and ideological vision as an alternative community in *the third space* beyond two cultural conventions and hegemonic entities. Through the bread metaphor, Matthew expands the socio-religious boundaries of the community, even its ethnic and political boundaries, while maintaining their Jewish heritage and their legitimacy. Further, Matthew clearly affirms that Jesus is the only agent of God and the only life-giving source and presents a new covenantal vision of Matthew as an alternative community, overcoming the Roman imperial ideology.

From this perspective, Matthew's Gospel uses the metaphor bread as a narrative strategy and a source of rhetorical claim for representing and reconstructing the communal identity in the Jewish and Graeco-Roman world. As discussed in James C. Scott's conceptions,[3] Matthew's community as a subordinate voluntary association or deviant group of formative Judaism creates its Gospel with the metaphor of bread as *hidden transcript* that indirectly or metaphorically represents a critique of the conventional perspective and identity of formative Judaism and the dominant imperial theology and ideology of the Roman Empire, while presenting and reproducing their own community identity. In this regard, Matthean bread as metaphor must be a source of the enunciation of the *Hybrid* identity of Matthew's community in-between formative Judaism and the Roman Empire.

This book brings another hermeneutic apparatus and lens to interpret the Matthean feeding narratives and the references to ingestion within the narrative context of Matthew's Gospel as a whole, beyond the traditional understandings. The book presents another way to see how the Matthean community represents an identity and communal vision amid the conflicts between formative Judaism and Roman imperialism in the first century C.E. The application of contemporary metaphor theory to the interpretation of the Gospel of Matthew provides numerous hermeneutic insights regarding: 1) the usage of cognitive conception and social memory, which are integrated in specific language and images, 2) the literary motif of a particular word as metaphor within the narrative plot and its strategic development, and 3) the analysis of social-cultural context and ideological vision, revealed by the metaphor and the text. As was presented, the metaphoric conception of a social memory reveals its own indigenous cultural identity; and the use of the metaphor within a narrative setting and plot development intensifies the meaning of the metaphor and re-presents the identity and ideological vision.

I hope the hermeneutic strategy in this book encourages further studies regarding the metaphor of bread or any food imagery in the other gospels and other metaphoric conceptions or descriptions in the New Testament, which are importantly intermingled within biblical literature.

Notes

Chapter 1: Introduction

1. Terry Eagleton, *Literary Theory: An Introduction* (Second Edition; Minnesota: Blackwell Publishers, 1996), 19–20.
2. Roland Boer, *Marxist Criticism of the Bible* (New York: T & T Clark, 2003), 15.
3. Graydon F. Snyder, *Inculturation of the Jesus Tradition—The Impact of Jesus on Jewish and Roman Cultures* (Harrisburg: Trinity Press, 1999), 129.
4. The book of Exodus describes manna as the "bread from heaven" (Exodus 16:4; cf. Psalms 78:24).
5. L. Juliana M. Claassens, *The God Who Provides: Biblical Images of Divine Nourishment* (Nashville: Abingdon, 2004), 16.
6. Ibid., xvi.
7. Francis Wright Beare, *The Gospel According to Matthew* (New York: Harper & Row, 1981), 326–328. Beare argues that from the earlier times bread and fish have been depicted on the table in symbolic representations of the Eucharist in the Synoptic accounts. See also John Nolland, *The Gospel of Matthew: A Commentary on the Greek Text* (NIGTC; Michigan: The Paternoster Press, 2005), 1073–1086; Daniel J. Harrington, S.J., *The Gospel of Matthew* (Sacra Pagina Series; Minnesota: The Liturgical Press, 1991), 366–371; I. H. Marshal, *Last Supper and Lord's Supper* (Grand Rapids: Eerdmans, 1981); Joachim Jeremias, *The Eucharistic Words of Jesus* (London: SCM Press, 1966).

8. Francis Wright Beare, *The Gospel According to Matthew*, 327.

9. See also, W. F. Albright and C. S. Mann, *Matthew* (AB; New York: Doubleday & Company, 1971), 178–179. The connection between the Kingdom, the New Covenant and the Eucharist is clearly made in Paul's first letter to the Corinthians. Many scholars see this as an already existing tradition.

10. Daniel J. Harrington, S.J., *The Gospel of Matthew*, 222. He thinks that the central theme of Matthew 14:13–21 is the banquet over which Jesus presides. See also Ulrich Luz, *Matthew 8–20* (Hermeneia; Minneapolis: Fortress, 2001), 314; Ulrich Luz, *Matthew 21–28*, 372–385.

11. For instance, Daniel Harrington argues that some literary settings and descriptions, such as "a deserted place" (ἔρημον τόπον), serve to remind the reader of Ancient Israel's sojourning in the wilderness of Sinai in Exodus. Reflecting on the journey in the wilderness, Matthew's Gospel recalls the memory of the Passover meal, particularly unleavened bread, and later the manna, which is "the bread of angels" (Psalm 78: 24–25) God provided. See Daniel J. Harrington, S.J., *The Gospel of Matthew* (Sacra Pagina Series; Minnesota: The Liturgical Press, 1991), 219; Joseph Grassi also affirms that many elements of the feeding narratives in the synoptic Gospels remind readers of the night of the Exodus and Jesus' Last Supper expression (Matthew 26:20). See Joseph A. Grassi, *Loaves and Fishes: The Gospel Feeding Narratives* (Minnesota: The Liturgical Press, 1991), 55.

12. Peder Borgen, *Bread from Heaven: An Exegetical Study of the Concept of Manna in the Gospel of John and the Writings of Philo* (SNT vol. 10; Leiden, 1981); Dennis E. Smith, *From Symposium to Eucharist: The Banquet in the Early Christian World* (Minneapolis: Fortress Press, 2003).

13. Jane S. Webster, *Ingesting Jesus: Eating and Drinking in the Gospel of John* (ABS. No. 6; Leiden: Brill, 2003).

14. However, Webster's study does not touch upon the rhetorical function of ingesting terms from a socio-cultural perspective, failing to acknowledge the role of meals and banquets in the ancient world and its relationship to the Johannine narrative, even though Webster recognizes that the metaphor is a cultural phenomenon.

15. Hal Taussig, *In the Beginning Was the Meal: Social Experimentation and Early Christian Identity* (Minneapolis: Fortress Press, 2009); Dennis E. Smith, *From Symposium to Eucharist: The Banquet in the Early Christian World* (Minneapolis: Fortress Press, 2003); See also Dennis E. Smith, and Hal Taussig, *Many Tables: The Eucharist in the New Testament and Liturgy Study* (London: SCM, 1990).

16. Daniel J. Harrington, S.J., *The Gospel of Matthew* (Sacra Pagina; Minnesota: The Liturgical Press, 1991).

17. Andrew J. Overman, *Matthew's Gospel and Formative Judaism* (Minneapolis: Fortress, 1990).

18. W. D. Davies and Dale C. Allison, Jr., *A Critical and Exegetical Commentary on the Gospel According to Saint Matthew*. 3 vols. (ICC; Edinburgh: T & T Clark, 1988).

19. Saldarini prefers the designation "group" rather than "community" because the more often-used "community" implies separation and independence from Judaism.
20. Anthony J. Saldarini, *Matthew's Christian-Jewish Community* (Chicago: The University of Chicago Press, 1994).
21. In the aftermath of the Jewish Revolt of 66–70 C.E. and the destruction of the temple, Pharisaic Judaism emerged as the dominant force within the Palestine Judaism in this period.
22. See Ulrich Luz, *Matthew 1–7* (Hermeneia; Minneapolis: Fortress Press, 2007); Graham N. Stanton, *A Gospel for a New People: Study in Matthew* (Westminster John Knox, 1992). Stanton argues there was a strident enmity that arose in the relationship between the parent body of Judaism and the Matthean community because there were clear distinctions and differentiation between them. He sees that the parent group of Judaism felt betrayed and understands the community's core values as being undermined believing that the parent group rejected any new relationship with the new group of Christianity. See also Donald Hagner, "Matthew: Christian Judaism or Jewish Christianity?" in *The Face of New Testament Studies: A Survey of Recent Research*, ed. S. Mcknight and G. Osborne (Grand Rapids: Baker Academic, 2004), 263–282.
23. Theissen argues that the ethos of the early Christian community was formed in a process of interaction with the dominant values of the pagan world, such as imperial ideology. Then many other scholars such as Richard Horsley and Peter Oakes seriously considered such questions in the relationship between Jesus/Paul and the Roman Empire. See Gerd Theissen, *A Theory of Christian Religion* (London: SCM Press, 1999), 81–117; Peter Oakes, ed., *Rome in the Bible and the Early Church* (Carlisle: Paternoster, 2002); John Riches and David C. Sim, eds. *The Gospel of Matthew in Its Roman Imperial Context* (JSNTS, 296; New York: T & T Clark, 2005).
24. Warren Carter, *Matthew and Empire: Initial Explorations* (Harrisburg: Trinity Press International, 2001).
25. Ibid., 170.
26. David Tracy, "Metaphor and Religion," in *Critical Inquiry* 5, no. 1 (1978), 106.
27. Ibid., 92.
28. George Lakoff and Mark Johnson, *Philosophy in the flesh: The embodied mind and its challenge to Western Thought* (New York: Basic Books, 1999), 19.
29. George Lakoff and Mark Johnson, *Metaphors We Live By* (Chicago: The University of Chicago Press, 1980); See also George Lakoff and Mark Turner, *More Than Cool Reason: A Field Guide to Poetic Metaphor* (Chicago: The University of Chicago Press, 1989); George Lakoff, "The Contemporary Theory of Metaphor," in *Metaphor and Thought*, ed. Andrew Ortony. Second Edition (Cambridge: Cambridge University Press, 1993), 202–251.
30. Lakoff and Johnson, *Metaphors We Live By*, 3.

31. Ibid., 3.

32. David E. Rumelhart, "Some Problems with the Notion of Literal Meanings," in *Metaphor and Thought*, ed. Andrew Ortony (Second Edition; Cambridge: Cambridge University Press, 1993), 81.

33. Ibid., 81.

34. The conventionalization/conceptualization is "to the extent that it is automatic, effortless, and generally established as a mode of thought among members of a linguistic community." Conventionalization can be a connection between the conceptual and linguistic levels because the conventionalized concepts can be applied to a wide range of linguistic expressions in many ways in common sense. See George Lakoff and Mark Turner, *More Than Cool Reason: A Field Guide to Poetic Metaphor* (Chicago: The University of Chicago Press, 1989), 55–56.

35. Lakoff and Johnson, *Metaphors We Live By*, 6.

36. George Lakoff, "The Contemporary Theory of Metaphor," in *Metaphor and Thought*, ed. Andrew Ortony (Second Edition; Cambridge: Cambridge University Press, 1993), 203.

37. Ibid., 204.

38. Ibid., 245.

39. Linguists use other terms, *tenor* and *vehicle*. *Tenor* refers to a word with "underlying idea or principal subject" in the literal frame, while *vehicle* refers to the figurative word. See I. A. Richards, *The Philosophy of Rhetoric* (London: Oxford University Press, 1936), 97.

40. Lakoff, "The Contemporary Theory of Metaphor," 210.

41. Here I quote the example of Dante's *Divine Comedy* from Lakoff and Turner's *More Than Cool Reason*, 9.

42. Lakoff and Johnson, *Metaphors We Live By*, 46–47.

43. Ibid., 52–55. "Extension" is to activate the previously *unused* parts of metaphor, that are normally not commonplace, to transform the metaphor and create new meaning.

44. Ibid., 47–48.

45. Paul Ricoeur, *The Rule of Metaphor: Multi-disciplinary Studies of the Creation of Meaning in Language*, translated by Robert Czerny (Toronto: University of Toronto Press, 1977), 247.

46. Ibid., 133.

47. George Lakoff and Mark Johnson, *Philosophy in the Flesh: The Embodied Mind and Its Challenge to Western Thought*, 13.

48. Ibid., 18.

49. Paul Ricoeur, "Biblical Hermeneutic." in *Semeia 4*, John Dominic Crossan, ed. (Missoula: The Society of Biblical Literature, 1975), 88.

50. J. L. Resseguie, *Narrative Criticism of the New Testament: An Introduction* (Grand Rapid: Baker Academic, 2005; Mieke Bal, *Narratology: Introduction to the Theory*

of Narrative (Second Edition; University of Toronto Press: Scholarly Publishing Division, 1997).

51. In the case of the conception of the implied reader, See W. Iser, *The Acts of Reading: A Theory of Aesthetic Response* (Baltimore: Johns Hopkins University, 1978).

52. Mark Allan Powell, "Literary Approaches and the Gospel of Matthew," in *Methods For Matthew*, ed. Mark Allan Powell (Cambridge: Cambridge University Press, 2009), 60.

53. Ibid., 60.

54. Karin Ikas and Gerhard Wagner, "Postcolonial Subjectivity and the Transclassical Logic of the Third," in *Communicating in the Third Space*, ed. Karin Ikas and Gerhard Wanger (New York: Routledge, 2009), 96.

55. Homi K. Bhabha, "The Third Space," in *Identity, Community, Culture, Difference*, ed. Jonathan Rutherford (London: Lawrence and Wishart, 1990), 209.

56. Homi K. Bhabha, *The Location of Culture* (Second Edition; New York: Routledge, 2004), 55.

57. Ibid., 54.

58. Homi K. Bhabha, "The Third Space," 211.

59. Homi K. Bhabha, *The Location of Culture*, 55.

60. Bhabha addresses those who live in border regions on the margins of different nations, in-between contrary homelands, in his book *The Location of Culture*. Here the borders are important thresholds of contradictions and ambivalence, which corroborate the third space of enunciation where the complex figures of difference and hybrid identity are produced.

61. Gina Wisker, *Key Concepts in Postcolonial Literature* (New York: Palgrave Macmillan, 2007), 189; See also Bill Ashcroft, Gareth Griffiths, and Helen Tiffin, eds., *The Postcolonial Studies: The Key Concepts* (New York: Routledge, 2000), 96.

62. Ibid., 189.

63. Homi Bhabha, *The Location of Culture*, 162.

64. Jenni Ramone, *Postcolonial Theories* (New York: Palgrave Macmillan, 2011), 112.

65. Bill Ashcroft, Gareth Griffiths, and Helen Tiffin, eds., *The Post-Colonial Studies Readers* (New York: Routledge, 2006), 158.

66. Ibid., 159.

67. Jenni Ramone, *Postcolonial Theories*, 112–113.

68. Homi K. Bhabha, *The Location of Culture*, 55.

69. In this book "the dominant group of formative Judaism" means the religious leader's group, the major group of formative Judaism that has hegemonic power, as well as the opponent group of Jesus in the account of the Gospel of Matthew, it also can be called the larger group or majority of formative Judaism; According to some aspects of life in Palestine from 165 BCE to 100 CE, Andrew Overman argues that Matthew's community was a sectarian minority group in struggle with formative Judaism, and he saw the opponent group of Matthew as a religious leadership group

or those who wield the power and authority within Judaism, which was emerging as a dominant group and forming a larger society within Palestine Judaism. See Andrew J. Overman, *Matthew's Gospel and Formative Judaism: The Social World of the Matthean Community* (Minneapolis: Fortress Press, 1990), 8–16, 23, 141–149; Anthony Saldarini also regarded Matthew's group as a minor group or sect within Judaism, which deviated from the major group of Judaism, which can be categorized as "leadership group of Jewish society" influenced by a rabbinic group or as the majority of Jews and the larger body of Judaism. See Anthony J. Saldarini, *Matthew's Christian Community* (Chicago: The University of Chicago Press, 1994), 85–87, 112–116; See also Petri Luomanen, "The 'Sociology of Sectarianism' in Matthew: Modeling the Genesis of Early Judaism and Christian Communities," in *Fair Play: Diversity and Conflicts in Early Christianity: Essays in Honor of Heikki Räisänen*, ed. Ismo Dunderburg and Christopher Tuckett (Netherland: Brill, 2002), 107–130; Although this article suggests the concept of "common Judaism" insisted by E. P. Sanders, it presents many aspects and arguments about sectarianism in formative Judaism; See also Petri Luomanen, *Recovering Jewish-Christian Sects and Gospels* (*SVC 10*; Leiden: Brill, 2012).

Chapter 2: *Bread/Meals* in Second Temple Judaism and Relevant Social Memories

1. George Lakoff and Mark Johnson, *Metaphors We Live By* (Chicago: The University of Chicago Press, 1980), 3–6.

2. L. Juliana M. Claassens, *The God Who Provides: Biblical Images of Divine Nourishment* (Nashville: Abingdon Press, 2004), 16.

3. David E. Sutton, *Remembrance of Repasts: An Anthropology of Food and Memory* (Oxford: Berg, 2001); See also David E. Sutton, *Memories Cast in Stone: The Relevance of the Past in Everyday Life* (New York: Berg, 1998).

4. Jewish independence was not realized until the time of the Maccabees, centuries later. Jewish territory also was ruled by foreigners—Persians and Greeks. After Greek and Roman rulers turned their attention to Jerusalem as a center of military and trade routes, significant numbers of foreigners came into Jewish territory; so that Jews struggled with the Hellenization of their indigenous culture. See Martin Hengel, *Judaism and Hellenism: Studies in their Encounter in Palestine During the Early Hellenistic Period*, trans. John Bowden (Philadelphia: Fortress Press, 1974); Lester L. Grabbe, *Judaic Religion in the Second Temple Period: Belief and Practice from the Exile to Yavneh* (New York: Routledge, 2000); George W. E. Nickelsburg and Michael E. Stone, *Faith and Piety in Early Judaism: Text and Documents* (Philadelphia: Fortress Press, 1983); Lester L. Grabbe, *An Introduction to Second Temple Judaism: History and*

<ol start="5">
<li></li>
</ol>

Religion of the Jews in the Time of Nehemiah, The Maccabees, Hillel and Jesus (New York: T & T Clark, 2010).

5. David Kraemer, *Jewish Eating and Identity through the Ages* (New York: Routledge, 2007), 25–37. Here Jewish people keep the persistence of the biblical law, especially for their eating dietary law, in light of Leviticus-Deuteronomy.

6. Many Jewish groups such as Pharisees, Sadducees, and Zealots held different views and observed different practices. In some other points, they condemned each other, even though they shared the origin of belief and some tradition within Judaism. In this sense, Philip Davies defines sect as "a social group that has socially segregated itself from its wider social matrix. A sect does not regard itself as merely a part of a wider society, but as the only legitimate representative, a microcosm." See Philip R. Davies, "Sect Formation in Early Judaism," in *Sectarianism in Early Judaism: Sociological Advances*, ed. David J. Chalcraft (London: Equinox, 2007), 134–137; Lester L. Grabbe, "When is a Sect a Sect—or Not? Groups and Movement in the Second Temple Period," in *Sectarianism in Early Judaism*, 114–132; Oskar Skarsavne, *In the Shadow of the Temple: Jewish Influences on Early Christianity* (Downers Grove, InterVarsity Press, 2002), 103–134.

7. Almost the same period as with Second Temple Period (530 BC to 70 AD), it is a period between the Hebrew Bible and the New Testament texts.

8. The sects must try to justify their existence on ideological grounds. Namely "the sect will (re)write its origins with the aim of establishing its identity claims, from a sectarian vantage point." At the same time the identity of sect and its reestablishment go back to the very beginning, which is the origin of its heritage. See Philip R. Davies, "Sect Formation in Early Judaism," 136.

9. Gillian Feeley-Harnik, *The Lord's Table: The Meaning of Food in Early Judaism and Christianity* (Washington: Smithsonian Book, 1994), 91.

10. Sinners were regarded as comparable to Gentiles in their lack of respect of the law (Torah).

11. In Second Temple times the entire system of ritual purity and impurity was in effect, based on the Levitical codes of Torah. Being impure means that one cannot approach the Temple and any holy things. Also pious Jews refused to eat Gentile food as they refused to eat with Gentiles, since Jews believe this means the assimilation to the Gentile way of life. Lawrence H. Schiffman, *From Text to Tradition: A History of Second Temple and Rabbinic Judaism* (New Jersey: Ktav Publishing House, 1991), 251–263; Gillian Feeley-Harnik, *The Lord's Table*, 97.

12. D. S. Russell, *From Early Judaism to Early Church* (Philadelphia: Fortress Press, 1986), 12.

13. Lawrence H. Schiffman, *From Text to Tradition: A History of Second Temple and Rabbinic Judaism* (New Jersey: Ktav Publishing House, 1991), 244–255.

14. Ritual purity remained in force in two matters: washing hands before meals and the observance of menstrual purification in marriage.

15. Luke 7:36–50; 11:37–52; 14:1–14.

16. Mark 1:31; 2:15–17; 7:2–23; 14:3–9; Matthew 8:13; 9:10–13; 15:1–20; Luke 5: 29–39; 10:38–42; 19:1–10.

17. Although there were various votive offerings and rituals, only on the pilgrim festivals is all Israel summoned to Jerusalem from all of Palestine and many places in the Diaspora, streaming to Jerusalem, in order to participate in this particular occasion, to serve God and to be the people of Israel.

18. Jacob Neusner, *Judaism When Christianity Began: A Survey of Belief and Practice* (Louisville: John Knox Press, 2002), 136.

19. Ibid., 135.

20. E.g., Exodus 23:17–19; Deuteronomy 16:13–17; See Jacob Neusner, *Judaism When Christianity Began*, 139.

21. Ibid., 144. Neusner argues that eating the meal is one of the most highlighted points in the festivals for the individual Israelite who offered the offerings and is atoned by God.

22. Bokser sees that Jewish people would regard Passover primarily as a national celebration of thanksgiving for the historic event of national freedom, when they had a national center. See Baruch M. Bokser, *The Origins of the Seder*, 83.

23. Josephus clearly describes the significance of Passover in light of the national function of the holiday, bonding people under the covenant of God. See Josephus, *Antiquities*, 4:203–204.

24. Josephus counts the number of pilgrims: two million seven hundred thousand. See Josephus, *The Jewish War*, 6.9.3: 422–427; E. P. Sanders estimates the actual number of attendees to be 300,000 to 500,000. The number of pilgrims could not be exact, but a huge number of people came to Jerusalem, so that the place of Jerusalem was fully crowed by the pilgrimage. E. P. Sanders, *Judaism: Practice and Belief 63 BCE-66 CE* (Philadelphia: Trinity Press International, 1992), 126.

25. Jordan D. Rosenblum, *Food and Identity in Early Rabbinic Judaism* (Cambridge: Cambridge University Press, 2010), 65, 73; Through the intersecting notions of the metonymy and embodiment of food, the practice on the food functions as part of a larger process of identity formation.

26. Ibid., 68. A non-Jew cannot/never eat the metonymic food of Israel except a circumcised convert.

27. Baruch M. Bokser, *The Origins of The Seder: The Passover Rite and Early Rabbinic Judaism* (Berkeley: University of California Press, 1984), 76–100.

28. Martin S. Jaffee, *Early Judaism: Religious Worlds of the First Judaic Millennium* (Second Edition; Bethesda: University Press of Maryland, 2006), 217–218; See also Baruch M. Bokser, *The Origins of the Seder*, 76–100.

29. Individual families or social units gather together at home with fewer distractions than in Jerusalem. This gathering has greater intimacy, bonding people in solidarity

with more effective ritual ceremonies. Baruch M. Bokser, *The Origins of the Seder*, 83–84.

30. Martin S. Jaffee, *Early Judaism*, 211–224.

31. Ibid., 218.

32. Nathan Macdonald, *Not Bread Alone: The Use of Food in the Old Testament* (Oxford: Oxford University Press, 2008), 198. He states the dietary laws and their final form were established in the exilic or probably post-exilic period. Torah's dietary laws must be strengthened and emphasized among the returnees.

33. E.g., Isaiah 65–66 reveals the prohibition of pork beyond Leviticus 11 and Deuteronomy 14: the prophet accuses the people "who sit inside tombs and spend the night in secret places; who eat swine's flesh with broth of abominable things in their vessels" (v. 4).

34. The text does not provide what was wrong with the food and the prior law or scripture to which Daniel was being obedient.

35. E.g., Tobit 1:10–11; Judith 10:5; 12:1–4; 1 Maccabees 1:63; Esther 4:16–17; one can see the revulsion and fear of defilement in the case of the righteous refusing to eat foreign and royal food. See W. Sibley Towner, *Daniel* (*IBCTP*; Louisville: John Knox Press, 1984), 24–25.

36. W. Sibley Towner, *Daniel*, 26.

37. Gillian Feeley-Harnik, *The Lord's Table: The Meaning of Food in Early Judaism and Christianity* (Washington: Smithsonian Books, 1981), 96–106 ; Nathan MacDonald, *Not Bread Alone*, 196–211.

38. The Assyrians' food is regarded as impure and incurs God's wrath (cf. 10:5; 12:5–9).

39. Nathan MacDonald, *Not Bread Alone*, 202.

40. To some Jews, Gentiles were regarded as the standard of evil kinless-ness and godlessness, or sinners (Deuteronomy 32:31), so any relationship with Gentiles, such as commensality and marriage, was prohibited—e.g., Exodus 34:14–16; Leviticus 7:7; 18–20; 20:5; Deuteronomy 31:16; Isaiah 52:1; 54:6–8; Jeremiah 3:1–20.

41. Gillian Feeley-Harnik, *The Lord's Table: The Meaning of Food in Early Judaism and Christianity* (Washington: Smithsonian Books, 1981), 85–91.

42. See also the Song of Songs; here the descriptions of food/drink and eating/drinking metaphorically signify a love relationship between female and male in line with the covenantal relationship between God and Israel. God gives food as loving husband; he also takes it away from his spouse when he thinks she does not love him anymore; and he will give it back to her after punishing her or when 'love' is restored (cf., Ezekiel 16; Hosea 2). See Athalya Brenner, "The Food of Love: Gendered Food and Food Imagery in the Song of Songs," in *Semeia 86: Food and Drink in the Biblcial World* (Atlanta: Society of Biblical Literature, 1999): 101–112.

43. Gillian Feeley-Harnik, *The Lord's Table: The Meaning of Food in Early Judaism and Christianity*, 90.

44. Ibid., 91.

45. Philip R. Davies, "Food, Drink, and Sects: The Question of Ingestion in the Qumran Texts," in *Semeia 86: Food and Drink in the Biblical Worlds*, ed. Athalya Brenner. (Atlanta: The Society of Biblical Literature, 1999), 156–157.

46. Schiffman affirms that while the messianic banquet of rabbinic source was to be a one-time affair inaugurating the messianic era, the Qumran community looked forward to a regular series of such banquets to be held in the days to come. So the Qumran communal meals were to be "a sample of the world to come." See Lawrence H. Schiffman, *Sectarian Law in the Dead Sea Scrolls: Courts, Testimony and the Penal Code* (Chino: Scholars Press, 1983), 197–200; James C. Vanderkam, *The Dead Sea Scrolls Today* (Grand Rapids: Eerdmans Publishing Company, 1994), 173–175.

47. Lawrence H. Schiffman, *Sectarian Law in the Dead Sea Scrolls: Courts, Testimony and the Penal Code*, 202.

48. After one year, one can first be allowed contact with the pure solid food of community. Then after two years, one is allowed contact with the liquid food, through which one becomes a full member with rights to the meal (1QS 6:13–23). Josephus also describes the procedures of the entrance of a new member at Qumran community, by contact with the communal meals. This is different from the description of the Rule of Community, but both seem to move through similar stages, centered on contact with the communal meal (Jewish War 2.137–139); See James C. Vanderkam, *The Dead Sea Scrolls Today*, 88–89.

49. Dennis E. Smith, *From Symposium to Eucharist*, 155.

50. The mechanism of "keeping apart" members from the common meal, who have not followed the rules, is entirely in keeping with the perception of the community as one "separated." The community creates its own set of symbolic boundaries through the food and meal. See Philip R. Davies, "Food, Drink and Sects: The Question of Ingestion in the Qumran Texts," in *Food and Drink in the Biblical Worlds, Semeia*. Vol. 86 (Atlanta: The Society of Biblical Literature, 1999), 151–163.

51. Nathan Macdonald, *Not Bread Alone*, 71.

52. David Sutton sees that the cycle of consumption of food works with the religious calendar. In fact, religion and ritual are naturalized through the practices of everyday life, but here the important point is the linking of past, present, and future in such practice. That is his conception of "prospective memory." David E. Sutton, *Remembrance of Repasts*, 28–29.

53. Nathan Macdonald, *Not Bread Alone*, 72–73.

54. See Baruch M. Bokser, *The Origins of the Seder: The Passover Rite and Early Rabbinic Judaism* (Berkeley: University of California Press, 1984), 1–28.

55. Baruch M. Bokser, *The Origins of the Seder: The Passover Rite and Early Rabbinic Judaism*, 15.

56. J. B. Segal sees this passage as a post-Exodus Passover direction. Although this passage is placed before the real Exodus, the scene of Moses' direction about children asking about Passover ritual observance itself seems to have happened after the real Exodus.

J. B. Segal, *The Hebrew Passover from the Earliest Times to A.D. 70* (London: Oxford University Press, 1963), 55.

57. Ibid., 47–65.

58. J. B. Segal, *The Hebrew Passover from the Earliest Times to A.D. 70,* 78–114; 155–188; Yehezkiel Kaufmann, *The Religion of Israel from Its Beginning to the Babylonian Exile* (Chicago: The University of Chicago, 1960).

59. Ruth Fredman Cernea, *The Passover Seder: An Anthropological Perspective on Jewish Culture* (New York: University Press of America, Inc., 1995), 2–3. See J. B. Segal, *The Hebrew Passover from the Earliest Times to A.D. 70,* 155–188.

60. Ruth Fredman Cernea, *The Passover Seder,* 2.

61. Mary B. Spaulding, *Commemorative Identities: Jewish Social Memory and the Johannine Feast of Booths* (LNTS 396; New York: T & T Clark, 2009), 39; See also Yael Zerubavel, *Collective Memory and Recovered: The Making of Israeli Roots National Tradition* (Chicago: The University of Chicago Press, 1995), 3–12; "Collective memory is substantiated through multiple forms of commemoration," and it dynamically connects the past to the presents, negotiating the shared memories of particular events.

62. Brevard S. Childs, *Memory and Tradition in Israel* (SBT 37; Naperville: A. R. Allenson, 1962), 84–85. Keeping the ceremony and its actualization is the process by which a past event is contemporized in every moment and place that it is practiced; See also Jacob Neusner, *Judaism When Christianity Began: A Survey of Belief and Practice* (Louisville: John Knox Press, 2002), 83–90.

63. Ibid., 84. He sees that the redemptive history continued in the sense that each generation of Israel, living in a concrete situation within history, through the commemorating process.

64. Mary B. Spaulding, *Commemorative Identity,* 15.

65. Paul Ricoeur, *Memory, History, Forgetting* (Chicago: University of Chicago Press, 2004), 84–85. Memory must be incorporated into the formation of identity. Brumberg-Kraus affirms that a ritual meal continues "to be palpable, concrete, experiential means for reinforcing or inculcating members with their distinctive religious identity." See Jonathan Brumberg-Kraus, "Not by bread alone…: The Ritualization of Food and Table Talk in the Passover Seder and in the Last Supper," in *Food and Drink in the Biblical Worlds. Semeia,* vol. 86. (Atlanta: The Society of Biblical Literature, 1999), 165–192.

66. In Jewish culture, the Passover meal and rituals as a symbolic action reveal an intrinsic attribute of God and function as a medium of relationship between man and God. Ruth Fredman Cernea, *The Passover Seder: An Anthropological Perspective on Jewish Culture* (New York: University Press of America, 1995), 4–9; Baruch M. Bokser, *The Origins of the Seder: The Passover Rite and Early Rabbinic Judaism.* 8–22.

67. Baruch M. Bokser, *The Origins of the Seder,* 16–17; J. B. Segal, *The Hebrew Passover from the Earliest Times to A.D. 70,* 55–61.

68. J. B. Segal, *The Hebrew Passover,* 61–62.

69. Baruch M. Bokser, *The Origins of the Seder*, 17.

70. 2 Kings 23:22 reports "no such Passover had been kept since the days of the judges." Here "no such Passover" does not mean that the Passover rite ceased temporarily, but rather it means that the Passover was not performed properly.

71. J. B. Segal, *The Hebrew Passover*, 87.

72. Bokser argues the quality of the Passover event in 2 Chronicles reflects its character of the "national holiday," rejoicing and praising to God. The Passover rite as a national celebration had a special function at the reconstruction of the Temple, when Israelites returned from the Exile (Ezra 6:19–20). See his book, *The Origin of the Seder*, 17–19.

73. William H. C. Propp, *Exodus 1–18: A New Translation with Introduction and Commentary* (AB; New York: Doubleday, 1998), 384.

74. He sees that Genesis contains the Priestly writer's interest about chronometry (e.g., Genesis 1:14–18) and shows God's establishment of the day and week. However, we cannot see any kind of calendarical measure by the month. About the calendar, refer to William H. C. Propp, *Exodus 1–18*, 384–387.

75. William H. C. Propp, *Exodus 1–18*, 384.

76. Ibid., 385.

77. J. B. Segal studied the aspects of the Passover in light of its analogies to the general pattern of New Year festivals in the Near East with various perspectives. For instance, he argues that "the destruction of the firstborn of Egypt and the redemption of the firstborn of Israel are a central feature of the Passover myth," opening a new era in Israelite history. J. B. Segal, *The Hebrew Passover: From the Earliest Time to A.D. 70*, 156–188.

78. J. B. Segal, *The Hebrew Passover*, 155.

79. Ibid., 148–151.

80. Ibid., 149.

81. Ruth Fredman Cernea, *The Passover Seder: An Anthropological Perspective on Jewish Culture* (New York: University Press of America, 1995), 24–25.

82. While God's relationship with Abraham in Genesis was an individual one, here in Exodus the relationship with God shifts to a communal one. Moses' role is just mediating between God and the Israelites.

83. Carol Meyers, *Exodus* (NCBT; New York: Cambridge University Press, 2005), 128.

84. In v. 31, the narrator also clearly names it *manna*.

85. *ABD*. vol. 4, 511.

86. Benno Jacog argued that there is an implicit connection between Manna and the Passover unleavened bread in light of the pure, simple form of bread. See Benno Jacob, *The Second of the Bible: Exodus*, trans. Walter Jacob (New Jersey: Ktav Publishing House, Inc, 1992, 471; See also Willian C. Propp, *Exodus 1–18*, 600–601.

87. The word appears seven times only in 16:1–12.

88. See Walter Brueggemann, "From Hurt to Joy, from Death to Life," *Int 28* (1974), 13–19. This thematic construction is constitutive for the life of Israel.

89. Carol Meyers, *Exodus,* 128: Water crisis (15:22–27), Food Crisis (16:1–36), Water and Military Crisis (17:1–16), Organizational crisis (18:1–27).

90. Walter Brueggemann, *The Land: Place as Gift, Promise, and Challenge in the Biblical Faith* (Second Edition; Minneapolis: Fortress Press, 2002), 29.

91. Carol Meyers, *Exodus,* 130.

92. Benno Jacob, *The Second Book of the Bible: Exodus,* 441.

93. James K. Bruckner, *New International Biblical Commentary: Exodus* (Massachusetts: Hendrickson Publishers, 2008), 150–151.

94. Walter Brueggemann contrasts two schema of life: (1) *Egypt/fullness, Wilderness/hunger/death* in their complaints: In the life of Egypt, they were filled with life-giving resource but destroyed life in slavery. (2) *Egypt/land/being destroyed as slavery, Wilderness/landless/being filled with free* in God's resolution: However, in the life of wilderness, they did not have any land and home, but they were filled with life-giving resource given by God. See Walter Brueggemann, *The Land.* 29–31.

95. Carol Meyers, *Exodus,* 130.

96. Walter Brueggemann, *The Land,* 32–33.

97. L. Juliana M. Claassens, *The God Who Provides–Biblical Images of Divine Nourishment* (Nashville: Abingdon, 2004) pp 1–22. Here, Claassens investigates nursing language, which is used to describe God's provisional care, related with manna in wilderness. For example, the verb "nurse" ינק (Deuteronomy 32:13–14), breast-shaped rocks, mother's milk and the like in Hebrew Scriptures.

98. Ibid., 2.

99. Timothy R. Ashley, *The Book of Numbers* (Michigan: Eerdmans Publishing company, 1993), 206.

100. Ibid., 210. Of course, it is possible to interpret this passage with the image of Moses as a "foster father." But Ashley favors the usual translation, nurse as a feminine meaning.

101. L. Juliana M. Claassens, *God Who Provides—Biblical Images of Divine Nourishment,* 6.

102. Ibid., 7.

103. Walter Brueggemann, *Deuteronomy* (Nashville: Abingdon Press, 2001), 279.

104. Graydon F. Snyder, *Inculturation of the Jesus Tradition—The Impact of Jesus On Jewish and Roman Cultures* (Harrisburg: Trinity Press, 1999), 129–145.

105. Dong-sun Kim, *The Bread for Today and the Bread for Tomorrow* (New York: Peter Lang, 2001), 38–39.

106. Miriam Feinberg Vamosh, *Food at the Time of the Bible from Adam's Apple to the Last Supper* (Herzlia: Abingdon, 2004), 15.

107. Ibid., 11.

108. Miriam Feinberg Vamosh, *Food at the Time of the Bible,* 15.

109. Joseph A. Grassi, *Loaves and Fishes* (Minnesota: The Liturgical Press, 1991), 17.

110. Victor P. Hamilton, *The Book of Genesis: Chapter 18–50* (NICOT; Michigan: Eerdmans Publishing Company, 1995), 207–208.

111. Graydon F. Snyder, *Inculturation of the Jesus Tradition*, 132.

112. Claassens affirms that "the memory of God's provision in the wilderness proved formative in Israel's religious Imagination." L. Juliana M. Claassens, *The God who Provides*, xvi.

113. Claassens' book, *The God who provides* clearly presents that the metaphor God who provides, based on Israel's wilderness experience, offers a striking illustration of God's relationship with Israel. See page 1–62.

114. Ibid., 144.

115. The terms "eschatological banquet" or "apocalyptic banquet" are more correct for the general phenomenon and the meaning of the banquet. The term "messianic banquet" refers primarily to the presence of messiah. See *ABD vol. 4.*, 788; However, in light of Jewish ideological thought and messianic expectation, the term "messianic banquet" is quite reasonable to cover the Jewish image of apocalyptic banquet.

116. This term can be used with eschatological banquet and apocalyptic banquet in the same sense. See Dennis E. Smith. *From Symposium to Eucharist: The Banquet in the Early Christian World*, 166.

117. Dennis E. Smith, *From Symposium to Eucharist: The Banquet in the Early Christian World*, 166–168; *ABD* vol. 4, 788–789.

118. Ibid., 167.

119. For instance, the Gospel of John describes Jesus as "a spring of water" or "living water" for giving an eternal life. The Book of Revelation 22:1–2, 6 and 17–19, the "water of life" also can be parallel to the "tree of life," bestowing the eternal life.

120. Exodus 16:1–17:7; Numbers 11; 20:2–13; cf., Psalm 78:25; 4 Ezra 1:19.

121. L. Juliana M. Claassens, *The God Who Provides*, 63–68.

122. In Joel 2:1–27, God enables his people to engage in agricultural activities, protects them from the enemy invasion, and makes a perfect environment with enough rain for great harvest.

123. Second Baruch 29:8, *APOTE* vol. 2, 498.

124. L. Juliana M. Claassens, *The God Who Provides*, 67.

125. Ibid., 67. The notion of God's presence is more clear in verses 28–29, in which God poured out the spirit upon "all flesh," sons, daughters, old men, and young men.

126. Dennis E. Smith, *From Symposium to Eucharist*, 168; See also T. H. Gaster, *Thespis: Ritual, Myth, and Drama in the Ancient Near East* (New York: Doubleday, 1961), 93–94.

127. Paul D. Hanson, *The Dawn of Apocalyptic* (Philadelphia: Fortress Press, 1975), 300–322; Paul D. Hanson, *Old Testament Apocalyptic* (Nashville: Abingdon Press, 1987).

128. *APOTE* vol. 2, 228.

129. John J. Collins, *The Apocalyptic Imagination: An Introduction to the Jewish Matrix of Christianity* (New York: Crossroad, 1984), 145–147.

130. Ibid., 146.

131. Judith E. Mckinlay, *Gendering Wisdom the Host—Biblical Invitations to Eat and Drink* (Sheffield: Sheffield Academic Press, 1996), 46.

132. "Seven" is a round or typological number. This number usually connotes completeness or appropriateness. The pillars of Solomon's temple had seven meshwork decorations (1 Kings 7:17). See Michael V. Fox, *Proverbs 1–9* (AB; New York: Doubleday, 2000), 297.

133. Leo G. Perdue, *Proverbs—Interpretation* (Louisville: John Knox Press, 2000), 151–152.

134. Here Woman Wisdom as the queen of heaven dispenses wisdom and life to her devotees and chooses kings to rule in justice. Through the righteous reign of the kings chosen by Wisdom, justice will permeate the cosmos and the social order; harmony and well being will be actualized in the kingdom. See Leo G. Perdue, *Wisdom Literature: A Theological History* (Louisville: John Knox Press, 2007), 74–75.

135. Michael V. Fox, *Proverbs 1–9*, 297–298.

136. Judith E. Mckinlay, *Gendering Wisdom the Host—Biblical Invitations to Eat and Drink*, 38–80.

137. Michael V. Fox, *Proverb 1–9*, 299. See also Judith E. Mckinlay, *Gendering Wisdom the Host*, 52–55.

138. In terms of giving life, the image of God who prepares a table can be found in Psalms 23:5; 146; Proverbs 9; Isaiah 25:6. See Judith E. Mckinlay, *Gendering Wisdom the Host*, 55.

139. L. Juliana M. Claassens, *The God Who Provides*, 88.

140. Gillian Feeley-Harnik, *The Lord's Table: The Meaning of Food in Early Judaism and Christianity*, 82.

141. Nathan Macdonald, *Not Bread Alone*, 205–207.

142. As Israelites commemorate the festival of unleavened bread, it serves the Israelites as a reminder of God's liberating power and complete care in the wilderness and teaches them knowledge of God. (Exodus 13:9–10).

143. Michael V. Fox, *Proverbs 1–9*, 297–298.

144. Terry Eagleton, *Literary Theory: An Introduction* (Second Edition; Minnesota: University of Minnesota Press, 1996).

145. Leo G. Perdue, *Wisdom Literature: A Theological History*, 75–76.

146. Moshe Greenberg, *Ezekiel 1–20, ABC.* (New York: Doubleday, 1983), 73.

147. Denis E. Smith, *From Symposium to Eucharist*, 133–144. He quotes from Ben Sira and finds a description of Jewish meals as "*symposirach,*" corresponding to general Greco-Roman customs. He found the relations between them in terms of the form of the meal, the types of etiquette discussed, the philosophical basis for etiquette, the similarities to the symposium literary tradition, and the function of the meal in the life and teaching of the stages. See also Michael V. Fox, *Proverbs 1–9, ABC.* 305–309.

148. Sirach chapters 31–32 clearly shows its parallelism to Greco-Roman symposium: general etiquette at the table (31:12–18), gluttony (31:19–22), liberality (31:23–24), wine (31:25–30), argument (31:31), presiding at the table (32:1–2), etc.
149. Michael V. Fox, *Proverbs 1–9*, 306.
150. L. Juliana M. Claassens, *The God Who Provides*, 16.

Chapter 3: The Metaphor of Bread in Feeding Narratives and Matthean Community

1. Many scholars see this narrative as primarily representing Jesus' identity and the motif of Jesus being greater than famous Israelite heroes and secular persons. In this regard, some scholars see this miraculous event corresponding to the miraculous events performed by Elijah in the Old Testament (the jar of meal: 1 Kings 17:8–16; the vessels of oil: 2 Kings 4:1–7; Elisha feeds one hundred men: 2 Kings 4:42–44), and it echoes the Passover meal and the image of Moses as prophet, expecting Jesus to redeem his people at Passover. See Roger David Aus, *Feeding the Five Thousand: Studies in the Judaic Background of Mark 6:30–44 par. And John 6:1–15* (SJ; Maryland: University Press of America, 2010), 19–40, 14–176; Dale C. Allison, Jr. *The New Moses: A Matthean Typology* (Minneapolis: Fortress Press, 1993).

2. Gerd Theissen, *The Miracle Stories of the Early Christian Tradition* (Edinburgh: Fortress, 1983), 103–106. Theissen categorizes this story as a "gift miracle" in which the main character shows the ability to handle some material goods in surprising ways, including exorcisms and healings. See also, John Nolland, *The Gospel of Matthew: A Commentary on the Greek Text* (*NIGTC*; Michigan: The Paternoster Press, 2005), 587; J. Billy, "Feeding the Multitude: Confronting the Mystery of Jesus," in *Emman* 108 (2002), 68–78; Dale C. Allison, Jr., *The New Moses: A Matthean Typology* (Minneapolis: Fortress Press, 1993); Robert H. Gundry, *Matthew: A Commentary on His Literary and Theological Art* (Grand Rapids: Eerdmans Publishing Company, 1982).

3. Davies and Allison, *The Critical and Exegetical Commentary on the Gospel According to Saint Matthew*. vol. 1. (*ICC*; Edinburgh: T & T Clark, 1991), 376; and see also volume 2: 486; Robert H. Gundry, *Matthew: A Commentary on His Literary and Theological Art* (Grand Rapids: Eerdmans Publishing Company, 1982), 290. According to Gundry, Matthew chose this verb, which is actually Matthew's favorite, for connoting "flight from danger." Interestingly, ἀναχωρέω appears 14 times in New Testament, of which 10 are in the Gospel of Matthew. *TDNT*. vol. 1, 95.

4. Matthew 4:21; 9:9, 27; 11:1; 12:9, 15; 13:53; 15:21, 29; 19:15.

5. Robert H. Gundry, *Matthew*, 290.

6. Deirdre Good, "The Verb ΑΝΑΧΩΡΕΩ In Matthew's Gospel," in *Novum Testamentum* XXXII, 1 (1990): 1–12.

7. *Ibid.*, 6–10. In 1 Maccabees 9:62 and 12:28; and 2 Maccabees 4:33; 5:27; 12:7; 13:16; 22, the verb is used to describe various military strategies. Good shows an example in 2 Maccabees 5:27 where Judas Maccabaeus and his follower withdraw into a deserted place in order to hide themselves, when Apollonius kills loyal Jews. So, basically the usage of ἀναχώρεω for hiding or retreat from danger or hostility occurs, even in Second Temple literature.

8. Ibid., 6.

9. Ibid., 12.

10. Ibid., 12.

11. Matthew 14:13, 15; Mark 1:35; 6:31, 32, 35; Luke 4:42; 9:12; Revelation 12:6; 12:14.

12. John Nolland, *The Gospel of Matthew*, 589; See also Davies and Allison, *The Gospel According to Saint Matthew*, vol. 2, 486.

13. This term does not have to indicate desert, but it is a place "without inhabitants," "empty," or "a lonely place." See *TDNT*. vol. 2, 657–660.

14. Daniel J. Harrington, S.J., *The Gospel of Matthew* (Sacra Pagina; Minnesota: Liturgical Press, 2007), 219; Allison sees this place may be the northwestern shore of the Sea of Galilee; Davies and Allison, vol. 2, 486.

15. Daniel J. Harrington, S.J., *The Gospel of Matthew*, 219.

16. John Nolland, *The Gospel of Matthew: A Commentary on the Greek Text*, 589.

17. The Old Testament has a number of Hebrew words to designate wilderness such as מִדְבָּר (midhbar), עֲרָבָה (aravah), חָרְבָּה (khorbah), שְׁמָמָה (shemamah), which mean "desolated place," "uncultivated land," "desolate wilderness." The Greek term ἔρημος is mostly used in the New Testament. *NIDB*. Vol 5, 848–852; *ABD*. Vol 6, 912–14.

18. For instance, Midhbar refers to semi-arid, unsettled and uncultivated land (e.g., Genesis 36:24), Aravah designates an infertile plain (e.g., Deuteronomy 3:17), and Shemamah refers to a wasteland or desolation, usually a destroyed land (e.g., 2 Kings 22:19); See *NIDB*. vol. 5. 848–852.

19. The wilderness accounts are found primarily in Exodus. 14; 15:22–17:15; Numbers. 10:33–22:1; 33:1–49; Deuteronomy 1:19–3:29; Psalm 78:105; 106; 81:7; 95:8–11; 135:10–12; 136:16–22; Jeremiah 2:2–6; Ezekiel 20:10–26; Hosea 2:14–15; 13:4–5; Amos 2:10; 5:25.

20. Daniel J. Harrington, S.J., *The Gospel of Matthew*, 219.

21. Donald A. Hanger. *Matthew 14–28* (WBC. vol. 33b; Dallas: Word Books, 1995), 417; Davies and Allison, 488.

22. John Nolland, *The Gospel of Matthew*, 590.

23. W. D. Davies and Dale C. Allison, *The Gospel According to Saint Matthew*, 488.

24. According to Exodus 12:18, the Feast of Unleavened Bread begins on the fourteenth "at evening." See William H. C. Propp, *Exodus 1–18: A New Translation with Introduction and Commentary* (AB; New York: Doubleday, 1998), 391.

25. Interestingly, Matthew's narrator omits the comparison between the crowds and "the sheep without a shepherd" in the first feeding scene (14:14), while the Markan narrative contains a comparison (Mk 6:24). However, there is no significant difference between two narratives because both narratives used the terms of σπλαγχνίζομαι to describe Jesus' emotion, and Matthew already expresses the comparison in the previous chapter in 9:35–36. So, in the case of Matthew's Gospel, the narrator does not need to repeat the comparison in the first feeding narrative.

26. *TDNT*. vol. 7, 554. In the synoptic tradition, σπλαγχνίζομαι is used for the Messiah in whom the divine mercy is present.

27. See previous chapter in the subsection titled *Manna: Bread from Heaven*. E.g., Exodus 2:9; 16:1–36; Numbers 11:1–15; Deuteronomy 32:7–14.

28. *TDNT*. vol. 5. 582–584.

29. Ibid., 586.

30. Anthony J. Saldarini, *Matthew's Christian-Jewish Community*, 37. Most of Matthew's crowds are Jesus' audience and followers who marveled at Jesus' teaching and miraculous deeds. However, they are not one single group or fixed unity. (e.g., 4:25; 5:1; 7:28–8:1; 9:8; 9:33, 36; 10:6; 11:1; 11:25–27;12:23, 46; 14:5;14:13–15; 15:10, 30–33; 17:14; 19:2; 20:29; 21:26; 22:33; 23:1).

31. In the case of Decapolis, John Nolland sees that the region of Decapolis was "reckoned to have been part of the Promised Land as originally given." John Nolland, *The Gospel of Matthew*, 185.

32. Robert H. Gundry, *Matthew*, 290–291. One of the interesting characteristics of Matthew's crowds is that they always follow Jesus.

33. Anthony J. Saldarini, *Matthew's Christian-Jewish Community*, 37–40; Saldarini sees that "ninety percent of the population were peasants and artisans," who had no direct access to social power.

34. Daniel Harrington, *The Gospel of Matthew*, 66.

35. Here one can compare Jesus with Moses' fasting on Mount Sinai (Exodus 34:28) and Moses as a leader can be regarded as a representative of Israel.

36. As Israel took a long period of testing before entering the Promised Land, Jesus had a similar testing period before the kingdom appears in his ministry. See B. Gerhardsson, *The Testing of God's Son* (Lund: Gleerup, 1966); David E. Holwerda, *Jesus and Israel: One Covenant or Two?* (Michigan: Eerdmans Publishing, 1995).

37. David E. Holwerda, *Jesus and Israel*, 47; R. T. France, *Jesus and the Old Testament Studies* (Downers Grove: InterVarsity, 1971), 50–53.

38. David E. Holwerda, *Jesus and Israel*, 66–69. Israel's wandering experience in the wilderness is expressed in terms of a test by God (Deut 8:2); and there Israel frequently failed the test, grumbling to God about the fact that they have no food.

39. Ulrich Luz, *Matthew 1–7: A Commentary*, trans. James E. Crouch. (Hermeneia; Minneapolis: Fortress Press, 2007), 152. Deuteronomy 8:2–5 presents the way in

which God led Israel during forty years in the wilderness to test whether it would keep his commandment.

40. Daniel J. Harrington, *The Gospel of Matthew*, 66.

41. Compared to the Markan feeding narrative 6:35–37, many scholars see that Matthew's narrator weakens the link with the two feeding miracles in Old Testament, associated with Elisha in 2 King 4:38–41 and 42–44. So, the narrative tries to remain to focused more on Jesus' identity or the discourse of faith and understandings of disciples. John Nolland, *The Gospel of Matthew*, 591; Davies and Allison, *Matthew.* vol. 2, 488–489.

42. Of course, the reader takes into account the amount of food here. However, what I mean by this is that Matthew's change from the Markan narrative has a narrative function to highlight the fact that the crowds eat the bread together and weaken the deficiency. Davies and Allison argue that this change shows the difference of the disciples' faith in Mark and Matthew. While Markan disciples fail to understand what Jesus has in mind, Matthew's disciples understand. Davies and Allison, *Matthew.* vol. 2, 489.

43. See the previous chapter about bread in Hebrew Scripture and Second Temple literature. Ancient Israel has kept commemorating Passover meal and the manna and made them a ritual for observing throughout the generations. All these commemorating and ritualizing processes functioned to formulate and maintain Israel's socio-religious communal identity.

44. Numbers 11:31 clearly describes the origin of quail as the living creature in the sea (Wisdom of Solomon 19:10–12). See Daniel J. Harrington, *The Gospel of Matthew*, 219; Davies and Allison, *Matthew.* vol. 2, 489; John Nolland, *The Gospel of Matthew*, 591. The fish also can be linked to the eschatological banquet through the expectation of eating the flesh of Leviathan (Bar. 29:3–8; 4 Ezra 6:49–52).

45. *TDNT.* vol. 2, 755.

46. In Matthew 15:36, the narrator used the verb εὐχαριστήσας, (give thanks), which is like the one used in Mark 8:6–7; 1 Cor. 14:16. In fact, there is the equation of the usage of εὐλογέω and εὐχριστέω in Mark 8:6–7 and 14:22 and John 6:11. Davies and Allison, *Matthew*, vol. 2, 490–491.

47. Daniel Harrington, *The Gospel of Matthew*, 219–220. Nolland sees the sequence of verbs as part of a normal Jewish meal pattern. John Nolland, *The Gospel of Matthew*, 592. Also refer to *TDNT.* vol. 2, 760.

48. In Jewish culture at Jesus' time, the main part of the meals is "opened with a blessing usually pronounced by the head of the house with a piece of bread in his hand. The others confirm it with Amen. After this the head of the house breaks the bread and distributes to those who sit at table with him. He himself eats first." *TDNT*, vol. 2, 760.

49. *TDNT.* vol. 2, 761.

50. Francis Wright Beare, *The Gospel According to Matthew* (New York: Harper & Row, 1981) 326–328. Beare argues that from the earlier times the bread and fish have been

depicted on the table in symbolic representations of the Eucharist in the Synoptic accounts.

51. Ulrich Luz, *Matthew 8–20*, 314.

52. The expression is normally used in reference to bread to describe the act of sharing a meal in the New Testament. (Mark 6:41; 14:22; Luke 9:16; Matthew 14:19; 15:36; Acts 2:42, 46; 20:7, 11). *NIDB*. vol. 1, 500.

53. *TDNT*. vol. 3, 728–729.

54. In the early Church, the communal meals are normally recognized as the ritual with the expression of "break bread" (Acts. 2:42, 46; 20:7, 11).

55. In an ancient Palestinian custom, the breaking of bread is enacted by the hands rather than cutting it with a knife (Jeremiah 16:7).

56. Source Domain = "the breaking of the bread." Target Domain = "the end of hostility, making a covenant, and the actual formation of new community." Refer to the part on methodologies in the introduction.

57. See Anthony J. Saldarini, *Matthew's Christian-Jewish Community*, 37–40.

58. In light of the Eucharistic overtones, many scholars see that the feeding narratives foreshadow the Last Supper meal. David. L. Turner, *Matthew* (BECNT; Michigan: Baker Academic, 2008), 369; Robert H. Gundry, *Matthew*, 292–294; Davies and Allison see the feeding scene as an "allegory of the Eucharist." Davies and Allison, vol. 2, 481.

59. Genesis 14:18–20; 26:26–31; 27–28; 29:22; 31:44–46; 51–54; Joshua 9:3–15; Judges 9:26–28; 2 Samuel 3:20; 9:7; 10–11; Proverbs 15:17; 17:1; See Gillian Feeley-Harnik, *The Lord's Table: The Meaning of Food in Early Judaism and Christianity* (Washington: Smithsonian Books, 1994), 85–87.

60. Numbers 18:19; 2 Chronicles 13:5; Ezra 4:14. Even in the relationship between Yahweh and Israelites, both identify and maintain their common obligation in the covenant through the common meal, "eating before God." (Exodus 18:12; Deut 12:7, 18). *Ibid.*, 87.

61. In the wisdom literatures, the Torah is described as bread (Proverbs 9). See Davies and Allison, *Matthew*. vol. 2, 489–490; Luz emphasizes that as far as the number five is concerned, some scholars affirm that the five loaves remind us that in rabbinic language bread may be a symbol for the Torah, so that one might think of the five books of Moses. Ulrich Luz, *Matthew 8–20*, 314; Davies and Allison see that two fishes can be applied for the Psalms and the prophets or the apostles and the gospel in New Testament. However, Luz sees that no symbolic connotation of two fishes is found.

62. Gillian Feeley-Harnik, *The Lord's Table*, 71–84. Conversely, the rejection of authority is symbolized by the refusal to participate in a meal or the prohibition of the food.

63. Ibid., 82–85.

64. The number itself can relate to the twelve disciples in the Gospels, who it symbolically reveals as representatives of the twelve tribes of Israel. As far as the new Israel is

concerned, the use of δώδεκα must be linked to the book of Revelation. In fact, the twelve tribes were a composition of the people of God in the Old Testament. This compositional number twelve occurs again in the measurements and arrangements of the New Jerusalem in the book of Revelation (12:1; 12:5; 21:12, 14, 16, 20). Here the number twelve is related to the plan of the city of God under the divine order and purpose. So, the twelve can remind the reader of the ancient constitution of Israel, and at the same time represents the eventual form of the Messianic community. See *TDNT*, 321–328; Daniel Harrington, *The Gospel of Matthew*, 220; John Nolland, *The Gospel of Matthew*, 594.

65. John Nolland, *The Gospel of Matthew*, 594.

66. E.g., Jeremiah 31:11–14; Amos 9:13–15; Joel 2:18–27; Isaiah 24–27 (eschatological banquet); Especially, in the prophetic literature God's miraculous provision presents Israel's vision and symbol of God's restoration. See L. Juliana M. Claassens, *The God Who Provides*, 64–75.

67. Both Moses and Jesus occupied several common features. Allison observes Matthew's "Moses typology"; Allison reads Matthew's Gospel and its portrait of Jesus as a typological frame in which Moses was described as "the paradigmatic prophetic-king, the Messiah's model, a worker of miracles, a giver of Torah, the mediator of Israel, and a suffering servant." See Dale C. Allison, Jr., *The New Moses: A Matthean Typology* (Minneapolis: Fortress Press, 1993); Terence L. Donaldson, *Jesus on the Mountain; A Study in Matthean Theology* (JSNTS 8; Sheffield: JSOT Press, 1985), 30–50.

68. Jesus cleanses a Leper (8:1–4); Jesus heals a Centurion's servant (8:5–13); Jesus heals Peter's mother in law and many others (8:14–17); Jesus stills a storm (8:23–27); Jesus heals the Gadarene Demoniacs (8:28–34); Jesus heals a paralytic (9:2–8); Jesus heals the woman with hemorrhages for twelve years (9:18–26); Jesus heals two blind men (9:27–31); Jesus heals one who was mute (9:32–34).

69. Numbers 27:17; "so that the congregation of the Lord may not be like sheep without a shepherd"; 1 Kings 22:17; 2 Chronicles 18:16; the prophets used flock-shepherd imagery for describing the exile (Ezekiel 34:5; Zechariah 13:7).

70. Daniel J. Harrington, *The Gospel of Matthew*, 138.

71. Ibid., 136.

72. Donald Senior, *The Gospel of Matthew* (IBT; Nashville: Abingdon Press, 1997), 114–115.

73. Deirdre Good, "The Verb ΑΝΑΧΩΡΕΩ In Matthew's Gospel," in *Novum Testamentum* XXXII, 1 (1990): 1–12. As was stated, Jesus' withdrawal is not just for fleeing from the potential persecution but also for an intentional moving and transition to fulfill what he is supposed to do. So, as Deirdre Good calls the motif of ἀναχώρεω "prophetic fulfillment," the reader can expect a kind of "prophetic fulfillment" in the first feeding story.

74. Davies and Allison, *Matthew*. vol. 2, 165; John Nolland sees that the phrase is influenced by the use of εἰς ὁδὸν in Mark 6:8, and matches it with the LXX, presenting "in the direction of the Gentile." John Nolland, *The Gospel of Matthew*, 415.

75. Dorothy Jean Weaver, *Matthew's Missionary Discourse–A Literary Critical Analysis* (JSNTS 38; Sheffield: JSOT Press, 1990), 84, 192; Daniel J. Harrington, *The Gospel of Matthew*, 140.

76. John Nolland, *The Gospel of Matthew*, 415.

77. Robert H. Gundry, *Matthew*, 185.

78. After Jesus had a debate with Pharisees and Scribes about the tradition of the Elders, he withdrew to the district of Tyre and Sidon. (15:21). Up to chapter 15, Jesus has never crossed the border of Israel, only the narrator places Jesus on the Gadarenes (8:28) for healing the demon possessed man.

79. Ulrich Luz, *Matthew 8–20*, 344.

80. Daniel J. Harrington, *The Gospel of Matthew*, 78.

81. In the LXX, הַר corresponds principally to ὄρος, the adjective ὀρενός (the hill country), or its substantive ὀρεινη (Mountainous region). There is no clear semantic difference between ὀρενός and ὄρος, so the phrase τὸ ὄρος can be used with the general meaning of הר. See Terence L. Donaldson, *Jesus on the Mountain—A Study in Matthean Theology* (JSNTSS 8; Sheffield: JSOT Press, 1985), 9–10.

82. *TDNT*. vol. 5, 475–487. God is exalted above the hills, the oldest, highest and most solid things on earth. (Psalms 90:2; 95:4; 65:5). God is described to grind and crush the earth, and the earthly things are nothing before God (Isaiah. 40:12; 40:4; Jeremiah. 4:24; Job 9:5; 28:9; Ezekiel. 38:20; Habakkuk. 3:6, etc).

83. Ibid., 281–282. The mountain shows God's blessing and curse to the Israelites (Deuteronomy 11:29; 27:12; Joshua 8:33). And the mountain is a dwelling place of Yahweh and the altar of burnt offering (1 Chronicles 16:39; 21:29; 2 Chronicles 1:3, 13). The Mount Sinai and Zion are the lawful places of revelation.

84. Terence L. Donaldson, *Jesus on the Mountain—A Study in Matthean Theology*, 30–86; 122–135.

85. Ibid., 31. The designation of the mountain of the law also appears with "Horeb." (Exodus 3:1; 17:6).

86. Ibid., 33. Yahweh comes in cloud and fire on Mount Sinai in order to meet with Moses. Here, Yahweh comes (Exodus 19:9) or descends (19:18; 34:5) to the mountain.

87. Ibid., 33.

88. Ibid., 35.

89. Ibid., 36.

90. Ibid., 36–37.

91. Such as Psalms 2, 18, 20, 21, 45, 72, 89, 101, 132.

92. Ibid., 37–40; Here the Mount Zion would be a secure stronghold, and it is eternal and immovable (Psalm 125:1).

93. Ibid., 41.

94. Ibid., 41–49.

95. Ibid., 42.

96. Ibid., 44.

97. In this case, Garland, Gnilka, Ulrich Luz, Daniel Patte, John Nolland, and J.R.C. Cousland basically identified the crowds as Jews and connect this scene to "the lost sheep of the house of Israel" (15:24) as an implementation of Jesus' vocational program.

98. Davies and Allison, Blomberg, D.A. Carson, France, Gundry, Robert H. Mounce, Daniel Harrington, Davis Turner see the crowd as Gentiles, connecting to Jesus' concern for the Gentile mission and the great commission (28:19–20).

99. Ulrich Luz, *Matthew 8–20*, 345.

100. Ibid., 345.

101. Robert H. Gundry, *Matthew*, 317–322; Daniel J. Harrington, *The Gospel of Matthew*, 239–240; Davies and Allison, *Matthew*. vol. 2, 561–566.

102. Daniel Harrington, *The Gospel of Matthew*, 240.

103. D. A. Carson, *Matthew 13–28* (EBC; Michigan: Zondervan, 1995), 357.

104. Fredrick. D. Bruner, *Matthew: The Chruchbook. Matthew 13–28* (Dallas: Word Books, 1990), 559.

105. Robert H. Mounce, *Matthew* (NIBC 1: Peabody: Hendrickson, 1991), 154. See also, L. Morris, *Matthew* (Grand Rapids: Eerdmans, 1992), 407; R. T. France, *Matthew* (NICNT; Grand Rapids: Eerdmans, 2007), 248.

106. Daniel J. Harrington, *The Gospel of Matthew*, p 239.

107. See J. R. C. Cousland, "The Feeding of the Four Thousand Gentiles in Matthew?– Matthew 15:29–39 as a Test Case," in *Novum Testamentum*, Vol. 41. (1999): 1–23. See also, W. D. Davies and Dale C. Allison, Jr., *The Gospel According to Saint Matthew*. vol. 2, 561–565.

108. J. R. C. Cousland, "The Feeding of the Four Thousand Gentiles in Matthew?– Matthew 15:29–39 as a Test Case," 18.

109. Ibid., 18.

110. Ibid., 19.

111. Janice Capel Anderson, *Matthew's Narrative Web: Over, and Over, and Over Again* (JSNTS 91; Sheffield: JSOT Press, 1994), 126–132.

112. Daniel J. Harrington, *The Gospel of Matthew*, 241. Also there is no mention of fish in the disciples' asking.

113. Ibid., 242.

114. In the first feeding narrative, the narrator used the verb εὐλογέω, which means "blessed" (Matthew 14:19; Mark 6:41), so the reader can recognize the different

usage of the Greek verb here. However, the verb εὐχαριστέω is also used as the word for grace at meals like εὐλογέω in Jewish culture. See *TDNT*, 803–806.

115. E.g., 4:23–25; 5:1; 8:1, 14–17, 23;14:13, 34–36; 15:30–31; 19:1–2.

116. Robert H. Gundry, *Matthew*, 317–319.

117. It is more appropriate that Jesus asks, "Do you have any food?" and "How much do you have?" But here Jesus specifically asked about the number of loaves the disciples have, not even talking about the fish. Here the narrator intentionally emphasizes the bread itself and its number.

118. Daniel J. Harrington, *The Gospel of Matthew*, 241. "The seventy nations of the world, the seven deacons of Acts 6:1–7," indicate the world-wide mission feature in early Christianity. Gundry see that the seven symbolizes that "the Gentile part of the church stumbles over the fact that the seven deacons" in Acts 6 were all Hellenistic Jews, not Gentiles. Robert H. Gundry, *Matthew*, 321; See also Davies and Allison, *Matthew*. vol. 2, 563; Hagner see that although the crowds in the second feeding narrative were Jews, the number seven points to fullness and perfection and "seventy" gentile nations. So the feeding itself symbolizes the meeting of the needs of the Gentiles as a fullness of messianic provision for the entire world. Donald A. Hagner, *Matthew 14–28*, 451–452.

119. Davies and Allison, *Matthew*. vol. 2, 563; Daniel J. Harrington, *The Gospel of Matthew*, 241.

120. *BDAG*. Second Edition, 447.

121. *BDAG*. Second Edition, 764; *NIDB*, vol. 1, 408; It was used in Acts 9:25; Paul was let down over the wall out of the city of Damascus in a basket; See also 2 Cor. 11:32–33. So, it is a basket large enough for carrying even people.

122. Donald A. Hagner, *Matthew 14–28*, 418; Daniel J. Harrington, *The Gospel of Matthew*, 241.

123. Contrast to Ulich Luz, who sees that Matthew is not interested in a feeding of the Jews or the Gentiles. He clearly affirms, "there is no advance in the second feeding over the first." Luz insists that Matthew's gospel does not highlight the difference, but it intends to use repetitious stories as "types," which present Jesus again and again dealing with only his people Israel. Ulrich Luz, *Matthew 8–20*, 345–346.

124. Terence L. Donaldson, *Jesus on the Mountain*, 30–50.

125. Francis Wright Beare, *The Gospel According to Matthew*, 327. Here, Beare also argues the feeding of the multitudes was an "eschatological sacrament."

126. Many commentaries mostly concentrate on the mountain setting in other narratives such as "the sermon on the mount," "the mountain of transfiguration," or "the scene of commissioning."

127. Based on the Sinai tradition and Mosaic covenant, which is basic motif of Israel's covenantal relationship with Yahweh, the Israel have established their own community and religious-political identity. (Exodus 3:1; 4:27; 17:6; 18:5; 19:10–15; 24:13; Numbers 10:33).

128. L. Juliana M. Claassens, *The God Who Provides*, 72–75; Terence L. Donaldson, *Jesus on the Mountain*, 35–43.

129. Terence L. Donaldson, *Jesus on the Mountain*, 35–38.

130. Ibid., 42.

131. L. Juliana M. Claassens, *The God Who Provides*, 73.

132. Terence L. Donaldson, *Jesus on the Mountain*, 128.

133. Donaldson argues that Matthew's mountain of feeding must be seen in a Zion perspective. So, he sees the feeding narrative as a Christological fulfillment of the expectations of Zion Eschatology. Terence L. Donaldson, *Jesus on the Mountain*, 131.

134. The narrative of the Canaanite woman whose faith is accepted by Jesus (15:21–28) functions as a transitional part between the first feeding narrative (14:13–21) and the second feeding narrative (15:29–39) in terms of Jesus' mission. In the Gospel of Matthew as a whole, the narrative of the Canaanite woman as a center of Gospel divides the first phase of Jesus' ministry and the second phase.

135. Daniel Harrington sees the story of the Centurion as Matthew's insertion of a prophecy about Gentiles sharing in a messianic banquet later while some Jews are shut out of it (8:11–12), *The Gospel of Matthew*, 117; Donald A. Hagner, *Matthew 1–13, WBC*, 203–206; Robert H. Gundry, *Matthew*, 140–147; Ulrich Luz, *Matthew 8–20*, 11; Luz argues that Jesus has seen many Gentiles having the faith in Jesus, so Jesus challenges his own church to become involved in the gentile mission.

136. This passage is also found in Luke 13:28–29, but the context is completely different from Matthew and Luke added "north and south."

137. See Davies and Allison, *Matthew*, vol. 2, 27–29; Dale C. Allison, Jr., "Who will Come from East and West? Observations on Matthew 8:11–12–Luke 13:28–29," in *IBS*, (1989): 158–170; E. P. Sanders, *Jesus and Judaism* (London: SCM Press, 1985), 219–220.

138. Davies and Allison, *Matthew*. vol. 2, 27–29.

139. Michael F. Bird, *Jesus and the Origins of the Gentile Mission* (LNTS 331; New York: T & T Clark, 2006), 87.

140. Davies and Allison, *Matthew*, vol. 2, 27–28.

141. The Parable of the lost sheep (18:10–14), the parable of the unforgiving servant (18:23–35), the parable of the laborers in the vineyard (20:1–16), the parable of the wicked Tenant (21:33–44), the parable of the Wedding Banquet (22:1–14).

142. In this section, I will draw the concept of the Third Space, which was mostly developed by Homi Bhabha, into my hermeneutic lens to see the context of Matthean community and its relevant identity.

143. Daniel Patte, *The Gospel According to Matthew: A Structural Commentary on Matthew's Faith* (Philadelphia: Fortress Press, 1987), 209. The place Jesus joined is "where one is free from social relationships; a place where social relationships do not and cannot play the central role they play in society."

144. Saldarini argues that members of Matthew's community as a fragile minority recognize themselves as Jews and follow Jewish heritage. At the same time, as a deviant sect or group, this community is alienated from the larger Jewish community that did not accept Jesus. See Anthony J. Saldarini, *Matthew's Christian-Jewish Community* (Chicago: The University of Chicago Press, 1994); "The Gospel of Matthew and Jewish-Christian Conflict," in *Social History of the Matthean Community: Cross-Disciplinary Approaches*, ed. D. L. Balch (Minneapolis: Fortress Press, 1991), 37–61; see also J. Andrew Overman, *Matthew's Gospel and Formative Judaism: The Social World of the Matthew Community* (Minneapolis: Fortress Press, 1990).

145. Refer to the previous section of Jesus' second feeding narrative.

146. The term "Magi" has been retained in the translation because modern language and other alternatives are not appropriate or accurate; Some interpret it as "wise men," "kings," or "astrologers." See Daniel J. Harrington, S.J., *The Gospel of Matthew*, 42. Harrington sees the term "Magi" to refer to a caste of Persian priests with expertise in the interpretation of dreams. Gundry argues that Matthew gets the Magi from Old Testament, in particular Dan 2:2, 10, which can infer the Magi as astrologers. Some other scholars see "from the East" as a representation of Arabia, which is 'east' in the biblical tradition (Genesis 10:30; Judge 6:3; Job 1:3; Isaiah 11:14) and Babylon, the land of the east.' See also Robert H. Gundry, *Matthew*, 26–27; Davies and Allison, *Matthew*, vol. 1, 227–231.

147. Davies and Allison, *Matthew*. vol. 1, 228.

148. If they were Jews, they must know where the messiah is to be born according to Jewish apocalyptic tradition. Daniel J. Harrington, *The Gospel of Matthew*, 42.

149. Ibid., 49.

150. There were many cases of the inclusion of Gentile proselytes in first-century Judaism. In fact, the inclusion of non-Jews is clearly reflected in the prophetic vision of Israel to share the banquet of God's kingdom with the nations (e.g., Isaiah 2:2–4; 42:6; 49:6–a light to the nations; 45:44–23; 51:4–5; 53:4; 56:7; 60:2; Zechariah 8:20–23). However, it just shows a vision of the inclusion of proselytes, not a vision of active mission and out-reach to the nations.

151. Davies and Allison, *Matthew*, vol. 2, 18–19.

152. E.g., Isaiah 2:2–4; 25:6; Micah 4:1–4; Zechariah 2:11–12; 8:20–23.

153. "Sons of the kingdom" appears in 13:38, which represents the actual heirs of the kingdom. However, in 8:12, this phrase means natural heirs of the kingdom. John Nolland, *The Gospel of Matthew*, 357; Allison, *Matthew*, vol. 2, 30–31; Daniel J. Harrington, *The Gospel of Matthew*, 114.

154. Daniel J. Harrington, *The Gospel of Matthew*, 117.

155. Philip A. Harland, *Dynamics of Identity in the World of the Early Christians: Associations Judeans, and Cultural Minorities* (New York: T & T Clark, 2009); Klaus

Berger, *Identity and Experience in the New Testament*. Trans. Charles Muenchow. (Minneapolis: Fortress Press, 2003).

156. Anthony J. Saldarini, *Matthew's Christian-Jewish Community*, 27–43.

157. See Anthony J. Saldarini, *Matthew's Christian-Jewish Community*; J. Andrew Overman, *Matthew's Gospel and Formative Judaism: The Social World of the Matthean Community* (Minneapolis: Fortress Press, 1990).

158. Anthony J. Saldarini, "Reading Matthew Without Anti-Semitism" in *The Gospel of Matthew In Current Study: Studies in Memory of William G. Thompson, S.J.*, ed. David E. Aune (Michigan: Eerdmans Publishing Company, 2001), 166–170; Anthony J. Saldarini, *Matthew's Christian-Jewish Community*, 44–67.

159. Most potential dangers are caused by the Jewish leaders. When Jesus heard John had been arrested right after the temptation story, Jesus withdrew into Galilee (ἀνεχώρησεν εἰς τὴν Γαλιλαίαν; 4:12). When the Pharisees plan to destroy Jesus at the counsel, Jesus withdrew from there (ἀνεχώρησεν ἐκεῖθεν;12:15). When he got the news of the death of John the Baptist, he withdrew from there (ἀνεχώρησεν ἐκεῖθεν; 14:13). Right after the big debate with some Pharisees and scribes, Jesus withdrew to the district of Tyre and Sidon (Ἰησοῦς ἀνεχώρησεν εἰς τὰ μέρη Τύρου καὶ Σιδῶνος; 15:21). Most uses of the term ἀναχώρεω occur in the face of potential hostility with Jesus' intentional move to somewhere else.

160. See the previous chapter of this book on the narrative features of ἀναχώρεω. See also Deirdre Good, "The Verb ΑΝΑΧΩΡΕΩ In Matthew's Gospel," in *Novum Testamentum* XXXII, 1 (1990): 1–12; The motif of ἀναχώρεω is a special feature of the Gospel of Matthew and presents a "three-fold pattern of hostility/withdrawal/ prophetic fulfillment."

161. Unlike the other gospels, Matthew makes Jesus refer to this term ἐκκλησία twice in 16:18 and 18:17.

162. Church as a Christian community is totally separated from Judaism and the Jewish Torah. It is an institutionalized organization in which the Gentile Christians are the main components. Also the Church communities, according to the Pauline letter and Acts, are placed outside of Israel and Syria, Antioch, and Western Asia Minor.

163. *Ekklesia* often translates the Hebrew קָהָל (qahal), meaning 'assembly, convocation, congregation.' This term is mostly found in postexilic writings, such as Chronicles, Ben Sira, and 1 Maccabees. Davies and Allison, *Matthew*, vol. 2, 629.

164. Anthony J. Saldarini, *Matthew's Christian-Jewish Community*, 116.

165. Ibid., 119.

166. In the synagogue (ἐν ταῖς συναγωγαῖς): General reference of synagogue as a common institution in Jewish villages (6:2, 5; 23:6); Their synagogue (ταῖς συναγωγαῖς αὐτῶν; 4:23; 9:35; 10:17; 12:9; 13:54), your synagogue (23:34).

167. "Their synagogue" might reflect a situation in which Jesus' followers no longer attended synagogue of any sort. In this way, "their synagogue" possibly corresponds to the synagogues of Pharisaic Judaism or other general institutionalized synagogues,

which were ruled by Jewish religious leaders. See Davies and Allison, *Matthew*, vol. 1, 413–414; Anthony J. Saldarini, *Matthew's Christian-Jewish Community*, 66–67. Daniel J. Harrington, S.J., *The Gospel of Matthew*, 72–75; Janice Capel Anderson, *Matthew's Narrative Web: Over, and Over, and Over Again* (JSNTS 91; Sheffield: Sheffield Academic Press, 1994), 56–59.

168. This does not mean also that the group was cut off from the Jewish community. Anthony J. Saldarini, *Matthew's Christian-Jewish Community*, 66–67.

169. Follower comes "from Galilee and the Decapolis and Jerusalem and Judea and from beyond the Jordan." (4:25).

170. A. Hultgren, *Jesus and His Adversaries: The Form and Function of the Conflict Stories in the Synoptic Tradition* (Minneapolis: Augsburg, 1979), 187.

171. Andrew J. Overman, *Matthew's Gospel and Formative Judaism*, 89.

172. Matthean scholars see that (1) it could be a reference to Jesus' obedience to the precepts in his life, or keeping the law; (2) Jesus' prophetic role in fulfilling the Scriptures revealed in Matthew 1–2, or (3) Jesus' teaching expressed in the love commandment (22:40). Daniel J. Harrington, S.J., *The Gospel of Matthew*, 81; Urich Luz, *Matthew 1–7*, 213–214.

173. Donald Senior, *The Gospel of Matthew* (IBT; Nashville: Abingdon Press, 1997), 39–41.

174. Ulrich Luz, *Matthew 1–7*, 232.

175. Luz sees that Matthew's community was a law-observant Christian group, even though some instructions indicate the Gentile mission. Urich Luz, *Matthew 1–7*, 211–225.

176. Daniel J. Harrington, *The Gospel of Matthew*, 84.

177. Aaron M. Gale, *Redefining Ancient Borders: The Jewish Scribal Framework of Matthew's Gospel* (New York: T & T Clark, 2005), 32–36. As far as the 5:19 is concerned, there are no other similar passages in the Synoptic Gospels. So this shows Matthew's own positive perspective on Jewish law and the Torah, not copying from other gospels. See also Douglas R. A. Hare, "How Jewish Is Matthew?" *CBQ* 62 (2002): 270–277.

178. Matthew 1:22; 2:5, 15, 17, 23; 3:3; 4:14; 8:17; 12:17; 13:14, 35; 21:4; 26:56; 27:9. Andrew J. Overman, *Matthew's Gospel and Formative Judaism*, 74. R. E. Brown sees how those citations emphasize that the whole of Jesus' life stands in God's preordained plan. Raymond E. Brown, *Birth of the Messiah*, 96–97.

179. Andrew J. Overman, *Matthew's Gospel and Formative Judaism*, 75–77.

180. Ibid., 76.

181. Saldarini argues that Matthew's alteration and deviance of the interpretation of the law is "not because of disagreement with a normative Judaism but because he is a minority against the majority and because he recommends a more fundamental reorientation of the tradition than many other Jewish movements. Anthony J. Saldarini, "The Gospel of Mattehw and Jewish-Christian Conflict," in *Social History*

of the Matthean Community, ed. David L. Balch. (Minneapolis: Fortress Press, 1991), 49–50. Also refer to his book, *Matthew's Christian-Jewish Community.*

182. Anthony J. Saldarini, *Matthew's Christian-Jewish Community*, 124.

183. Daniel J. Harrington, *The Gospel of Matthew*, 90. Davies and Allison, *Mathew,* vol. 1, 505–509.

184. Matthew 5:21–26: new interpretation about murder; 5:27–30: new interpretation about adultery; 5:31–32: new interpretation about divorce; 5:33–37: new interpretation about oaths; 5:38–42: new interpretation about retaliation; 5:43–48: new interpretation about love for enemies.

185. Also there is a tense dichotomy between the past and present: "you have heard" is past tense; "I say to you" present tense. Here the tense dichotomy shows two authorities separated in time. So here Jesus reveals a new authoritative teacher and interpreter of the law, corresponding with Moses. See Davies and Allison, *Matthew 1*, 506.

186. Daniel J. Harrington, *The Gospel of Matthew*, 90. Here the six antitheses can be regarded as examples of the principle that Jesus came not to abolish but to fulfill the law. So the antitheses are intended to illustrate the contents of Jesus' fulfillment of law.

187. Anthony J. Saldarini, *Matthew's Christian-Jewish Community*, 131. Saldarini sees that Jesus rather affirms the binding force of Jewish law and then argues for an interpretation of the law modified with the principle of mercy.

188. Andrew J. Overman, *Matthew's Gospel and Formative Judaism*, 81.

189. This value continues to apply following debates in 12:9–14 that one may violate the Sabbath law in order to fulfill a more important task of the compassion and mercy. Healing a man with a withered hand is more important than the strict observance of the Sabbath law.

190. Matthew seems to disagree with Mark that Jesus abolished the Jewish dietary laws regarding unclean food. See Daniel J. Harrington, *The Gospel of Matthew*, 230. As far as food is concerned, Early Christianity had been debated (Galatians 2:11–14; Romans 14:19–20; Colossians 2:20–23; Acts 10:14–17; etc.).

191. Saldarini sees that "Matthew supports the purity and dietary laws as part of biblical law but rejects traditions and practices which are not found in the Bible." Anthony J. Saldarini, *Matthew's Christian-Jewish Community*, 134.

192. Anthony J. Saldarini, *Matthew's Christian-Jewish Community*, 140.

193. Ibid., 141.

194. James C. Scott, *Domination and the Arts of Resistance* (New Haven: Yale University Press, 1990).

195. See further Warren Carter, *Matthew and Empire: Initial Explorations* (Harrisburg: Trinity Press International, 2001).

196. Warren Carter, *The Roman Empire and the New Testament: An Essential Guide* (Nashville: Abingdon, 2006) 1–26.

197. Ibid., 96.

198. Richard A. Horsley, *Jesus and the Powers: Conflict, Covenant, and the Hope of the Poor* (Minneapolis: Fortress Press, 2011), 37–41; Warren Carter, *Matthew and Empire: Initial Explorations*, 20–34.

199. There is no separation between the religious and political spheres in the Roman world, especially in Roman imperial ideology. They claimed that most political power and societal well-being must be sanctioned by the gods' blessings. Warren Carter observed, "religious rituals and theological words were used by emperors and their officials, as well as by loyal supporters in Rome and in the provinces, to evoke "a picture of the relationship between the emperor and the gods" and "impose a definition of the world." Warren Carter, *Matthew and Empire*, 9–30.

200. Warren Carter, *The Roman Empire and the New Testament*, 100–114; See also Warren Carter, *Matthew and Empire*, 9–19.

201. Warren Carter, *Matthew and the Margins: A Sociopolitical and Religious Reading* (New York: Orbis Books, 2000), 307–308.

202. Dennis E. Smith, *From Symposium to Eucharist: The Banquet in the Early Christian World* (Minneapolis: Fortress Press, 2003), 220.

203. Ibid., 234. Dennis Smith sees that, in many cases in Gospel narratives, Jesus' meal or the expression of messianic banquet does not present historical data but is part of the interpretive matrix provided by the author or the narrator.

204. See Dennis E. Smith, *From Symposium to Eucharist*, 9; Hal Taussig, *In the Beginning Was the Meal: Social Experimentation and Early Christian Identity* (Minneapolis: Fortress Press, 2009), 26–32.

205. L. Juliana M. Claassens, *The God Who Provides*, 72–75; Terence L. Donaldson, *Jesus on the Mountain*, 35–43.

206. T. H. Gaster, *Thespis: Ritual, Myth, and Drama in the Ancient Near East* (New York: Doubleday, 1961), 93–94; Isaiah 34:5–7; Zechariah 9:15.

207. Dennis E. Smith, *From Symposium to Eucharist: The Banquet in the Early Christian World*, 168.

208. Terence L. Donaldson, *Jesus on the Mountain*, 35–38.

209. Ibid., 42.

210. A widespread expectation that the messiah would invite the people to participate in a messianic banquet was found in the Second Temple period. (e.g., 1QS 6:4–5; 1QSa 2:11–22; 2 Baruch 29:4–10; 4 Ezra 6:52; 1 Enoch 60:24; 62:1–16).

211. Terence L. Donaldson, *Jesus on the Mountain*, 128.

212. Warren Carter, *The Roman Empire and the New Testament: An Essential Guide*, 83–85.

213. Dennis E. Smith, *From Symposium to Eucharist*, 276–277.

214. Ibid., 1–46.

215. Ibid., 2. According to Smith, although there were minor differences in the meal customs by the regions and the character of social groups, meals took similar forms, procedures, and meaning across a broad range of the ancient world.

216. There are more common features: the transition from *deipnon* to *symposion* with a ceremonial libation with wine; the meal was led by a "president" (*symposiarch*); and it included a variety of marginal participants including servants, uninvited guests, and even dogs. See Hal Taussig, *In the Beginning Was the Meal: Social Experimentation and Early Christian Identity* (Minneapolis: Fortress Press, 2009), 21–26; Dennis E. Smith, *From Symposium to Eucharist*, 13–46.

217. Matthias Klinghardt, *Gemeinschaftsmahl und Mahlgemeinschaft: Soziologie und Liturgie Frühchristlicher Mahlfeiern* (Tübingen: Francke Verlag, 1996).

218. Hal Taussig, *In the Beginning was the Meal*, 26–32.

219. Dennis E. Smith, *From Symposium to Eucharist*, 8–12.

220. Ibid., 12.

221. Dennis E. Smith and Hal Taussig, *Many Tables: The Eucharist in the New Testament and Liturgy Today* (London: SCM, 1990), 56.

222. Dennis E. Smith, *From Symposium to Eucharist*, 240.

223. The semiprivate nature means that people are individually invited to the meals, however, the meal gathering itself functions as a social association, which commonly opens the issue of the larger society with similar experiences and perspectives.

224. Ibid., 34.

225. Ibid., 118.

226. Wendy Cotter, "The Collegia and Roman Law: State Restrictions on Voluntary Associations, 61BCE-200CE," in *Voluntary Associations in the Graeco-Roman World*, ed. John S. Kloppenborg and Stephen G. Wilson (New York: Routledge, 1996), 74–89.

227. Philip Harland noted association gatherings in Asia Minor during Hellenistic era, especially synagogues and Christian gatherings. In this work, he found both Jewish and Christian associations sometimes have shown respect to imperial domination, even though some other cases were anti-imperial. Here his overall idea is that there was a range of attitudes toward the Roman Empire in general. See Philip Harland, *Associations, Synagogues, and Congregations: Claiming a Place in Ancient Mediterranean Society* (Minneapolis: Fortress, 2003). Hal Taussig briefly introduces Philip Harland's observation about the associations in his work. See the book, *In the Beginning was the Meal*, 120–125.

228. Hal Taussig, *In the Beginning was the Meal*, 129.

229. Ibid., 54.

230. In the early Church, the communal meals are normally recognized as a ritual with the expression of three verbs εὐλογέω (bless), κλάω (break) and δίδωμι (give), (Acts. 2:42, 46; 20:7, 11).

231. Richard A. Horsley, *Jesus and the Power: Conflict, Covenant, and the Hope of the Poor*, 58–61.

232. Richard A. Horsley, *Jesus and Empire*, 81–85.

233. Richard A. Horsley, *Jesus and the Powers* 43–50. Horsley argues that messianic movements in Israel had two interrelated goals: "to attain from Roman and Herodian rule and to restore a more egalitarian social-economic order." See his book, *Jesus and Empire*, 50–52.

234. Warren Carter, *Matthew and the Margins: A Sociopolitical and Religious Reading*, 307.

235. Ibid., 306. Ezekiel 34 declares that God will do these tasks with Davidic dynasty (34:10, 14, 23–29). Here Jesus can be described as a son of David who fulfills God's will.

236. Ibid., 307.

237. Philip A. Harland, *Dynamics of Identity in the World of the Early Christians* (New York: T & T Clark, 2009), 25–46.

238. Voluntary associations were represented by numerous designations such as *thiasos, synodos, philosophiai*, and *eranos* in the Greco-Roman world. All are gatherings of people and organizations, extending family groups for common purposes such as athletics, rituals, meals, and the like for socializing.

239. Philip A. Harland, *Dynamics of Identity in the World of the Early Christians*, 26.

240. Stephen G. Wilson, "Voluntary Associations: An Overview," in *Voluntary Associations in the Graeco-Roman World*, ed. John S. Kloppenborg and Stephen G. Wilson (New York: Routledge, 1996), 1.

241. Philip A. Harland, *Dynamics of Identity*, 32–35. Kloppenborg sees three groups of social networks: association with a household; with common trade (and civic locale); and around the cult of a deity. See John S. Kloppenborg, "Collegia and THIASOI," in *Voluntary Associations in the Graeco-Roman World*, ed. John S. Kloppenborg and Stephen G. Wilson (New York: Routledge, 1996), 16–27.

242. Anthony J. Saldarini, *Matthew's Christian-Jewish Community*, 84–116.

243. Ibid., 37. Most of Matthew's crowds are Jesus' audience and followers who marveled at Jesus' teaching and miraculous deeds. However, they are not one single group or fixed unity. (e.g., 4:25; 5:1; 7:28–8:1; 9:8; 9:33, 36; 10:6; 11:1; 11:25–27;12:23, 46; 14:5; 14:13–15; 15:10, 30–33; 17:14; 19:2; 20:29; 21:26; 22:33; 23:1).

244. Wayne O. McCready, "*EKKLESIA* and Voluntary Associations," in *Voluntary Associations in the Graeco-Roman World*. ed. John S. Kloppenborg and Stephen G. Wilson (New York: Routledge, 1996), 60.

245. Matthew's community intentionally differentiates from the Jewish Synagogue, choosing *ekklesia* for designating their community. See Anthony J. Saldarini, *Matthew's Christian-Jewish Community*, 116–120; Richard S. Ascough, "Matthew and Community Formation," 112–114.

246. Richard S. Ascough, "Matthew and Community Formation," 114.

247. Dennis C. Duling, "The Matthean Brotherhood and Marginal Scribal Leadership," in *Modelling Early Christianity: Social-Scientific Studies of the New Testament in Its Context*, ed. Philip F. Esler (London: Routledge, 1995), 178.

248. Anthony J. Saldarini, *Matthew's Christian-Jewish Community*, 116–120.

249. Homi K. Bhabha, *The Location of Culture* (Second Edition; New York: Routledge, 2004), 55.

250. Ibid., 53.

251. Ibid., 55.

252. Ibid., 54.

253. Philip A. Harland, *Dynamics of Identity*, 47–59, 161–181.

254. Making boundaries between "us" and "them" in terms of socio-cultural, religious, and even political parameters is central to a process of identity formation. See Philip A. Harland, Dynamics of Identity, 176–178. In the case of identity formation and group formation, Bruce Malina presents in light of socio-scientific perspective with the following stages: forming, storming, norming, performing and adjourning. These stages mostly concentrate on internal dynamics of the group formation. However, from the perspective of the broader contexts, interaction between groups within larger society would be crucial in the process to legitimize the identity of a particular group or association. See Bruce J. Malina, *The New Testament World: Insights from Cultural Anthropology* (Third Edition; Louisville: Westminster John Knox Press, 2001), 206–217; Richard S. Ascough, "Matthew and Community Formation," in *The Gospel of Matthew In Current Study*, ed. David E. Aune (Michigan: Eerdmans Publishing Company, 2001), 96–126.

255. Matthew uses the source of Jewish teachings and prophetic heritage so that they can achieve legitimacy among other Jewish groups in the formative Judaism.

256. Anthony J. Saldarini, *Matthew's Christian-Jewish Community*, 107–123.

257. Homi Bhabha, *The Location of Culture*, 28–56.

Chapter 4: The Metaphor of Bread toward All Nations: New Covenant and Ideology in *Hybridity*

1. As was studied in previous chapter, Deirdre Good observes the motif of ἀναχώρεω as a special feature of the Gospel of Matthew, presenting a "three-fold pattern of hostility/withdrawal/prophetic fulfillment," with which Matthew seems to create. See Deirdre Good, "The Verb ANAXΩPEΩ In Matthew's Gospel," in *Novum Testamentum* XXXII, 1 (1990): 1–12.

2. E.g., Matthew 4:21; 9:9, 27; 11:1; 12:9, 15; 13:53; 15:21, 29; 19:15.

3. John Nolland, *The Gospel of Matthew*, 611–615. Washing one's hands before eating is difficult to find in Scripture. Leviticus 15:11 relatively presents the appropriate point of view about washing hands. Here God is surely being more honored if the ritual purity is maintained.

4. According to the context of Matthew's account, the cleanliness under discussion is not so much a matter of physical hygiene as it is ritual cleanliness. It is rather

concerned with participation in the cultic life associated with the Jerusalem Temple. Daniel J. Harrington, S.J., *The Gospel of Matthew*, 232.

5. For example, Matthew 11:21 shows the two woes against two pairs of cities; Chorazin and Bethsaida comparing with Tyre and Sidon. Robert H. Gundry, *Matthew*, 214. 310.

6. "Sidon" in the Old Testament is described as "the first born of Canaan" and placed at the border of Canaan (Genesis 10:19; 10:15; 1 Chronicles 1:13). So, Sidon has never been recognized as a part of the territory of Ancient Israel (Judge 1:1), rather the city served as a fixed point for the territory of Canaan. See *NIDB*. vol. 5, 248–250; *ABD*. vol. 6, 17–18.

7. Isaiah 23:1–12; Jeremiah 25:22; 27:3; 47:4; Ezekiel 26–28:11–23; Joel 3:3–4; Amos 1:9–10; Zechariah 9:2–4.

8. Davies and Allison see that "it evidently became common for the two cities, which were thought of as arrogant centres of wealth, to be spoken of together." Davies and Allison, *Matthew*, vol. 2, 267.

9. Daniel J. Harrington, *The Gospel of Matthew*, 235.

10. Many scholars agree that Jesus' exact location and whether Jesus actually entered the Gentile territory are very ambiguous and either way is possible. Among Matthean scholars, Daniel Harrington, and Terence L. Donaldson denied Jesus' actual entrance and ministry in Jewish territory.

11. Daniel J. Harrington, *The Gospel of Matthew*, 236; Davies and Allison, *Matthew*, vol. 2, 546.

12. Amy-Jill Levine, *The Social and Ethnic Dimensions of Matthean Salvation History* (Lewiston: Edwin Mellen, 1988), 138.

13. Gundry argues that Matthew changes the ambiguous terms ὅρια in Mark 7:24 to μέρη in order to "forestall an inference that Jesus went up to the borders of Gentile territory but did not enter." See Robert H. Gundry, *Matthew*. 310.

14. *BDAG*, Third Edition, 723. This term can also be identified with the "region" or "district." But it basically and literally means a boundary or marker of division between two regions. See also *TDNT*. vol. 2, 531.

15. μέρος means "part" as distinct from the whole (e.g., "part of the body, of building, or a city"—Luke 11:36; 15:12; Acts 5:2; John 19:23). τα μέρη can be translated "the territory, country, district" (e.g., Matthew 2:22; 15:21; 16:13; Mark 8:10; Acts 2:10; 19:1). See *TDNT*, vol. 4. 594–598. John Nolland sees that τα μέρη "probably meant the rural territory controlled by the cities." John Nolland, *The Gospel of Matthew*. 631.

16. Most Matthean scholars agree that the conversation between Jesus and the Canaanite woman in Matthew's account is a significant factor, with Jesus' healing miracle gradually diluting into the dialogue. (e.g., Gail R. O'Day, Elaine M. Wainwright, Stephenson Humphries-Brooks, Janice Capel Anderson, Robert H. Gundry, Daniel Hagner, Urich Luz, Daniel Patt, Daniel Harrington, Davies and Allison).

17. Rudolf Bultmann had classified the narrative of the Canaanite woman in Matthew as an apophthegm or controversy dialogue, rather than a miracle story. Although the story itself contains a miraculous act of Jesus, the miracle has been subordinated to Jesus' teaching, apophthegm, which the early churches ascribed to Jesus. See Rudolf Bultmann, *History of the Synoptic Tradition* (New York: Harper & Row, 1963), 38, 21, 63. Davies and Allision, *Matthew*, vol. 2, 544. See also Gail R. O'Day, "Surprised by Faith: Jesus and the Canaanite Woman," in *A Feminist Companion to Matthew*, ed. Amy-Jill Levine and Marianne Blickenstaff (Sheffield: Sheffield Academic Press, 2001), 114–125; Gerd Theissen, *The Gospel in Context: Social and Political History in the Synoptic Tradition* (Minneapolis: Fortress Press, 1991), 112–122.

18. Frances Taylor Gench, *Back to the Well: Women's Encounters with Jesus in the Gospel* (Louisville: John Knox Press, 2004), 2–3. Gail R. O'Day, "Surprised by Faith: Jesus and the Canaanite Woman," 118–123.

19. In particular, he sees that v. 28 has been rewritten and v. 24 is probably redactional composition based on the traditional saying in 10:5–6. He also sees that the structure of this narrative is reminiscent of Mark 10:46–52. In this sense, Luz regards Matthew's treatment as a literary artistry. Ulrich Luz, *Matthew 8–20*, 336–337.

20. While the Gospel of Mark clearly describes that the woman found her daughter was healed and the demon was gone (7:30) when she got at home, Matthew's narrator simply informs that her daughter was healed (15:28).

21. Donald A. Hagner, *Matthew 14–28*, 440.

22. Davies and Allison, *Matthew*, vol. 2, 541. Each dyadic unit "consists in turn of words addressed to Jesus followed by his reaction."

23. Ibid., 541. See also Donald A. Hagner, *Matthew 14–28*, 440.

24. Daniel J. Harrington, *The Gospel of Matthew*, 235. Sometimes the word "dog" is used as an appellation for Gentiles. Davies and Allison, *Matthew*. vol. 2, 553.

25. Elisabeth S. Fiorenza, *In Memory of Her: A Feminist Theological Reconstruction in Christian Origins* (New York: Crossroad, 1994), 137.

26. Dogs, like pigs, lived as scavengers. "Feral pariah dogs roamed in packs on the outskirts of town (Psalm 59:6, 14; cf. Revelation 22:15)." Refer to *ABD*, vol. 6, 1143; *NIDB*, vol. 2, 155–156.

27. E.g., 2 Kings 8:13; Exodus 22:30; 1 Samuel 16:9; 24:15; 2 Samuel 3:8; 9:8; Proverb 26:11.

28. Winton Thomas presents the spectrum of the meaning in the Hebrew term, *keleb*, dogs in a very broad sense, from "slave" to faithful servant in David's confession. For example, Davies refers to himself as Yahweh's dog, signifying a sense of humility before God. Sometimes *keleb* refers to temple servants that have attained the idea of the faithful dog of God. D. Winton Thomas, "KELEBH 'Dog': Its Origin and Some Usages of It in the Old Testament," *Vetus Testamentum* 10 (1960), 410–427.

29. Glenna S. Jackson observes the usage of κυων and *keleb* in other biblical literature and argues that the term is clearly "a literary metaphor fashioned from common sources to distinguish persons outside the Jewish faith or the established in-group." See Glenna S. Jackson, *'Have Mercy on Me': The Story of the Canaanite Woman in Matthew 15:21–28* (JSNTS 228; Sheffield: Sheffield Academic Press, 2002), 48–58; Robert H. Dundry, *Matthew*, 315.

30. *TDNT*. vol. 3, 1101; *BDAG*, Third Edition, 575.

31. Robert H. Gundry, *Matthew*, 314–315; Davies and Allison, *Matthew*, vol. 2, 554; Daniel Harrington, *The Gospel of Matthew*, 235.

32. John Nolland indicates that "Canaanites" is used eighty-seven times in the LXX. The word appears in close connection with Sidon (Genesis 10:19) and with Tyre (2 Samuel 24:7), which normally represents the result of ethnic stereotype. John Nolland, *The Gospel of Matthew*, 632.

33. Niels Peter Lemche, *The Canaanites and Their Land* (JSOTSup 110; Sheffield: JSOT Press, 1991). Glenna Jackson also observed the history of Canaanite and mostly follows the works of Lemche. See also Glenna Jackson's book, *'Have Mercy on Me,'* 60–82.

34. Niels Peter Lemche, *The Canaanites and Their Land*, 154.

35. Ibid., 165–166.

36. Gail R. O'Day, "Surprised by Faith: Jesus and the Canaanite Woman," in *A Feminist Companion to Matthew*, ed. Amy-Jill Levine and Marianne Blickenstaff (Sheffield: Sheffield Academic Press, 2001), 114. Of course, she does not touch upon the metaphor in this text, but she clearly informs that the text must be read to see how it is constructed as well as layered by a multifold narrative strategy and device.

37. Gerd Theissen, *The Miracle Stories of the Early Christian Tradition*, trans. Francis McDonagh (Philadelphia: Fortress Press, 1983), 53–54.

38. Davies and Allison were intrigued by this title υἱὸς Δαυίδ, which was used for Solomon who was later renowned as a mighty healer, exorcist, and magician in the Old Testament. In this regard, the title "son of David" functions not only as a messianic title but also to clarify Jesus' ability to heal. So they assumed that the author of Matthew probably knew the Jewish legends about Solomon's power and presented Jesus in this light. Davies and Allison, *Matthew*, vol. 2, 135–136, 548.

39. Ἀπόλυσον αὐτήν can be translated as "dismiss her," "send her away," "release her," so the disciple's request can be interpreted in both ways, in which disciples are simply ignoring her or they ask Jesus to give her what she wants. On the one hand, Ἀπόλυσον αὐτήν can be understood in light of the similar phrase and disciples' character appear in 14:15: "send the crowds away" and 19:13–15. Here the disciples are described as the negative characters that do not understand what Jesus would do. On the other hand, according to Jesus' negative answer, "I was not sent except to the lost sheep of the house of Israel," the reader can infer that the disciples actually urged Jesus to give

her what she wants. See Frances Taylor Gench, *Back to the Well: Women's Encounter with Jesus in the Gospels*, 7; Davies and Allison, *Matthew* vol. 2, 549.

40. Many English bibles translate the ἄρτος as "food" in v. 26, but its actual literal meaning is bread. So it should be translated as bread; "it is not right to throw the children's bread to the dogs."

41. According to the continuation of ὁ δὲ or ἡ δὲ εἶπεν, the reader recognizes that the woman is debating with Jesus. See Davies and Allison, *Matthew*, vol. 2, 555.

42. Kathleen E. Corley, *Private Woman Public Meal–Social Conflict in the Synoptic Tradition* (Massachusetts: Hendrickson Publishers, 1993), 168.

43. Davies and Allison, *Matthew*, vol. 2, 554–555.

44. As far as the bread is concerned, the reader may not only take into account the unleavened bread in the Passover meal (Exodus 12 and 13) and manna, the bread from heaven (Exodus 16:4), signifying beyond the food to the experience of God's action and salvation, but also conjecture the socio-political and religious meaning around those experiences, which had significant roles for forming and sustaining the community of Israel and communal identity throughout the history of Israel. So, in this narrative, when Jesus metaphorically affirms that the children's bread (τὸν ἄρτον τῶν τέκνων) can be shared with the Gentiles, the reader naturally applies one's conceptual knowledge about bread into the interpretation of this narrative.

45. In this debate, the main issue is the relation between pure and impure; tradition and word of God; and internal and external sources of defilement.

46. Gail R. O'Day, "Surprised by Faith: Jesus and the Canaanite Woman," 115.

47. Ibid., 116–118.

48. Gail R. O'Day, "Surprised by Faith," 114–125; See also Gundry, *Matthew*, 314.

49. In the lament Psalms such as Psalm 86, 88 and 109, the Psalm normally contains words of lament, petition, and complaint. Furthermore the words reflect actual change and transformation of God's plan. In particular, the Psalmists present the motivation with his/her petitions, giving a reason to God to change and act. Likewise, Matthew 15:21–28 contains elements and forms similar to lament psalms. The Canaanite woman presents the motivation to Jesus with reasons to change his mind and act. Gail R. O'Day, "Surprised by Faith," 118–123.

50. Ibid., 125. Gail O'Day argues that Matthew uses the form of the lament Psalm to shape this narrative unit by presenting the woman's persistent, vigorous and confident faith in God's promise for the salvation of Israel and the dramatic change of Jesus' mind, like God's.

51. Tamar in Genesis 38 was not given her ethnic origin. However many scholars referred to early Jewish literature, such as Jubliee 41:1–7, and inferred that she was from Canaanite. Rahab is from Canaanite Jericho. Ruth is Moabite, and Bathsheba probably is Hittite according to Uriah.

52. In Matthew's account, the woman is called a "Canaanite" instead of "Syro-Phoenician" as in the Gospel of Mark.

53. Daniel J. Harrington, *The Gospel of Matthew*, 235. The appearance of women's names is very rare in Jewish genealogies, and exceptions can be found in cases of irregularity of decent or the noteworthy reputation of a special woman who is different from others. See Marshall D. Johnson, *The Purpose of the Biblical Genealogies: with Special Reference to the Setting of the Genealogies of Jesus* (SNTSMS 8, Second Edition; New York: Cambridge University, 1988), 153.

54. If Matthew's Gospel wanted to present four great ancestral mothers of Israel, it probably would have to be Sarah, Rebecca, Leah, and Rachel, as was in the history of Israel in Old Testament references such as Genesis 38:12–26; Joshua 2:1–21; Ruth 4:13–17; 2 Samuel 11:2–27. However, the four women in Matthew's genealogy were regarded as problematic figures in moral and ethical perspective. See Herman C. Waetjen, "The Genealogy as the Key to the Gospel According to Matthew," in *Journal of Biblical Literature*, Vol. 95, No. 2 (Jun, 1976), 215.

55. This idea, espoused by Jerome, highlights the sinful background of the women in order to show God's saving grace and sovereignty in fulfilling the Davidic promise. However, some other scholars argue that the characters of the four women cannot be recognized as sinful, even in Old Testament accounts. For example, Bathsheba was a victim of David's sexual harassment, and Tamar and Rahab were recognized as proselytes and heroines in the history of Israel, and it is also very unclear that Ruth sinned against Boaz. See Raymond E. Brown, *The Birth of the Messiah: A Commentary on the Infancy Narratives in the Gospels of Matthew and Luke* (New York: Doubleday, 1993), 71–72; John C. Hutchison, "Women, Gentiles, and the Messianic Mission in Matthew's Genealogy," in *Bibliotheca Sacra*, vol. 158 (2001), 153–154; see also Wim J. C. Weren, "The Five Women in Matthew's Genealogy," in *Catholic Biblical Quarterly* 59 (April 1997), 296–301.

56. This argument, which has been popularized by Martin Luther and still valuable, concentrates on women as foreigners and the inclusion of the women in the messianic history of Israel. This inclusion advocates and foreshadows the Gentile inclusion and mission. However, it is not clear that all women were recognized as Gentile for the first century Jews. Tamar and Rahab were not presented as Gentiles but proselytes to Judaism. Also it could still be a questionable about "why woman? Does it concern only ethnic status?" See Raymond E. Brown, *The Birth of the Messiah*, 72–72; John C. Hutchison, "Women, Gentiles, and the Messianic Mission in Matthew's Genealogy," 154–156; Ulrich Luz, *Matthew 1–7*, 84–85. Luz regards this idea as the best choice, although it is uncertain.

57. Raymond E. Brown, *The Birth of the Messiah*, 73.

58. Ulirich Luz, *Matthew 1–7*, 84. This irregular divine providence permits a connection between four women to the Virgin Mary. Raymond Brown sees that these women were presented as examples of how God planned the way of messiah beyond human obstacles. Raymond E. Brown, *The Birth of the Messiah*, 71–74; See also Marshall D. Johnson, *The Purpose of Biblical Genealogies*, 157–158. Johnson sees that all

genealogies have apologetic purposes, and Matthew's genealogy also advocates Priestly messiah by calling attention to the irregularities in the Davidic line.

59. Herman C. Waetjen, "The Genealogy as the Key to the Gospel According to Matthew," 216; Wim J. C. Weren, "The Five Women in Matthew's Genealogy," 289. Weren sees the irregularity in genealogy as a deviation from the current pattern for the fulfillment of Israel's history.

60. Wim J. C. Weren, "The Five Women in Matthew's Genealogy," 296–305.

61. Ibid., 303.

62. Ibid., 297; Marshall D. Johnson, *The Purpose of the Biblical Genealogies*, 159–162.

63. Raymond E. Brown, *The Birth of the Messiah*, 73.

64. Wim J. C. Weren, "The Five Women in Matthew's Genealogy," 301.

65. Many scholars concentrate on the issue of the mission to the Gentiles in the light of salvation history. So the religious-ethnic boundary was naturally highlighted, but the other issues that the bread metaphor contains have been blurred.

66. Gail R. O'Day, "Surprised by Faith: Jesus and the Canaanite Woman," 114.

67. See Kathleen E. Corley, *Private Woman Public Meal—Social Conflict in the Synoptic Tradition* (Massachusetts: Hendrickson Publishers, 1993); Elaine M. Wainwright, "The Gospel of Matthew," in *Searching the Scriptures: A Feminist Commentary* vol. 2, ed. Elisabeth Schüssler Fiorenza (New York: The Crossroad Publishing Company, 1994), 635–677; Elaine M. Wainwright, *Toward a Feminist Critical Reading of the Gospel according to Matthew* (New York: Walter De Gruyter, 1991); Gail R. O'Day, "Surprised by Faith: Jesus and the Canaanite Woman," in *A Feminist Companion to Matthew*, ed. Amy-Jill Levine and Marianne Blickenstaff (Sheffield: Sheffield Academic Press, 2001); 114–125; another article in this volume by Stephenson Humphries-Brooks, "The Canaanite Women in Matthew," 138–156; Frances Taylor Gench, *Back to the Well: Women's Encounters with Jesus in the Gospel* (Lousville: Westminster John Knox Press, 2004), 1–28; Elisabeth S. Fiorenza, *In Memory of Her: A Feminist Theological Reconstruction in Christian Origins* (New York: Crossroad, 1994); Musa W. Dube, "Rahab Says Hello to Judith: A Decolonizing Feminist Reading." in *The Postcolonial Biblical Reader*, ed. R. S. Sugirtharajah (Massachusetts: Blackwell Publishing, 2006), 142–158; Musa W. Dube, *Postcolonial Feminist Interpretation of the Bible* (St. Louis: Chalice Press, 2000); Stuart L. Love, "Jesus, Healer of the Canaanite Woman's Daughter in Matthew Gospel: A Social-Scientific Inquriy," in *BTB* 32 (2002), 11–20; Stuart L. Love, "The Household: A Major Social Component for Gender Analysis in the Gospel of Matthew," in *BTB* 23 (Spring 1993), 21–31.

68. Elaine M. Wainwright, "The Gospel of Matthew," in *Searching the Scriptures: A Feminist Commenary*. vol. 2. ed. Elisabeth Schüssler Fiorenza (New York: The Crossroad Publishing Company, 1994), 670.

69. Elain M. Wainwright, "The Gospel of Matthew," 650–654. See three articles in *Feminist Companion to Matthew*. ed. Amy-Jill Levine with Marianne Blickenstaff

(Sheffield: Sheffield Academic Press, 2001): Gail R. O'Day, "Surprised by Faith: Jesus and the Canaanite Women," 114–125; Elaine Wainwright, "Not Without My Daughter: Gender and Demon Possession in Matthew 15:21–28," 126–137; Stephenson Humphries-Brooks, "The Canaanite Women in Matthew," 138–156; Frances Taylor Gench, *Back to the Well: Women's Encounters with Jesus in the Gospel* (Louisville: Westminster John Knox Press, 2004), 1–28.

70. In the Gospel of Mark, the woman who is a "Greek, a Syrophoenician by birth" (7:26) simply approaches Jesus inside a house, so the woman's appearance is not public affair. Also most of her actions are indirectly described by the narrator's explanation, rather than in dialogues.

71. Gail O'Day sees the woman as a protagonist who initiates the conversation. By contrast Jesus initiates nothing in this story. Her bold initiation and daring insistence are key points. O'Day connects the character of the Canaanite woman to the Lament Psalm. Gail R. O'Day, "Surprised by Faith: Jesus and the Canaanite Woman," 116–125.

72. Frances Taylor Gench, *Back to the Well*, 14; Elaine M. Wainwright, "The Gospel of Matthew," 670; Karen Jo Torjesen, "Reconstruction of Women's Early Christian History," in *Searching the Scriptures: A Feminist Introduction*, vol. 1, ed. Elisabeth Schüssler Fiorenza (New York: Crossroad, 1993), 290–310.

73. The terms and phrases, "Lord," "Son of David," and "have mercy on me," appear many times within Matthew's Gospel (e.g., 9:27; 20:30–31; 17:15), and these liturgical terms and formula are based in Jewish tradition, especially founded in Psalms (6:2; 9:13; 30:10; 41:4, etc). According to Wainwright, Matthean community has traditionized these terms as their own liturgical and theological formulation. Elaine M. Wainwright, "The Gospel of Matthew," 670.

74. Wainwright interprets the narrative and the dialogue (or debate) in light of the context of the Matthean community rather than the general or traditional miracle aspect of the story. She concentrates on how Matthew has traditionized the theological discourse within the Matthean house-churches and focuses on its possible encoding of women's perspectives. Elaine Wainwright, "The Gospel of Matthew," 667–673.

75. Musa W. Dube, "Rahab Says Hello to Judith: A Decolonizing Feminist Reading." in *The Postcolonial Biblical Reader*, ed. R. S. Sugirtharajah (Massachusetts: Blackwell Publishing, 2006), 142–158. See also Musa W. Dube, *Postcolonial Feminist Interpretation of the Bible* (St. Louis: Chalice Press, 2000).

76. Musa W. Dube, *Postcolonial Feminist Interpretation of the Bible*, 146–147.

77. Jerusalem, represented as the main city of Jesus' own land, reveals Israel's political and cultural center. Canaan recalls memories of conquering and possessing a foreign land. In this regard, Jesus' encountering with the Canaanite woman possibly recalls the colonial relation in the history of Israel.

78. Ibid., 147–153. The woman can survive only as a colonized mind and a subjugated person. Otherwise she must accept the superiority of the colonizer and betray her own people and land.

79. Ibid., 153–155. In this respect, Musa Dube sees that the Gospel of Matthew upholds the imperialistic values and strategies, which advocate the superiority of some races, classes, and the colonizer.

80. The structure that I observed presents a chiastic pattern. Janice Capel Anderson also presents a chiastic structure, centered on the Canaanite woman. While I see a chiastic structure in the light of the metaphor of bread, she observs a structure in which the three healings form a triad: two blind men (9:29–31; 20:29–34), Sing of Jonah (12:28–42; 16:1–4), and the Canaanite woman (15:21–28). See Janice Capel Anderson, *Matthew's Narrative Web: Over, and Over, and Over Again* (JSNTS 91; Sheffield: Sheffield Academic Press, 1994), 179–191.

81. In the first century of Jesus' time, the Passover sacrifice and meal were celebrated only in Jerusalem because the animal eaten had to be slaughtered in the Temple. So as a pilgrimage festival, many people were gathered in Jerusalem at the season of the Passover. See Anthony J. Saldarini, *Jesus and Passover* (New York: Paulist Press, 1984).

82. In order to determine whether Jesus' Last Supper was the Passover meal, one need to observe all accounts of Jesus' Last Supper in the Bible: Mark 14:12–16; Matthew 26:17–27; Luke 22:14–23 ; and 1 Corinthians 11:23–26. See B. M. Bokser, "Was the Last Supper a Passover Seder?" in *Bible Review* 3/2 (1987): 24–33; Joachim Jeremias, *The Eucharistic Words of Jesus* (London: SCM Press, 1966), 15–88.

83. These texts contains an account of events which took place in Egypt and concrete instructions for celebrating Passover, the feast of Unleavened Bread and the consecration of the first-born.

84. Anthony J. Saldarini, *Jesus and Passover*, 31.

85. Exodus 12:8. According to the halakah the Passover meal is to end before midnight. Ulrich Luz, *Matthew 21–28*, 359; Davies and Allison, *Matthew*, vol. 3, 460.

86. At the Passover meal, people should recline to eat, signifying that they have passed from slavery to freedom. See Joachim Jeremias, *The Eucharistic Words of Jesus* (London: SCM Press, 1966), 48–49; Davies and Allison, *Matthew*. vol. 3, 460.

87. The four required cups of wine were central to the later Passover Seder, which indicates a shift in emphasis from public ritual to family celebration. Joachim Jeremias, *Eucharistic Words of Jesus*, 50–53; Anthony J. Saldarini, *Jesus and Passover*, 34.

88. Joachim Jeremias, *The Eucharistic Words of Jesus*, 54–55; 84–88; Gillian Feeley-Harnik, *The Lord's Table*, 117.

89. Joachim Jeremias, *The Eucharistic Words of Jesus*, 84–88, 111–115.

90. The account of Jesus' supper begins with an expression of Jesus' command for the Passover on "the first day of Unleavened Bread" (26:17). This expression not only signifies the time of Passover and the unleavened bread ancient Israelites had taken, but also reminds the reader of the metaphor of *bread* in two feedings scenes (14:13–21;

15:29–39), the Canaanite woman (15:21–28), and Jesus' warning of the Yeast of the Pharisees and Sadducees (16:11); and other relevant discourses on bread. So, the reader can link all previous discourses on the bread as metaphor to Jesus' last meal gathering.

91. At the beginning of Passover, for a week people eat dough which has not been leavened as a sign that the old is finished and the new is about to come.

92. Saldarini insists, "the unleavened bread and bitter herbs expresses Israel's danger and suffering in Egypt as well as its eschatological hope for salvation." The rituals of Passover extend God's salvation and care from the past to now and the end of the world. Anthony J. Saldarini, *Jesus and Passover*, 44–50.

93. William H. C. Propp, *Exodus 1–18: A New Translation with Introduction and Commentary* (AB; New York: Doubleday, 1998), 384.

94. Anthony J. Saldarini, *Jesus and Passover*, 7.

95. Not only the event in Egypt, but its commemoration process as a ritual festival contributed to form the identity and character of the Jewish people. In fact the communal identity was preserved by the Passover celebration. Ibid., 37–40.

96. While τοῦτο is neuter, ἄρτος is masculine.

97. Davies and Allison, *Matthew* vol. 3, 471; *NIDB*, vol. 1, 484.

98. In Greek and Roman culture of the period from 100 B.C. to 100 A.D., the term σῶμα primarily means "person," or man that is made up of body and soul. So here the body cannot move without the sour nor vice versa. So the σῶμα can even be man's ego, which is the whole being and its life. See *TDNT.* vol. 7, 1025–1041; *NIDB.* Vol. 1, 484.

99. Joachim Jeremias, *The Eucharistic Words of Jesus.* 220–225.

100. Ulrich Luz, *Matthew 21–28*, 374–381. Luz see this as a prophetic symbolic action, identifying his soma (body) with the meaning of his symbolic actions such as the event of breaking, distributing, and eating.

101. Gillian Feeley-Harnik, *The Lord's Table*, 82–85.

102. Davies and Allision, *Matthew*, vol. 3, 470; As people who partook of Passover shared in the redemption from Egypt, Jesus' command to eat implies participation in the death of Jesus and sharing its effect and benefits.

103. In the standard practice of Passover, there was question-and-answer session about the redemptive story from Egypt which the Passover meal liturgically restaged. Normally the interpretation on the bread could have occurred as early as after the distribution of the unleavened bread (Exodus 12:26–27; 13:6). See John Nolland, *The Gospel of Matthew*, 1074; Anthony J. Saldarini, *Jesus and Passover*, 35–36.

104. Joachim Jeremias, *The Eucharistic Words of Jesus*, 54. The bread was the 'bread of affliction' of Deuteronomy16:3.

105. Nolland sees that "my body" in place of "bread of affliction" implicitly relocates the affliction of the ancestors of Israel to the one who is the bread, Jesus. John Nolland, *The Gospel of Matthew*, 1075.

106. A Community's history, experience, self-awareness and continuity lie embedded in the religious rituals, festivals, and the process of commemoration. In this process, private ideals and ideology of community merge "in the symbols and metaphors spoken and ritually enacted by the participants." These phenomenon are revealed in the Jewish Passover. See Anthony J. Saldarini, *Jesus and Passover*, 1–4.

107. Most scholars see that "the blood" signifies Jesus' fate on the cross, his sacrificial death, alluding to the out-poured blood of the paschal lamb. See Joachim Jeremias, *The Eucharistic Words of Jesus*, 220–225; Daniel J. Harrington, *The Gospel of Matthew*, 368.

108. Some scholars also connect this passage with Jeremiah 31:31–34 or Isaiah 53:12. However, the lack of the verbal connections with "covenant" and "sins" in Matthew's Gospel deteriorate the value of convince for me. See, Davies and Allison, *Matthew*, vol. 3, 475.

109. John Nolland, *The Gospel of Matthew*, 1079.

110. Davies and Alison, *Matthew*. vol. 3, 473.

111. E.g., 6:12, 14–15; 12:31–32; 18:27, 35.

112. *NIDB*, vol. 2., 483. Given human sinfulness, admission to the kingdom is not possible apart from divine forgiveness. See also *ABD*. Vol. 2., 835–838,

113. Isaiah 2:2–4; 25:6; Micah 4:1–4; Zechariah 2:11–12; 8:20–23.

114. Davies and Allison, *Matthew*, vol. 2, 480–482; vol. 3, 464–469; Dale C. Allison, *The New Moses*, 238–242.

115. Dale C. Allison, *The New Moses*, 242.

116. Janice Capel Anderson, *Matthew's Narrative Web: Over and Over, and Over Again* (JSNTS 91; Sheffield: JSOT Press, 1994).

117. "Go therefore and make disciples of all nations, baptizing them in the name of the Father and of the Son and of the Holy Spirit, teaching them to observe all that I have commanded you; and I am with you always, to the end of the age" Matthew 28:19–20.

118. Refer to Gerd Theissen, *The Gospel in Context: Social and Political History in the Synoptic Tradition* (Minneapolis: Fortress Press, 1991); Amy-Jill Levine, *The Social and Ethnic Dimensions of Matthean Salvation History* (Lewiston: Edwin Mellen, 1988); Gene R. Smille, "Even the Dogs: Gentiles in the Gospel of Matthew," in *JETS* 45 (2002): 73–97; E. P. Sanders, *Jesus and Judaism* (Philadelphia: Fortress, 1985); John P. Meier, *Law and History in Matthew's Gospel: A Redactional Study of Mt 5:17–48* (*ABc 71*; Rome: Biblical Institute Press, 1976); John P. Meier, "Salvation History in Matthew: In Search of a Starting Point," in *CBQ* 37 (1975): 203–215; and *A Marginal Jew: Rethinking the Historical Jesus*. 3 vols (Anchor Bible Reference Library; New York: Doubleday, 1991–2001); Rudolf Schnackenburg, *The Gospel of Matthew*, trans. Robert R. Barr (Michigan: Eerdermans Publishing Company, 2002).

119. John P. Meier, *Law and History in Matthew's Gospel: A Redactional Study of Mt 5:17–48*. (Analecta Biblica 71; Rome: Biblical Institute Press, 1976), 27; John P. Meier.

"Salvation History in Matthew: In Search of a Starting Point," in *CBQ* 37 (1975): 203–215; See also Meier, *The Vision of Matthew* (New York: Paulist, 1978), 26–41.

120. Some scholars divide salvation history into two stages. For instance Kingsbury sees the time of Israel to the Messiah Jesus and the time of the post-Easter Jesus until the end of time. See also Donald A. Hagner, *Matthew*, vol. 1, 271.

121. Terence L. Donaldson, *Jews and Anti-Judaism in the New Testament: Decision Points and Divergent Interpretations* (Waco: SPCK, 2010), 37–38.

122. "The heirs of the kingdom will be thrown into the outer darkness" (8:12); "the kingdom of God will be taken away from you and given to the people that produces the fruits of the kingdom" (21:43); "your house is left to you, desolate" (23:38), etc.

123. Lloyd Gaston, "The Messiah of Israel as Teacher of the Gentiles: The Setting of Matthew's Christology," in *Interpretation* 29 (1975), 32–33.

124. Anthony J. Saldarini, *Matthew's Christian-Jewish Community* Andrew J. Overman, *Matthew's Gospel and Formative Judaism: The Social World of the Matthean Community* (Minneapolis: Fortress Press, 1990).

125. Anthony J. Saldarini, *Matthew's Christian-Jewish Community*, 109.

126. Ibid., 44.

127. Ibid., 45.

128. Ibid., 46–48.

129. Here the narrator reminds the reader of the number of leaves of bread, of people who are fed, and of the baskets left over. As I studied in the previous chapter, the number and bread represents the restoration of Israel, the inclusion of the Gentile and Jesus' actual formation of community. Furthermore, the bread as a metaphor presents the basic ideology and teaching for forming a new communal identity in Jesus' community.

130. Daniel J. Harrington, *The Gospel of Matthew*, 244.

131. Davies and Allison, *Matthew*, vol. 2, 588. Leaven must take negative connotations because of Jesus' preceding warning "Watch and beware."

132. Warren Carter, *The Roman Empire and the New Testament: An Essential Guide* (Nashville: Abingdon Press, 2006), 69–70.

133. Matthew 21–22 contains the scene of Jesus' entry into Jerusalem and the Temple with five controversy stories and three parables for accusing the Jerusalem leadership. The very next chapter 24 presents Jesus' prediction that Temple will be destroyed and the end of the world will come. So, many commentators see chapter 23 is a summary of the previous conflicts between Jesus and his opponents.

134. Daniel J. Harrington, *The Gospel of Matthew*, 320.

135. Several scholars see the affirmation of the authority of Scribes and Pharisees as a projection of the power dynamics in Jewish society after 70 A.D. Matthew may admit the official position of the dominant Jewish leadership group and their influential power. At the same time, Matthew is faced with a kind of competition and a threat of

rejection from the dominant group. See Anthony J. Saldarini, *Matthew's Christian-Jewish Community*, 46–48; Daniel J. Harrington, *The Gospel of Matthew*, 230.

136. Anthony J. Saldarini, *Matthew's Christian-Jewish Community*, 46.

137. In fact, Matthew uses the biblical tradition of public denunciation that can be found in the prophetic literature. E.g., Amos 5:18–20; 6:1–7; Isaiah 5:8–10, 11–24; 10: 1–3; 28:1–4; 29:1–4; 30:1–3; 31:1–4; Micah 2:1–4). This form of woe oracle is usually addressed to people with power or influence. See Daniel J. Harrington, *The Gospel of Matthew*, 326–327.

138. Garland argues that the intention of Matthew's denunciation in chapter 23 is "an attempt to provide a solution for the Christian problem of Israel's rejection of the Jewish Messiah and the increasing takeover of the kingdom of heaven by Gentiles, in addition to the problem of explaining the recent destruction of the Temple." His in-depth study in Matthew chapter 23 presents convincing arguments, concentrating on the fact that chapter 23 has essentially a pedagogical function for the Matthean community. Among the many possible contextual problems, Israel's rejection of Jesus as Messiah and the crisis of the rejection of the Matthean community among the Jewish groups.

    David E. Garland, *The Intention of Matthew 23*. (*STNT* Vol 22; Leiden: Brill, 1979).

139. Anthony J. Saldarini, *Matthew's Christian-Jewish Community*, 46–55. Saldarini uses a sociological theory of the process of legitimation, developed by Peter Ludwig Berger and Thomas Luckmann, and applies this ideal for the process of the establishment of Matthean community. Through the delegitimizing of the Jewish leader and their interpretation of the Jewish symbol, Matthew legitimates and institutionalizes its own community.

    See also Anthony J. Saldarini, "The Gospel of Matthew and Jewish-Christian Conflict," in *Social History of The Matthean Community*, ed. David L. Balch (Minneapolis: Fortress Press, 1991), 38–54; Daniel J. Harrington, *The Gospel of Matthew*, 323.

140. Matthew's denunciation to the Jewish leader served to illustrate how the Jewish leaders had failed in vital matters, especially the interpretation of the law and God's will. In this regard, the responsibility of Israel's fate and the destruction of the Temple must be in the false leader of Jews. At the same time, Matthew presents the appropriate leader, Jesus the Messiah. David E. Garland, *The Intention of Matthew 23*, 213.

141. Jack Dean Kingsbury, *Matthew: Structure, Christology, Kingdom* (Philadelphia: Fortress, 1975), 40–83. The reason for his argument is not because of the number of appearance of the title, but because of the meaning, which can cover the whole portrait of Jesus in Matthew.

142. Right after the miracle of walking on the sea, the disciples confess Jesus as "son of God" (14:33), and Peter makes a confession of Jesus at Caesarea Philippi (16:16).

143. Jack Dean Kingsbury, *Matthew: Structure, Christology, Kingdom*, 128–149.

144. Dale C. Allison, Jr., *The New Moses: A Matthean Typology* (Minneapolis: Fortress, 1993). Moses as an epic character can be identified with the portrait of Jesus in Matthew's Gospel. E.g., the wicked king attempts to slaughter the children of Israel (Matthew 1–2; Exodus 1:1–2:10), Temptation in the desert (Matthew 4:1–11; Exodus 16:1–17:7), Teaching and giving the law (Matthew 5–7; Moses' law), etc.

145. Warren Carter, *Matthew and Empire: Initial Explorations*, 57–74; See also "Matthean Christology in Roman Imperial Key: Matthew 1:1," in *The Gospel of Matthew in its Roman Imperial Context,* ed. John Rich and David C. Sim (JSNTS 276; New York: T & T Clark, 2005), 143–164.

146. Warren Carter, *Matthew and Empire*, 67–69.

147. Ibid., 68.

148. Warren Carter sees the disciples' confession of Jesus as God's son shows their recognition of Jesus' agency in agreement with God's verdict on him (14:33; 16;16).

149. Warren Carter, *Matthew and Empire: Initial Explorations*, 57–74.

150. Warren Carter, *The Roman Empire and the New Testament: An Essential Guide*, 110.

151. So-called "bread and circuses," made famous by the satirist Juvenal (*Sat.* 10. 77–81), has an important role to maintain the imperial ideology, providing adequate food with entertainment. See Paul Veyne, *Bread and Circuses: Historical Sociology and Political Pluralism* (London: Penguin, 1990); Peter Garnsey and Richard Saller, *The Roman Empire: Economy, Society, and Culture* (Berkeley: University of California Press, 1987), 83–85, 95–96.

152. Along with the pyramids of patronage, elites built up vast personal empires of wealth from the practices of imperialism that made them wealthy and powerful while impoverishing and ruining the Roman citizen and soldiers. Richard A. Horsley, *Jesus and the Powers: Conflicts, Covenant, and the Hope of the Poor* (Minneapolis: Fortress Press, 2011), 29–31. See also Richard A. Horsley, *Jesus and Empires: The Kingdom of God and the New World Disorder* (Minneapolis: Fortress Press, 2003), 24–26.

153. Ibid., 30.

154. *NIDB*, vol. 2., 483; *ABD.* vol. 2., 835–838. See foot note number 112 in this chapter.

155. Horsley sees Jesus' healing ministry is both for the healing of a particular person and a continuing transformation of the social "body" of subsequent communities of healers. See Richard A. Horsley, *Jesus and Empire*, 108–109.

156. Warren Carter, *Matthew and Empire*, 88.

157. The blood alludes that the people had to smear blood from the lamb on the doorpost of their house at the night of Exodus, so that they can be safe from God's judgment (Exodus 12:1–13). See Warren Carter, *Matthew and the Margins: A Sociopolitical and Religious Reading*, 506–507; see also *Matthew and Empire*, 88.

158. Warren Carter, *Matthew and Empire*, 88–89.

159. Warren Carter, *The Roman Empire and the New Testament*, 3.

160. The small of the elites used taxes, rests, loans, interest, tribute, and trade to redistribute production from peasant farmers artisans and other lower groups of people. So the cities were normally centers of elite power, which extended the political, societal, economic and religious control over surrounding areas and villages. See Warren Carter, *The Roman Empire and the New Testament*, 1–12; 45–52; 100–101.

161. Ibid., 110.

162. Rodney Stark, *The Rise of Christianity: How the Obscure, Marginal Jesus movement Became the Dominant Religious Force in the Western World in a Few Centuries* (San Francisco: Harper Collins, 1996). Leif Vaage sees that the resistance to Roman rule itself and its manner could be a factor of the success of early Christianity in the Roman Empire. Leif E. Vaage, "Why Christianity Succeeded (in) the Roman Empire," in *Religious Rivalries in the Early Roman Empire and the Rise of Christianity. ESCJ* vol. 18. ed., Leif E. Vaage (Canada: Wilfrid Laurier University Press, 2006).

163. John Riches, "Matthew's Missionary Strategy in Colonial Perspective," in *The Gospel of Matthew in Its Roman imperial Context*, 140–141. Riches argues the Gospel adopts a counter-cultural idiom found both in the Hellenistic cults and in Jewish apocalypse in order to present the polemics against the Greek and Roman political powers. These counter-cultural claims are developed in territorial claims for the expansion of sacred space.

164. Robert J. C. Young, *Colonial Desire: Hybridity in Theory, Culture, and Race* (New York: Routledge, 1995), 25; Bill Ashcroft, Gareth Griffiths, and Helen Tiffin, eds. *The Post-Colonial Studies Readers* (New York: Routledge, 2006), 158.

165. Robert J. C. Young, *Colonial Desire*, 25.

166. Anthony J. Saldarini, *Matthew's Christian-Jewish Community*, 46–55. See also Anthony J. Saldarini, "The Gospel of Matthew and Jewish-Christian Conflict," in *Social History of The Matthean Community*, ed. David L. Balch (Minneapolis: Fortress Press, 1991), 38–54; Daniel J. Harrington, *The Gospel of Matthew*, 323. Refer to foot note number 139 in this chapter.

167. Matthew's denunciation to the Jewish leader served to illustrate how the Jewish leaders had failed in vital matters, especially the interpretation of the law and God's will. In this regard, the responsibility of Israel's fate and the destruction of the Temple must be in the false leader of Jews. At the same time, Matthew presents the appropriate leader, Jesus the Messiah. David E. Garland, *The Intention of Matthew 23*, 213.

168. Warren Carter, *The Roman Empire and the New Testament*, 3.

Chapter 5: Conclusion

1. George Lakoff and Mark Johnson, *Metaphors We Live By* (Chicago: The University of Chicago Press, 1980), 3–6.

2. David E. Sutton, *Remembrance of Repasts: An Anthropology of Food and Memory* (Oxford: Berg, 2001); See also Davie E. Sutton, *Memories Cast in Stone: The Relevance of the Past in Everyday Life* (New York: Berg, 1998).

3. James C. Scott, *Domination and the Arts of Resistance* (New Haven: Yale University Press, 1990).

Bibliography

Abegg, Martin G. "The Covenant of the Qumran Sectarian," in *The Concept of the Covenant in the Second Temple Period*, edited by Stanley E. Porter and Jacqueline C.R. De Roo. Boston: Brill (2003): 81–98.

Albright, W. F., and C. S. Mann. *Matthew. AB.* vol 26; New York: Doubleday & Company, 1971.

Allison, Dale C., Jr. *The New Moses: A Matthean Typology.* Minneapolis: Fortress Press, 1993.

———. "Who will Come from East and West? Observations on Matthew 8:11–12–Luke 13:28–29," in *IBS* (1989): 158–170.

Anderson, Janice Capel. *Matthew's Narrative Web: Over, and Over, and Over Again. JSNTS 91;* Sheffield: JSOT Press, 1994.

Ascough, Richard S. "Matthew and Community Formation," in *The Gospel of Matthew in Current Study*, edited by David E. Aune. Michigan: Eerdmans Publishing Company, 2001.

Ashcroft, Bill, Gareth Griffiths, and Helen Tiffin, eds. *The Post-Colonial Studies Readers.* New York: Routledge, 2006.

———. *The Empire Writes Back: Theory and Practice in Post-colonial Literatures.* Second Edition. New York: Routledge, 2002.

Ashley, Timothy R. *The Book of Numbers.* Michigan: Eerdmans Publishing Company, 1993.

Asu, Roger David. *Feeding the Five Thousand: Studies in the Judaic Background of Mark 6:30–44 par. And John 6:1–15.* Studies in Judaism; Maryland: University Press of America, 2010.

Aune, David E., ed. *The Gospel of Matthew in Current Study: Studies in Memory of Willam G. Thompson, S.J.* Michigan: Eerdmans Publishing Company, 2001.

Bach, Alice. "Eating Their Words," in *Food and Drink in the Biblical World, Semeia 86;* Atlanta: The Society of Biblical Literature, 215–222.

Bal, Mieke. *Narratology: Introduction to the Theory of Narrative.* Second Edition; University of Toronto Press: Scholarly Publishing Division, 1997.

Balch, David L., ed. *Social History of the Matthean Community: Cross-Disciplinary Approaches.* Minneapolis: Fortress Press, 1991.

Balentine, Samuel E. *The Torah's Vision of Worship.* Minneapolis: Fortress Press, 1989.

Banks, Robert. "Matthew's Understanding of the Law: Authenticity and Interpretation in Matthew 15:17–20," in *JBL.* Vol 93. No. 2 (Jun 1974): 226–242.

Bauer, David R. *The Structure of Matthew's Gospel: A Study in Literary Design. JSNTS 31;* New York: The Almond Press, 1988.

Beare, Francis Wright. *The Gospel According to Matthew.* New York: Harper & Row, 1981.

Beaty, James M. "Was the Last Supper a Passover Seder?" in *Passover, Pentecost, and Parousia— Studies in Celebration of the Life and Ministry of R. Hollis Gause,* edited by S. J. Land, R. D. Moore, and J. C. Thomas—Journal of Pentecostal Theology Supplement Series. Vol. 35. Deo Publishing, 2010.

———. "The Mission of the Disciples and the Mission Charge: Matthew 10 and Parallels," in *JBL.* Vol 99. No. 1 (March 1970): 1–13.

Berger, Klaus. *Identity and Experience in the New Testament.* Translated by Charles Muenchow. Minneapolis: Fortress Press, 2003.

Bhabha, Homi. K. *The Location of Culture,* Second Edition; New York: Routledge, 2004.

Bird, Michael F. *Jesus and the Origins of the Gentile Mission. LNTS 331;* New York: T & T Clark, 2006.

———. "The Third Space," in *Identity, Community, Culture, Difference,* edited by Jonathan Rugherford. London: Lawrence and Wishart (1990): 207–221.

Boer, Roland. *Marxist Criticism of the Bible.* New York: T & T Clark, 2003.

Bokser, Baruch. M. "Was the Last Supper a Passover Seder?" in *BR 3/2* (1987): 24–33.

———. *The Origins of the Seder: The Passover Rite and Early Rabbinic Judaism.* London: University of California Press, 1984.

Bokser, Baruch M. *The Origins of the Seder: The Passover Rite and Early Rabbinic Judaism.* Berkeley: University of California Press, 1984.

Borgen, Peder. *Bread from Heaven: An Exegetical Study of the Concept of Manna in the Gospel of John and the Writings of Philo.* SNT vol 10. Leiden, 1981.

Boyarin, Daniel. "A Question of Theory or Experimentality," in *Semeia: Food and Drink in the Biblical World, Semeia 86;* Atlanta: The Society of Biblical Literature, 223–226.

Brenner, Athalya. "The Food of Love: Gendered Food and Food Imagery in the Song of Songs," in *Semeia: Food and Drink in the Biblical World, Semeia 86;* Atlanta: The Society of Biblical Literature, 101–112.

Brown, Raymond E. *The Birth of the Messiah: A Commentary on the Infancy Narratives in the Gospels of Matthew and Luke.* New York: Doubleday, 1993.

Brumberg-Kraus, Jonathan. "Not by bread alone…: The Ritualization of Food and Table Talk in the Passover Seder and in the Last Supper," in *Food and Drink in the Biblical Worlds. Semeia, 86;* Atlanta: The Society of Biblical Literature, 1999.

Bruner, Fredrick. D. *Matthew: The Churchbook. Matthew 13–28.* Dallas: Word Books, 1990.

Brooks, Stephenson H. *Matthew's Community: The Evidence of His Special Sayings Material. JSNTS* 16; Sheffield: Sheffield Academic Press, 1987.

Broshi, Magen. *Bread, Wine, Walls, and Scroll. JSPS 36*; New York: Sheffield Academic Press, 2001.

Brueggemann, Walter. *The Land: Place as Gift, Promise, and Challenge in Biblical Faith.* Second Edition. Minneapolis: Fortress Press, 2002.

———. "From Hurt to Joy, from Death to Life," *Interpretation 28* (1974): 13–19.

———. *Deuteronomy.* Nashville: Abingdon Press, 2001.

Bultmann, Rudolf. *History of the Synoptic Tradition.* New York: Harper & Row, 1963.

Carroll, Robert P. "YHWH's Sour Grapes: Images of Food and Drink in the Prophetic Discourses of the Hebrew Bible," in *Semeia: Food and Drink in the Biblical World, Semeia 86*; Atlanta: The Society of Biblical Literature, 113–134.

Carson, D. A. *Matthew 13–28. EBC. Vol. 2*; Michigan: Zondervan, 1995.

Caster, Theodor Herzl. *Passover: Its History and Traditions.* Westport: Greenwood Press, 1949.

Carter, Warren. *Matthew and Empire: Initial Explorations.* Harrisburg: Trinity Press International, 2001.

———. *The Roman Empire and the New Testament: An Essential Guide.* Nashville: Abingdon, 2006.

———. *Matthew and the Margins: A Sociopolitical and Religious Reading.* New York: Orbis Books, 2000.

———. "Matthean Christology in Roman Imperial Key: Matthew 1:1," in *The Gospel of Matthew in its Roman Imperial Context*, edited by John Rich and David C. Sim *JSNTS 276*; New York: T & T Clark, 2005.

———. "Matthew's Gospel: Jewish Christianity, Christian Judaism, or Neither?" in *Jewish Christianity Reconsidered: Rethinking Ancient Groups and Texts.* edited by Matt Jackson-McCable. Minneapolis: Fortress Press, 2007.

———. "Matthew and the Gentiles: Individual Conversion and/or Systemic Transformation?" in *JSNT* 26.3 (2004): 259–282.

Cernea, Ruth Fredman. *The Passover Seder: An Anthropological Perspective on Jewish Culture.* New York: University Press of America, 1995.

Childs, Brevard S. *Memory and Tradition in Israel. SBT 37*; Naperville: A. R. Allenson, 1962.

Chilton, Bruce D., and Jacob Neusner. *Classical Christianity and Rabbinic Judaism: Comparing Theologies.* Michigan: Baker Academic, 2004.

Chilton, Bruce D. *A Feast of Meanings: Eucharistic Theologies from Jesus through Johannine Circles. SNT 72*; New York: Brill, 1994.

Claassens, L. Juliana M. *The God Who Provides: Biblical Images of Divine Nourishment.* Nashville: Abingdon Press, 2004.

Clark, Gillian. *Christianity and Roman Society.* Cambridge: Cambridge University Press, 2004.

Clarke, Howard. *The Gospel of Matthew and Its Reader: A Historical Introduction to the First Gospel.* Indianapolis: Indiana University Press, 2003.

Clements, Ronald E. *Wisdom in Theology.* Michigan: Eerdmans Publishing Company, 1992.

Collins, John J. *The Apocalyptic Imagination: An Introduction to the Jewish Matrix of Christianity.* New York: Crossroad, 1984.

Corley, Kathleen E. *Private Woman Public Meal—Social Conflict in the Synoptic Tradition.* Massachusetts: Hendrickson Publishers, 1993.

Cotter, Wendy. "The Collegia and Roman Law: State Restrictions on Voluntary Associations, 61BCE-200CE," in *Voluntary Associations in the Geaeco-Roman World*, edited by John S. Kloppenborg and Stephen G. Wilson. New York: Routledge, 1996.

Couland, J. R. C. "The Feeding of the Four Thousand Gentiles in Matthew?—Matthew 15:29–39 as a Test Case," in *NT, Vol. 41* (1999): 1–23.

Crenshaw, James L. *Old Testament Wisdom: An Introduction*. Third Edition. Louisville: Westminster John Knox Press, 2010.

Crown, Alan D. "Judaism and Christianity: The Parting of the Ways," in *When Judaism and Christianity Began: Essays in Memory of Anthony J. Saldarini*, edited by Alan J. Avery-Peck and Jacob Neusner. *SJSD 85*; Leiden: Brill, 2004.

Davies, W. D., and Dale C. Allison, Jr. *A Critical and Exegetical Commentary on the Gospel According to Saint Matthew*. 3 volumes. The International Critical Commentary; Edinburgh: T & T Clark, 1991.

Davies, Philip R. "Food, Drink and Sects: The Question of Ingestion in the Qumran Texts," in *Food and Drink in the Biblical World, Semeia 86*; Atlanta: The Society of Biblical Literature, 151–164.

Davila, James R. "Ritual in the Old Testament Apocrypha," in *With Wisdom As a Robe: Qumran and Other Jewish Studies in Honour of Ida Frohlich*. Edited by Karoly Daniel Dobos and Miklos Koszeghy. Sheffield: Sheffield Phoenix Press, 2009: 123–145.

Dearman, Andrew J. *Religion and Culture in Ancient Israel*. Massachusetts: Hendrickson Publishers, 1992.

Deutsch, Celia M. *Lady Wisdom, Jesus, and the Sages: Metaphor and Social Context in Matthew's Gospel*. Pennsylvania: Trinity Press International, 1996.

———. "Wisdom in Matthew: Transformation of a Symbol," in *NT* Vol. 32. Fasc 1 (January 1990): 13–47.

Donaldson, Terence L. *Jesus on the Mountain: A Study in Matthean Theology*. JSNTS 8; Sheffield: JSOT Press, 1985.

———. *Jews and Anti-Judaism in the New Testament: Decision Points and Divergent Interpretations*. Waco: SPCK, 2010.

Downing, F. Gerald. *Making Sense in (and of) the First Christian Century*. *JSNTS 197*; Sheffield: Sheffield Academic Press, 2000.

Dube, Musa W. "Rahab Says Hello to Judith: A Decolonizing Feminist Reading," in *The Postcolonial Biblical Reader*, edited by R. S. Sugirtharajah Massachusetts: Blackwell Publishing, 2006.

———. *Postcolonial Feminist Interpretation of the Bible*. St. Louis: Chalice Press, 2000.

Duling, Dennis C. "The Matthean Brotherhood and Marginal Scribal Leadership," in *Modelling Early Christianity: Social-Scientific Studies of the New Testament in Its Context*, edited by Philip F. Esler. London: Routledge, 1995.

Eagleton, Terry. *Literary Theory: An Introduction*. Second Edition. Minnesota: University of Minnesota Press, 1996.

Edwards, Douglas R. *Religion and Power: Pagans, Jews and Christians in the Greek East*. New York: Oxford University Press, 1996.

Ermatinger, James W. *Daily Life of Christians in Ancient Rome*. Westport, CT: Greenwood Press, 2007.

Evans, Craig A. "Covenant in the Qumran Literature," in *The Concept of the Covenant in the Second Temple Period*, edited by Stanley E. Porter and Jacqueline C. R. De Roo. Boston: Brill, (2003): 55–80.

Fanon, Frantz. *Black Skin, White Masks*. Translated by Charles Lam Markmann. New York: Grove Weidenfield, 1991.

Feeley-Harnik, Gillian. *The Lord's Table: The Meaning of Food in Early Judaism and Christianity*. Washington: Smithsonian Book, 1994.

Fiorenza, Elisabeth Schüssler. *In Memory of Her: A Feminist Theological Reconstruction in Christian Origins*. New York: Crossroad, 1994.

Ford, Desmond. *Daniel*. Nashville: Southern Publishing Association, 1978.

Foster, Paul. *Community, Law and Mission in Matthew's Gospel. WUNT2. 177*; Tübingen: Mohr Siebeck, 2004.

Fox, Michael V. *Proverbs 1–9, AB*; New York: Doubleday, 2000.

France, R. T. *Jesus and the Old Testament Studies*. Downers Grove: InterVarsity, 1971.

———. *Matthew. NICNT*; Grand Rapids: Eerdmans, 2007.

Gale, Aaron M. *Redefining Ancient Borders: The Jewish Scribal Framework of Matthew's Gospel*. New York: T & T Clark, 2005.

Garland, David E. *Reading Matthew: A Literary and Theological Commentary on the Fist Gospel*. New York: Crossroad, 1993.

———. *The Intention of Matthew 23. STNT* 52; Leiden: Brill, 1979.

Garnsey, Peter and Richard Saller. *The Roman Empire: Economy, Society, and Culture*. Berkeley: University of California Press, 1987.

Gaster, T. H. *Thespis: Ritual, Myth, and Drama in the Ancient Near East*. New York: Doubleday, 1961.

Gaston, Lloyd. "The Messiah of Israel as Teacher of the Gentiles: The Setting of Matthew's Christology," in *Interpretation* 29 (1975).

Gene R, Simille. "Even the Dogs: Gentiles in the Gospel of Matthew," in *JETS* 45 (2002): 73–97.

Gench, Frances Taylor. *Back to the Well: Women's Encounters with Jesus in the Gospel*. Louisville: John Knox Press, 2004.

Gerhardsson, B. *The Testing of God's Son*. Lund: Gleerup, 1966.

Good, Deirdre. "The Verb ANACWREW In Matthew's Gospel," in *Novum Testamentum XXXII*, 1 (1990): 1–12.

Goodenough, Erwin R. *Jewish Symbols in the Greco-Roman Period*. New Jersey: Princeton University Press, 1988.

Gowan, Donald E. *The Bible on Forgiveness. PTMS 133;* Eugene: Pickwick Publications, 2010.

Grabbe, Lester L. *Judaic Religion in the Second Temple Period: Belief and Practice from the Exile to Yavneh*. New York: Routledge, 2000.

———. *An Introduction to Second Temple Judaism: History and Religion of the Jews in the Time of Nehemiah, The Maccabees, Hillel and Jesus*. New York: T & T Clark, 2010.

Grams, Rollin G. "Narrative Dynamics in Isaiah's and Matthew's Mission Theology," in *Transformation* 21/4 (October 2004): 238–255.

Grassi, Joseph A. *Loaves and Fishes: The Gospel Feeding Narratives*, Minnesota: The Liturgical Press, 1991.

Gundry, Robert H. *Matthew: A Commentary on His Literary and Theological Art*. Grand Rapids: Eerdmans Publishing Company, 1982.

Hagner, Donald A. *Matthew—Word Bible Commentary*, 2 vols. (vol. 33a–b). Dallas: Word Books, 1995.

———. "Matthew: Christian Judaism or Jewish Christianity?" in *The Face of New Testament Studies: A Survey of Recent Research*, edited by S. Mcknight and G. Osborne. Grand Rapids: Baker Academic, 2004, 263–282.

Ham, Caly. "The Last Supper in Matthew," in *Bulletin for Biblical Research*. 10.1 (2000): 53–69.

Hamilton, Victor P. *The Book of Genesis: Chapter 18–50*. New International Commentary on the Old Testament; Michigan: Eerdmans Publishing Company, 1995.

Hannan, Margaret. *The Nature and Dreams of the Sovereign Rule of God in the Gospel of Matthew*. *LNTS 308*; New York: T & T Clark, 2006.

Hanson, K. C., and Douglas E. Oakman. *Palestine in the Time of Jesus: Social Structures and Social Conflicts*. Minneapolis: Fortress Press, 1998.

Hanson, Paul D. *The Dawn of Apocalyptic*. Philadelphia: Fortress Press, 1975.

———. *Old Testament Apocalyptic*. Nashville: Abingdon Press, 1987.

Hare, Douglas R. A. "How Jewish Is Matthew?" *CBQ* 62 (2002): 270–277.

Harland, Philip A. *Dynamics of Identity in the World of the Early Christians: Associations Judeans, and Cultural Minorities*. New York: T & T Clark, 2009.

———. *Associations, Synagogues, and Congregations: Claiming a Place in Ancient Mediterranean Society*. Minneapolis: Fortress, 2003.

Harrington, Daniel J., S.J. *The Gospel of Matthew—Sacra Pagina Series*. Minnesota: The Liturgical Press, 1991.

Hengel, Martin. *Judaism and Hellenism: Studies in Their Encounter in Palestine During the Early Hellenistic Period*. Translated by John Bowden. Philadelphia: Fortress Press, 1974.

Hill, Jonathan. *Christianity: How a Despised Sect from a Minority Religion Came to Dominate the Roman Empire*. Minneapolis: Fortress Press, 2011.

Holwerda, David E. *Jesus and Israel: One Covenant or Two?* Michigan: Eerdmans Publishing, 1995.

Hood, Jason B. *The Messiah, His Brothers, and the Nations: Matthew 1:1–17. LNTS. 441*; New York: T & T Clark, 2011.

Horsley, Richard A., ed. *Paul and Empire: Religion and Power in Roman Imperial Society*. Harrisburg: Trinity Press International, 1997.

———. *Jesus and the Powers: Conflict, Covenant, and the Hope of the Poor*. Minneapolis: Fortress Press, 2011.

———. *Jesus and Empires: The Kingdom of God and the New World Disorder*. Minneapolis: Fortress Press, 2003.

———. *Religion and Empire: People, Power, and the Life of the Spirit*. Minneapolis: Fortress, 2003.

———. *Sociology and the Jesus Movement*. New York: Crossroad, 1990.

Hultgren, A. *Jesus and His Adversaries: The Form and Function of the Conflict Stories in the Synoptic Tradition*. Minneapolis: Augsburg, 1979.

Hutchison, John C. "Women, Gentiles, and the Messianic Mission in Matthew's Genealogy," in *Bibliotheca Sacra*, Vol. 158 (2001).

Ikas, Karin, and Gerhard Wagner. "Postcolonial Subjectivity and the Transclassical Logic of the Third," in *Communicating in the Third Space*, edited by Karin Ikas and Gerhard Wanger. New York: Routledge, 2009.

Iser, Wolfgang. *The Acts of Reading: A Theory of Aesthetic Response*. Baltimore: Johns Hopkins University, 1978.

Jackson, Glenna S. *'Have Mercy on Me': The Story of the Canaanite Woman in Matthew 15:21–28*. *JSNTS* 228; Sheffield: Sheffield Academic Press, 2002.

Jackson-McCable, Matt, ed. *Jewish Christianity Reconsidered: Rethinking Ancient Groups and Texts*. Minneapolis: Fortress Press, 2007.

Jacob, Benno. *The Second Book of the Bible: Exodus*. Translated by Walter Jacob. New Jersey: Ktav Publishing House, Inc, 1992.

Jaffee, Martin S. *Early Judaism: Religious World of the First Judaic Millennium*. Bethesda: University Press of Maryland, 2006.

Janes, Dominic. *Romans and Christians*. Charleston: Tempus Publishing, 2002.

Jeremias, Joachim. *The Eucharistic Words of Jesus*. London: SCM Press, 1966.

Johnson, Marshall D. *The Purpose of the Biblical Genealogies: With Special Reference to the Setting of the Genealogies of Jesus*. SNTSMS 8; Second Edition; New York: Cambridge University, 1988.

Kaufmann, Yehezkiel. *The Religion of Israel from its Beginning to the Babylonian Exile*. Chicago: The University of Chicago Press, 1960.

Kim, Dong-sun. *The Bread for Today and the Bread for Tomorrow*. New York: Peter Lang, 2001.

Kingsbury, Jack Dean. *Matthew: Structure, Christology, Kingdom*. Philadelphia: Fortress, 1975.

Klauck, H. J. *The Religious Context of Early Christianity: A Guide to Graeco-Roman Religions*. Edinburgh: T & T Clark, 2000.

Kloppenborg, John S. "Collegia and THIASOI," in *Voluntary Associations in the Graeco-Roman World*, edited by John S. Kloppenborg and Stephen G. Wilson. New York: Routledge, 1996.

Kraemer, David. *Jewish Eating and Identity Through the Ages*. New York: Routledge Taylor & Francis Group, 2007.

Kunin, S. D. *We Think What We Eat: Neo-Structuralist Analysis of Israelite Food Rules and Other Cultural and Textual Practices*. JSOTSup, 412. London: Continuum, 2004.

Lakoff, George. "The Contemporary Theory of Metaphor," in *Metaphor and Thought*, edited by Andrew Ortony. Second Edition. Cambridge: Cambridge University Press, 1993.

Lakoff, George and Mark Johnson. *Metaphors We Live By*. Chicago: The University of Chicago Press, 1980.

———. *Philosophy in the Flesh: The Embodied Mind and Its Challenge to Western Thought*. New York: Basic Books, 1999.

Lakoff, George, and Mark Turner. *More Than Cool Reason: A Field Guide to Poetic Metaphor*. Chicago: The University of Chicago Press, 1989.

Lawrence, Louise J. *Reading with Anthropology: Exhibiting Aspects of New Testament Religion*. Waynesboro: Paternoster Press, 2005.

Lemche, Niels Peter. *The Canaanites and Their Land*. JSOTSup 110; Sheffield: JSOT Press, 1991.

Levine, Amy-Jill. *The Social and Ethnic Dimensions of Matthean Salvation History*. Lewiston: Edwin Mellen, 1988.

————. *The Misunderstood Jew: The Church and the Scandal of the Jewish Jesus*. New York: Harper-Collins Publishers, 2006.

———— and Marianne Blickenstaff, eds. *A Feminist Companion to Matthew*. Sheffield: Sheffield Academic Press, 2001.

Lieu, Judith M. *Christian Identity in the Jewish and Graeco-Roman World*. New York: Oxford University Press, 2004.

Lieu, Judith M., John North, and Tessa Rajak, eds. *The Jews Among Pagans and Christians in the Roman Empire*. New York: Routledge, 1994.

Lkarsavne, Oskar. *In the Shadow of the Temple: Jewish Influences on Early Christianity*. Downers Grove, IL: Intervarsity Press, 2002.

Loomba, Ania. *Colonialism/Postcolonialism: The New Critical Idiom*. Second Edition. New York: Routledge, 2005.

Love, Stuart L. "Jesus, Healer of the Canaanite Woman's Daughter in Matthew Gospel: A Social-Scientific Inquiry," in *BTB* 32 (2002), 11–20.

————. "The Household: A Major Social Component for Gender Analysis in the Gospel of Matthew," in *BTB* 23 (Spring 1993), 21–31.

Luomanen, Petri. *Recovering Jewish-Christian Sects and Gospels*. SVC 10; Leiden: Brill, 2012.

————. "The 'Sociology of Sectarianism' in Matthew: Modeling the Genesis of Early Judaism and Christian Communities," in *Fair Play: Diversity and Conflicts in Early Christianity: Essays in Honor of Heikki Räisänen*, edited by Ismo Dunderburg and Christopher Tuckett. Netherland: Brill (2002): 107–130.

Luz, Ulrich. *Matthew in History: Interpretation, Influence, and Effects*. Minneapolis: Fortress Press, 1994.

————. *Matthew: A Commentary*. 3 vols. Translated by James E. Crouch. Hermeneia—A Critical and Historical Commentary on the Bible, edited by Helmut Koester. Minneapolis: Fortress Press, 2007.

————. *New Testament Theology: The Theology of the Gospel of Matthew*. Translated by J. Bradford Robinson. Cambridge: Cambridge University Press, 1993.

MacDonald, Nathan. *What Did the Ancient Israelites Eat? Diet in Biblical Times*. Michigan: Eerdmans Publishing Company, 2008.

Magness, Jodi. *Stone and Dung, Oil and Spit: Jewish Daily Life in the Time of Jesus*. Michigan: Eerdmans Publishing, 2011.

————. *Not Bread Alone: The Uses of Food in the Old Testament*. New York: Oxford University Press, 2008.

Marshall, I. Howard, *Last Supper and Lord's Supper,* Grand Rapids: Eerdmans, 1981.

Malina, Bruce J. *The New Testament World: Insights from Cultural Anthropology*. Third Edition. Louisville, KY: Westminster John Knox Press, 2001.

Mattern, S. *Rome and the Enemy: Imperial Strategy in the Principate*. Berkeley: University of California Press, 1999.

Matthews, Victor H. *Manners and Customs in the Bible*. Massachusetts: Henderickson Publishers, 1988.

McCready, Wayne O. "*EKKLESIA* and Voluntary Associations," in *Voluntary Associations in the Graeco-Roman World*, edited by John S. Kloppenborg and Stephen G. Wilson. New York: Routledge, 1996.

McKinlay, Judith E. "To Eat or Not to Eat: Where Is Wisdom in This Choice?" in *Food and Drink in the Biblical World, Semeia 86*; Atlanta: The Society of Biblical Literature, 73–84.

―――. *Gendering Wisdom the Host: Biblical Invitations to Eat and Drink. JSOTsup 216*; Sheffield: Sheffield Academic Press, 1996.

McLoad, John. *Beginning Postcolonialism.* New York: Manchester University Press, 2000.

Meier, John P. *Law and History in Matthew's Gospel: A Redactional Study of Mt 5:17–48. ABc 71*; Rome: Biblical Institute Press, 1976.

―――. "Salvation History in Matthew: In Search of a Starting Point," in *CBQ 37* (1975): 203–215.

―――. *The Vision of Matthew.* New York: Paulist, 1978.

Menninger, Richard E. *Israel and the Church in the Gospel of Matthew.* New York: Peter Lang, 1994.

Meyers, Carol. *Exodus.* The New Cambridge Bible Commentary; New York: Cambridge University Press, 2005.

Moore, Stephen D., and Fernando F. Segovia, eds. *Postcolonial Biblical Criticism: Interdisciplinary Intersections.* New York: T & T Clark, 2005.

Mounce, Robert H. *Matthew.* New International Biblical Commentary; Peabody: Hendrickson, 1991.

Murphy, Frederick J. "The Jewishness of Matthew: Another Look," in *When Judaism and Christianity Began: Essays in Memory of Anthony J. Saldarini*, edited by Alan J. Avery-Peck and Jacob Neusner. SJSD 85; Leiden: Brill, 2004.

Murphy-O'Connor, Jerome. "Miracles in Matthew," in *The Furrow*, Vol. 19, No. 3, Supplement: The Bible, No. 4 (Spring, 1968): 7–13.

Nestor, Dermot Anthony. *Cognitive Perspectives On Israelite Identity.* New York: T & T Clark, 2010.

Neusner, Jacob. *Judaism When Christianity Began: A Survey of Belief and Practice.* Louisville: John Knox Press, 2002.

Newman, Robert C. "Breadmaking with Jesus," in *JETS.* 40/1 (March, 1997): 1–11.

Newport, Kenneth G. C. *The Sources of Sitz im Leben of Matthew 23. JSNTS 117*; Sheffield: Sheffield Academic Press, 1995.

Nickelsburg, George W. E., and Michael E. Stone. *Faith and Piety in Early Judaism: Text and Documents.* Philadelphia: Fortress Press, 1983.

Nolland, John. *The Gospel of Matthew: A Commentary on the Greek Text. NIGTC*; Michigan: The Paternoster Press, 2005.

Novak, Ralph Martin. *Christianity and the Roman Empire: Background Texts.* Pennsylvania: Trinity Press International, 2001

O'Day, Gail R. "Surprised by Faith: Jesus and the Canaanite Woman," in *A Feminist Companion to Matthew*, edited by Amy-Jill Levine and Marianne Blickenstaff. Sheffield: Sheffield Academic Press, 2001.

Oakes, Peter. Edited. *Rome in the Bible and the Early Church.* Grand Rapid: Baker Academic, 2002.

Overman, J. Andrew. *Matthew's Gospel and Formative Judaism: The Social World of the Matthew Community.* Minneapolis: Fortress Press, 1990.

Parkinson, Jim. "A Canaanitic Word in the Logos of Christ; or The difference the Syro-Phoenician Woman Makes to Jesus." *Semeia* 75 (1996): 61–85.

Patte, Daniel. *The Gospel According to Matthew: A Structural Commentary on Matthew's Faith.* Philadelphia: Fortress Press, 1987.

Perdue, Leo G. *Wisdom Literature: A Theological History.* Louisville: Westminster John Knox Press, 2007.

————. *Wisdom and Creation: The Theology of Wisdom Literature.* Nashville: Abingdon Press, 1994.

————. *Proverbs—Interpretation.* Louisville: John Knox Press, 2000.

Pfoh, Emanuel. *The Emergence of Israel in Ancient Palestine: Historical and Anthropological Perspectives.* London: Equinox Publishing Ltd., 2009.

Pitre, Brant. *Jesus and the Jewish Roots of the Eucharist—Unlocking the Secrets of the Last Supper.* New York: Doubleday, 2011.

Pitzparick, P. J. *In Breaking of Bread: The Eucharist and Ritual.* Cambridge: Cambridge University Press, 1993.

Powell, Mark Allan, ed. *Methods for Matthew.* New York: Cambridge University Press, 2009.

Priest, John F. "The Messiah and the Meal in 1QSa," in *JBL.* Vol. 82. No. 1 (March 1963): 96–100.

Propp, Willam H. *Exodus 1–18: A New Translation with Introduction and Commentary.* The Anchor Bible. New York: Doubleday, 1998.

Ramone, Jenni. *Postcolonial Theories.* New York: Palgrave Macmillan, 2011.

Reed, Stephen A. "The Role of Food as Related to Covenant in Qumran Literature," in *The Concept of the Covenant in the Second Temple Period*, edited by Stanley E. Porter and Jacqueline C. R. De Roo. Boston: Brill (2003): 129–166.

Reinhartz, Adele. "Reflections on Table Fellowship and Community Identity," in *Food and Drink in the Biblical World, Semeia 86*; Atlanta: The Society of Biblical Literature, 227–233.

Richards, I. A. *The Philosophy of Rhetoric.* London: Oxford University Press, 1936.

Riches, John. *Matthew.* Sheffield: Sheffield Academic Press, 1996.

————. "Matthew's Missionary Strategy in Colonial Perspective," in *The Gospel of Matthew in Its Roman Imperial Context,* edited by John Rich and David C. Sim. JSNTS 276; New York: T & T Clark, 2005.

Ricoeur, Paul. *Memory, History, Forgetting.* Chicago: University of Chicago Press, 2004.

————. *The Rule of Metaphor: Multi-disciplinary Studies of the Creation of Meaning in Language,* Translated by Robert Czerny. Toronto: University of Toronto Press, 1977.

————. "Biblical Hermeneutic" in *Semeia 4*, edited by John Dominic Crossan. Missoula: The Society of Biblical Literature, 1975.

Rosenblum, Jordan D. *Food and Identity in Early Rabbinic Judaism.* New York: Cambridge University Press, 2010.

Rodriguez, Jeanette, and Ted Fortier. *Cultural Memory: Resistance, Faith, and Identity.* Austin: University of Texas Press, 2007.

Rouwhorst, Gerard. "Table Community in Early Christianity," in *A Holy People: Jewish and Christian Perspectives on Religious Communal Identity,* edited by Marcel Poorthuis and Joshua Schwartz. Boston: Brill, 2006, 69–84.

Resseguie, James L. *Narrative Criticism of the New Testament:* An Introduction. Grand Rapids: Baker Academic, 2005.

Roy, Anindyo. "Postcoloniality and the Politics of Identity in the Diaspora: Figuring 'Home,' Locating Histories," in *Postcolonial Discourse and Changing Cultural Contexts: Theory and Criticism,* edited by Rajan Gita and Mohanram Radhika. Westport, CT: Greenwood Press, 1995.

Rumelhart, David E. "Some Problems with the Notion of Literal Meanings," in *Metaphor and Thought,* edited by Andrew Ortony. Second Edition. Cambridge: Cambridge University Press, 1993.

Said, Edward W. *Orientalism.* London: Penguin, 2003.

Saldarini, Anthony J. *Matthew's Christian-Jewish Community*. Chicago: The University of Chicago Press, 1994.

———. "Reading Matthew Without Anti-Semitism" in *The Gospel of Matthew in Current Study: Studies in Memory of William G. Thompson, S.J.*, edited by David E. Aune. Michigan: Eerdmans Publishing Company, 2001:166–170.

———. "The Gospel of Mattehw and Jewish-Christian Conflict," in *Social History of the Matthean Community*, edited by David L. Balch. Minneapolis: Fortress Press, 1991.

———. *Jesus and Passover*. New York: Paulist Press, 1984.

Sanders, E. P. *Judaism: Practice and Belief 63 BCE–66–CE*. London: SCM Press, 1992.

———. *Jesus and Judaism*. Philadelphia: Fortress, 1985.

Sanders, Jack T, Charisma. *Converts, Competitors: Societal and Sociological Factors in the Success of Early Christianity*. London: SCM Press, 2000.

Schiffman, Lawrence H. *Sectarian Law in the Dead Sea Scrolls: Courts, Testimony and the Penal Code*. Chino: Scholars Press, 1983.

Schnackenburg, Rudolf. *The Gospel of Matthew*. Translated by Robert R. Barr. Michigan: Eerdermans Publishing Company, 2002.

Schweid, Eliezer. *The Jewish Experience of Time: Philosophical Dimensions of the Jewish Holy Days*. Translated by Amnon Hadary. New Jersey: Jason Aronson Inc, 2000.

Scott, James C. *Domination and the Arts of Resistance*. New Haven: Yale University Press, 1990.

Scott, J. Martin C. "Matthew 15:21–28: A Test-Case for Jesus' Manners," in *JSNT 63* (1996): 21–44.

Scott, J. Julius. "Gentiles and the Ministry of Jesus: Further Observation on Matthew 10:5–6; 15:21–28," in *JETS*, 33/2 (June, 1990): 161–169.

Segal, Alan F. "Matthew's Jewish Voice," in *Social History of the Matthean Community*, edited by David L. Balch. Minneapolis: Fortress Press, 1991.

Segal, J. B. *The Hebrew Passover from the Earliest Times to A.D. 70*. New York: Oxford University Press, 1963.

Segovia, Fernando F. *Decolonizing the Biblical Studies: A View From the Margins*. Orbis Books, 2000.

———. "Biblical Criticism and Postcolonial Studies: Toward a Postcolonial Optic," in *The Postcolonial Bible*, edited by R. S. Sugirtharajah. Sheffield: Sheffield Academic Press, 1998.

Senior, Donald. *The Gospel of Matthew. IBT*; Nashville: Abingdon Press, 1997.

Setzer, J. Claudia. *Jewish Responses to Early Christians: History and Polemics, 24–150 C.E.* Minneapolis: Fortress Press, 1994.

Sharon, Diane M. "When Fathers Refuse to Eat: The Trope of Rejecting Food and Drink in Biblical Narrative," in *Food and Drink in the Biblical World, Semeia 86*; Atlanta: The Society of Biblical Literature, 135–150.

Skarsaune, Oskar. *In the Shadow of the Temple: Jewish Influences on the Early Christianity*. Downers Grove: InterVarsity Press, 2002.

Slee, Michelle. *The Church in Antioch in the First Century CE: Communion and Conflict. JSNTS 244*; Sheffield: Sheffield Academic Press, 2003.

Smith, Dennis E. *From Symposium To Eucharist: The Banquet in the Early Christian World*. Minneapolis: Fortress Press, 2003.

———. and Hal Taussig. *Many Tables: The Eucharist in the New Testament and Liturgy Today*. London: SCM, 1990.

Snyder, Graydon F. *Inculturation of the Jesus Tradition—The Impact of Jesus on Jewish and Roman Cultures*. Harrisburg: Trinity Press, 1999.

Soggin, Alberto J. *Israel in the Biblical Period: Institutions, Festivals, Ceremonies, Rituals*. Translated by John Bowden. New York: T & T Clark, 2001.

Sordi, Marta. *The Christians and the Roman Empire*. Translated by Annabel Bedini. Norman: University of Oklahoma, 1986.

Spaulding, Mary B. *Commemorative Identities: Jewish Social Memory and the Johannine Feast of Booths. LNTS 369*; New York: T & T Clark, 2009.

Stanton, Graham N. *A Gospel for a New People: Study in Matthew.* Westminster John Knox, 1992.

Stark, Rodney. *The Rise of Christianity: How the Obscure, Marginal Jesus Movement Become the Dominant Religious Force in the Western World in a Few Centuries*. San Francisco: Harper Collins, 1996.

Strecker, Jeorg. "The Concept of History in Matthew," in *JAAR*. Vol. 35, No. 3 (Sept., 1967): 219–230.

Sugirtharajah, R. S. *Postcolonial Criticism and Biblical Interpretation*. New York: Oxford University Press, 2002.

———, ed. *The Postcolonial Biblical Reader*. Malden: Blackwell Publishing Ltd., 2006.

———. "Charting the Aftermath: A Review of Postcolonial Criticism," in *The Postcolonial Biblical Reader*, edited by R. S. Sugirtharahah. Oxford: Blackwell Publishing, 2006.

Taussig, Hal. *In the Beginning Was the Meal: Social Experimentation and Early Christian Identity*. Minneapolis: Fortress Press, 2009.

Theissen, Gerd. *The Miracle Stories of the Early Christian Tradition*. Translated by Francis. Philadelphia: Fortress Press, 1983.

———. *The Gospel in Context: Social and Political History in the Synoptic Tradition*. Minneapolis: Fortress Press, 1991.

Theissen Gerd, *A Theory of Primitive Christian Religion*. London: SCM Press, 1999.

Thomas, D. Winton. "KELEBH 'Dog': Its Origin and Some Usages of It in the Old Testament," *Vetus Testamentum* 10 (1960), 410–427

Thompson, J. A. *Handook of Life in Bible Times*. Downers Grove: Inter-Varsity Press, 1986.

Tilborg, Sjef Van. *The Jewish Leaders in Matthew*. Leiden: Brill, 1972.

Tomson, Peter J. "Jewish Food Laws in Early Christian Community Discourse," in *Food and Drink in the Biblical World, Semeia 86*; Atlanta: The Society of Biblical Literature, 193–214.

Torjesen, Karen Jo. "Reconstruction of Women's Early Christian History," in *Searching the Scriptures: A Feminist Introduction*, Volume 1, edited by Elisabeth Schüssler Fiorenza. New York: Crossroad, 1993.

Towner, W. Sibley. *Daniel. IBCTP*; Atlanta: John Knox Press, 1984.

Tracy, David. "Metaphor and Religion." *Critical Inquiry* 5, no. 1 (1978)

Trebilco, Paul. *Self-Designations and Group Identity in the New Testament*. Cambridge: Cambridge University Press, 2012.

Turner, David L. *Matthew*. Baker Exegetical Commentary on the New Testament; Michigan: Baker Academic, 2008.

Vaage, Leif E., ed. *Religious Rivalries in the Early Roman Empire and the Rise of Christianity. SCJ 18*; Wilfrid Laurier University Press, 2006.

———. "Why Christianity Succeeded (in) the Roman Empire," in *Religious Rivalries in the Early Roman Empire and the Rise of Christianity, SCJ* 18, edited by Leif E. Vaage. Canada: Wilfrid Laurier University Press, 2006.

Vanderkam, James C. *An Introduction to Early Judaism.* Grand Rapids, MI: Eerdmans Publishing Company, 2001.

———. *The Dead Sea Scrolls Today.* Grand Rapids, MI: Eerdmans Publishing Company, 1994.

Vamosh, Miriam Feinberg. *Food at the Time of the Bible: From Adam's Apple to the Last Supper.* Herzlia; Israel: Abingdon Press, 2004.

Verseput, Donald J. "Jesus' Pilgrimage to Jerusalem and Encounter in the Temple: A Geographical Motif in Matthew's Gospel," in *NT.* XXXVI, 2 (1994): 105–121.

———. "The Faith of the Reader and the Narrative of Matthew 13:53–16:20," in *JSNT* 46 (1992): 3–24.

Veyne, Paul. *Bread and Circuses: Historical Sociology and Political Pluralism.* London: Penguin, 1990.

Waetjen, Herman C. "The Genealogy as the Key to the Gospel According to Matthew," in *JBL.* Vol. 95, No. 2 (Jun. 1976).

Wainwright, Elaine. "The Gospel of Matthew," in *Searching the Scriptures: A Feminist Commentary.* vol. 2, edited by Elisabeth Schüssler Fiorenza. New York: Crossroad, 1994.

———. *Women Healing/Healing Women: The Genderization of Healing in Early Christianity.* London: Equinox, 2006.

———. *Toward a Feminist Critical Reading of the Gospel according to Matthew.* New York: Walter De Gruyter, 1991.

Weaver, Dorothy Jean. *Matthew's Missionary Discourse—A Literary Critical Analysis. JSNTS 38*; Sheffield: JSOT Press, 1990.

Webster, Jane S. *Ingesting Jesus: Eating and Drinking in the Gospel of John.* Academia Biblica Series. No. 6. Leiden: Brill, 2003.

Werbner, Pnina, and Modood Tariq, eds. *Debating Cultural Hybridity: Multi-Cultural Identities and the Politics of Anti-Racism.* New Jersey: Zed Books, 1997.

Weren, Wim J. C. "The Five Women in Matthew's Genealogy. *CBQ 59* (April 1997).

Westermann, Claus. *Roots of Wisdom: The Oldest Proverbs of Israel and Other Peoples.* Louisville: Westminster John Knox Press, 1995.

Williams, P. J. "Bread and the Peshitta in Matthew 16:11–12 and 12:4." *NT* XLIII. Vol. 4. (2001): 331–334.

Wilson, Stephen G. "Voluntary Associations: An Overview," in *Voluntary Associations in the Graeco-Roman World*, edited by John S. Kloppenborg and Stephen G. Wilson. New York: Routledge, 1996.

Wisker, Gina. *Key Concepts in Postcolonial Literature.* New York: Palgrave Macmillan, 2007.

Young, Robert J. C. *Colonial Desire: Hybridity in Theory, Culture, and Race.* New York: Routledge, 1995.

———. "The Void of Misgiving," in *Communicating in the Third Space*, edited by Karin Ikas and Gerhard Wagner. New York: Routledge, 2009.

Zeitlin, Irving M. *Ancient Judaism: Biblical Criticism from Max Weber to the Present.* Cambridge: Polity Press, 1984.

Zerubavel, Yael. *Collective Memory and Recovered: The Making of Israeli Roots National Tradition.* Chicago: The University of Chicago Press, 1995.

Zetterholm, Magnus. *The Formation of Christianity in Antioch: A Social-Scientific Approach to the Separation Between Judaism and Christianity.* London: Routledge, 2003.

Studies in Biblical Literature

This series invites manuscripts from scholars in any area of
biblical literature. Both established and innovative methodologies, covering general and particular areas in biblical study, are
welcome. The series seeks to make available studies that will
make a significant contribution to the ongoing biblical discourse.
Scholars who have interests in gender and sociocultural
hermeneutics are particularly encouraged to consider this series.

For further information about the series and for the submission of
manuscripts, contact:

> Peter Lang Publishing
> Acquisitions Department
> 29 Broadway, 18th floor
> New York, NY 10006

To order other books in this series, please contact our Customer
Service Department:

> (800) 770-LANG (within the U.S.)
> (212) 647-7706 (outside the U.S.)
> (212) 647-7707 FAX

or browse online by series at:

WWW.PETERLANG.COM